"A deeply learned yet highly accessible exp journey, and most compellingly, the living mystical, and sacramental sources that not to death. Gregory Hillis brings wonderful t̲ ...., ..., and fresh insight to every facet of the irrepressible mosaic that is Thomas Merton and, yes, his capaciously Catholic theological and apologetic literary genius. Without avoiding critical assessments of its famous subject, *Man of Dialogue* should put to rest every superficial dismissal of Merton's legacy—and, sadly, they are 'legion'—that downplays or denies Merton's extraordinary witness as a Catholic Christian monk and priest of Gethsemani, to the day of his death and well beyond."

> —Christopher Pramuk, University Chair of Ignatian Thought and
> Imagination, Regis University

"Thomas Merton counted his Catholic faith, along with his monastic vocation and calling to be a writer, as three gifts for which he would be ever grateful. In this exceptionally informative and insightful study, Gregory Hillis illuminates Merton's Catholic vision and the ways in which it informed his identity, shaped his spirituality, inspired his prophetic witness, and made him, in the words of Pope Francis, a 'man of dialogue.' A significant contribution to Merton studies and a must read!"

> —Christine M. Bochen, Professor Emerita, Nazareth College,
> Rochester, New York

"Professor Hillis engages the reader with a compelling introduction to the life and thought of the Trappist who spent his time in prayerful dialogue with God and the world around him. He demonstrates with ease through the lens of Merton's many published works and personal journals that the great man was from the early days of his conversion totally immersed in and utterly loyal to Catholic thought, tradition, prayer, liturgy and lived this authentically in his monastic vocation and in dialogue with the modern world."

> —Bishop Fintán Monahan, author of *Peace Smiles, Rediscovering
> Thomas Merton*

"For all that has been written about the fine innerworkings of Merton's expansive mind, most have missed what Hillis demonstrates as the mainspring—his identification with the priesthood and the universalism of the Eucharist, the principle part of his everyday life."

> —Br. Paul Quenon, Abbey of Gethsemani, author of *How to Live,
> and In Praise of the Useless Life*

"In *Man of Dialogue*, Dr. Gregory Hillis unpacks the gift of Thomas Merton as a true man of dialogue and finds his own faith journey in the life of his subject. While acknowledging Merton's complexities and fallible experiences, Dr. Hillis seeks to set the record straight about Thomas Merton's identity throughout his life as a thoroughly and deeply rooted Catholic. This book includes a compelling account of Merton as an active contemplative seeking to be engaged in the joys, sufferings, anguish, and grief of this world and Merton's rich insights and fascinating encounters with a wide array of individuals. *Man of Dialogue* provides a path that diverges from soundbites and quick solutions to the courageous and intelligent path of dialogue so desperately needed by our world."

—Most Reverend Joseph E. Kurtz, Archbishop of Louisville

"Beautifully written, this book paints an engaging, instructive, even inspiring picture of a unique twentieth-century American Catholic. And the undertones of its argument reverberate beyond Merton himself. Who indeed is a Catholic? Someone who fits into the tight confines of a group narrowly defined? Or one who senses the presence of God in the truth, beauty, and goodness of other religious traditions, who finds a world of grace in the struggle for justice, who sees the image of God in everyone walking around at Fourth and Walnut? While focused with great insight on Thomas Merton, this book shines helpful light on the current tension about Catholic identity in the church."

—Elizabeth A. Johnson, CSJ, Distinguished Professor of
Theology Emerita, Fordham University

"Thomas Merton was a faithful Catholic. But his interest in Eastern religions, his challenges to the status quo in the church, and even his ideas about monasticism, have made his Catholicism suspect in some quarters. Greg Hillis's beautifully written and expertly researched book restores Merton's Catholicism to where it should be in studies of his remarkable life: at the center."

—James Martin, SJ, author of *Learning to Pray* and *Jesus:
A Pilgrimage*

"His Holiness the Dalai Lama praised Thomas Merton for introducing him to 'the real meaning of the word "Christian".' In *Man of Dialogue*, for the first time, Gregory Hillis comprehensively mines the breadth and depth of Merton's Catholic Christianity and shows the profound extent of Merton's embrace and commitment to his Catholic faith, his vocation as a Trappist monk at the Abbey of Gethsemani, and as a priest of the Catholic Church."

—Paul M. Pearson, Director, Thomas Merton Center

Man of Dialogue

Thomas Merton's Catholic Vision

Gregory K. Hillis

LITURGICAL PRESS
Collegeville, Minnesota

www.litpress.org

1   2   3   4   5   6   7   8   9

Library of Congress Cataloging-in-Publication Data

Names: Hillis, Gregory K., 1975– author.
Title: Man of dialogue : Thomas Merton's Catholic vision / Gregory K. Hillis.
Description: Collegeville, Minnesota : Liturgical Press, [2021] | Includes index. | Summary: "Illustrates how Merton was fundamentally shaped by his identity as a Roman Catholic"— Provided by publisher.
Identifiers: LCCN 2021025160 (print) | LCCN 2021025161 (ebook) | ISBN 9780814684603 (paperback) | ISBN 9780814684856 (epub) | ISBN 9780814684856 (pdf)
Subjects: LCSH: Merton, Thomas, 1915-1968. | Catholics—Religious identity.
Classification: LCC BX4705.M542 H555 2021 (print) | LCC BX4705.M542 (ebook) | DDC 248.4/82—dc23
LC record available at https://lccn.loc.gov/2021025160
LC ebook record available at https://lccn.loc.gov/2021025161

For Kim

A century ago, at the beginning of the Great War, which Pope Benedict XV termed a "pointless slaughter," another notable American was born: the Cistercian monk Thomas Merton. He remains a source of spiritual inspiration and a guide for many people. In his autobiography he wrote: "I came into the world. Free by nature, in the image of God, I was nevertheless the prisoner of my own violence and my own selfishness, in the image of the world into which I was born. That world was the picture of Hell, full of men like myself, loving God, and yet hating him; born to love him, living instead in fear of hopeless self-contradictory hungers." Merton was above all a man of prayer, a thinker who challenged the certitudes of his time and opened new horizons for souls and for the Church. He was also a man of dialogue, *a promoter of peace between peoples and religions.*

—*Pope Francis, Address to the United States Congress,*
September 24, 2015

CONTENTS

Acknowledgments

I have been reading and working on Thomas Merton for many years, and over the past four years I have had the opportunity to teach an undergraduate class on Merton at Bellarmine University. I am grateful to my students for their insights, observations, and particularly their penetrating questions about Merton. These students influenced my understanding of Merton in a myriad of ways, and their influence is on display on almost every page of this book.

I am fortunate to belong to an academic department that is both collegial and supportive. To my colleagues in the department of theology at Bellarmine University—Hoon Choi, Joseph Flipper, Elizabeth Hinson-Hasty, Justin Klassen, and Deborah Prince—thank you for your kindness and friendship. I'm grateful to have you as colleagues and friends.

Paul Pearson and Mark Meade, respectively director and assistant director of the Merton Center at Bellarmine University, provided assistance to me along the way, particularly in terms of finding material. Both also were consistently available for my questions and queries.

A number of people read through various parts of the book. I am grateful to Renée Roden, Christine Bochen, Elizabeth Johnson, and Paul Pearson for their feedback and encouragement. The esteemed Merton scholar, Patrick F. O'Connell, gave me pre-publication access to three edited volumes of Merton's novitiate conferences.

Faculty at various institutions asked me to give lectures on Merton, and these invitations gave me the opportunity to work through some of my thoughts on Merton's Catholic vision. I am grateful to Timothy O'Malley at the University of Notre Dame, David Hunter at Boston College, Micah Kiel at St. Ambrose University, and Fr. Christian Raab, OSB, at St. Meinrad Seminary. My parish in Louisville, Epiphany Catholic Church, likewise asked me to present some of my research, and the feedback and encouragement from my fellow parishioners was a boon.

I owe a debt of gratitude to my editor at Liturgical Press, Hans Christoffersen. He was receptive to my book from the beginning, and he has been invariably patient when I hit various snags along the way. His encouragement regarding the worth of my project helped me persevere. Stephanie Lancour was likewise patient with me when I felt certain changes needed to be made.

Bellarmine University awarded me a Faculty Development Fellowship to work on this project. This opened up time for writing that I wouldn't otherwise have had, and made it possible to finish the project.

Although the pandemic temporarily put a stop to my visits, I am a regular visitor to the Abbey of Gethsemani. I presented early drafts of two of the chapters at the monastery, and received helpful feedback from the monks, many of whom knew Merton. I want especially to express my gratitude to Fr. Michael Casagram, Br. Frederic Collins, Fr. Lawrence Morey, and Br. Paul Quenon for their hospitality and friendship. I have learned a great deal from each of them, not only about Merton, but also about the contemplative life.

My father, Bruce Hillis, is a constant support, and has been ever since I decided to pursue the academic life. He dutifully reads everything that I publish, and knowing of my interest in Merton, he read through *The Seven Storey Mountain*. I value his love and support more than he could ever know. My mother-in-law, Laura Kauffeldt, has likewise been a wonderful support. She too reads everything that I publish, and isn't shy about telling me how proud she is of me.

Kim Hillis is my spouse and my best friend. She has been on this academic path with me since the very beginning, and has been unfailing in her love for me, even at my most unlovable. She has been a constant fount of encouragement, love, and support. I can't fully express how grateful I am to have you in my life, Kim.

My sons—Isaac, Sam, and Leo—enrich my life in innumerable ways. I have learned through them what it means truly to love unconditionally and to receive unconditional love. Their lives are a gift for which I am eternally grateful. Thank you for being.

As I was writing this book, two close family members passed away suddenly and unexpectedly—my mother, Jeanne Hillis, and my father-in-law, Wayne Kauffeldt. My mom wore her love for me on her sleeve, and she always went out of her way to tell me how proud she was of me. I wish that she were around to see this book in print. I owe her so much. Wayne always made sure to ask me about what I was working on, and I would have loved to talk to him about this book.

> Saints of God, come to their aid! Hasten to meet them, angels of the Lord!
> May Christ, who called them, take them to himself;
> May angels lead them to the bosom of Abraham.
> Eternal rest, grant unto them, O Lord, and let perpetual light shine upon them.
> May they rest in peace.

Gregory K. Hillis
Louisville, Kentucky
December 10, 2020
Feast of Our Lady of Loreto
52nd anniversary of the death of Thomas Merton

Permissions

ABBREVIATIONS TO TITLES
BY THOMAS MERTON

Novitiate Conference Notes

Ci — *Cassian and the Fathers*, Volume 1 of *Initiation into the Monastic Tradition*, Patrick F. O'Connell, ed. (Kalamazoo, MI: Cistercian Publications, 2005)

Cii — *Pre-Benedictine Monasticism*, Volume 2 of *Initiation into the Monastic Tradition*, Patrick F. O'Connell, ed. (Kalamazoo, MI: Cistercian Publications, 2006)

Ciii — *An Introduction to Christian Mysticism*, Volume 3 of *Initiation into the Monastic Tradition*, Patrick F. O'Connell, ed. (Kalamazoo, MI: Cistercian Publications, 2008)

Civ — *The Rule of Saint Benedict*, Volume 4 of *Initiation into the Monastic Tradition*, Patrick F. O'Connell, ed. (Collegeville, MN: Liturgical Press, 2009)

Cv — *Monastic Observances*, Volume 5 of *Initiation into the Monastic Tradition*, Patrick F. O'Connell, ed. (Collegeville, MN: Liturgical Press, 2010)

Cvi — *The Life of the Vows*, Volume 6 of *Initiation into the Monastic Tradition*, Patrick F. O'Connell, ed. (Collegeville, MN: Liturgical Press, 2012)

Cvii — *Charter, Customs, and Constitutions of the Cistercians*, Volume 7 of *Initiation into the Monastic Tradition*, Patrick F. O'Connell, ed. (Collegeville, MN: Liturgical Press, 2015)

Cviii — *The Cistercian Fathers and Their Monastic Theology*, Volume 8 of *Initiation into the Monastic Tradition*, Patrick F. O'Connell, ed. (Collegeville, MN: Liturgical Press, 2016)

Cix   *Medieval Cistercian History*, Volume 9 of *Initiation into the Monastic Tradition*, Patrick F. O'Connell, ed. (Collegeville, MN: Liturgical Press, 2016)

NCi   *A Monastic Introduction to Sacred Scripture*, Volume 1 of *Novitiate Conferences on Scripture and Liturgy*, Patrick. F. O'Connell, ed. (Eugene, OR: Cascade, 2020)

NCii   *Notes on Genesis and Exodus*, Volume 2 of *Novitiate Conferences on Scripture and Liturgy*, Patrick F. O'Connell, ed. (Eugene, OR: Cascade, 2021)

NCiii   *Liturgical Feasts and Seasons*, Volume 3 of *Novitiate Conferences on Scripture and Liturgy*, Patrick F. O'Connell, ed. (Forthcoming from Cascade)

Private Journals

Ji   *Run to the Mountain: The Story of a Vocation*, Volume 1 of *The Journals of Thomas Merton*, Patrick Hart, ed. (San Francisco: HarperSanFrancisco, 1995)

Jii   *Entering the Silence: Becoming a Monk and Writer*, Volume 2 of *The Journals of Thomas Merton*, Jonathan Montaldo, ed. (San Francisco: HarperSanFrancisco, 1996)

Jiii   *A Search for Solitude: Pursuing the Monk's True Life*, Volume 3 of *The Journals of Thomas Merton*, Lawrence Cunningham, ed. (San Francisco: HarperSanFrancisco, 1996)

Jiv   *Turning Toward the World: The Pivotal Years*, Volume 4 of *The Journals of Thomas Merton*, Victor A. Kramer, ed. (San Francisco: HarperSanFrancisco, 1996)

Jv   *Dancing in the Waters of Life: Seeking Peace in the Hermitage*, Volume 5 of *The Journals of Thomas Merton*, Robert E. Daggy, ed. (San Francisco: HarperSanFrancisco, 1997)

Jvi   *Learning to Love: Exploring Solitude and Freedom*, Volume 6 of *The Journals of Thomas Merton*, Christine M. Bochen, ed. (San Francisco: HarperSanFrancisco, 1997)

Jvii   *The Other Side of the Mountain: The End of the Journey*,
         Volume 7 of *The Journals of Thomas Merton*, Patrick
         Hart, ed. (San Francisco: HarperSanFrancisco, 1998)

Letters

Li   *The Hidden Ground of Love: The Letters of Thomas Mer-
         ton on Religious Experience and Social Concerns*, William
         H. Shannon, ed. (New York: Farrar, Straus and Giroux,
         1985)
Lii   *The Road to Joy: The Letters of Thomas Merton to New and
         Old Friends*, Robert E. Daggy, ed. (New York: Farrar,
         Straus and Giroux, 1989)
Liii   *The School of Charity: The Letters of Thomas Merton on
         Religious Renewal and Spiritual Direction*, Patrick Hart,
         ed. (New York: Farrar, Straus and Giroux, 1990)
Liv   *The Courage for Truth: Letters to Writers*, Christine M.
         Bochen, ed. (New York: Farrar, Straus and Giroux,
         1993)
Lv   *Witness to Freedom: Letters in Times of Crisis*, William H.
         Shannon, ed. (New York: Farrar, Straus and Giroux, 1994)

Books

AJ   *The Asian Journal of Thomas Merton* (New York: New Di-
         rections, 1973)
BW   *Bread in the Wilderness* (New York: New Directions,
         1953)
CGB   *Conjectures of a Guilty Bystander* (Garden City, NY: Dou-
         bleday, 1966)
CP   *The Collected Poems of Thomas Merton* (New York: New
         Directions, 1977)
HR   *"Honorable Reader": Reflections on My Work* (New York:
         Crossroads, 1989)

LB	*The Living Bread* (New York: Farrar, Straus and Cudahy, 1956)
LH	*Life and Holiness* (New York: Herder, 1963)
NM	*The New Man* (New York: Farrar, 1961)
NSC	*New Seeds of Contemplation* (New York: New Directions, 1961)
PFP	*Passion for Peace: The Social Essays*, William H. Shannon, ed. (New York: Crossroad, 1995)
PPCE	*Peace in the Post-Christian Era* (Maryknoll, NY: Orbis, 2004)
SC	*Seeds of Contemplation* (New York: New Directions, 1949)
SCel	*Seasons of Celebration: Meditations on the Cycle of Liturgical Feasts* (New York: Farrar, Straus and Giroux, 1965).
SD	*Seeds of Destruction* (New York: Farrar, Straus and Giroux, 1964)
SSM	*The Seven Storey Mountain* (New York: Harcourt, Brace and Company, 1948)
TMA	*Thomas Merton in Alaska: The Alaskan Conferences, Journals, and Letters* (New York: New Directions, 1988)
TMSE	*Thomas Merton: Selected Essays*, Patrick F. O'Connell, ed. (Maryknoll, NY: Orbis, 2013)
ZBA	*Zen and the Birds of Appetite* (New York: New Directions, 1968)

Brief Note on References
Citations to Merton's journal will include the journal volume and the page number, followed by the date of the journal entry.

Citations to Merton's letters will include the volume in which the letter was published, a reference to the writer and recipient of the letter, followed by the date the letter was written.

Brief Note on the Text
Unless otherwise noted, all emphases in quotations from Merton are by Merton himself.

Introduction

MERTON THE CATHOLIC?

Merton was above all a man of prayer, a thinker who challenged the certitudes of his time and opened new horizons for souls and for the Church. He was also a man of dialogue, a promoter of peace between peoples and religions.

—Pope Francis, Address to the United States Congress,
September 24, 2015

Merton and Me

I have a tattoo of a Thomas Merton drawing on my shoulder. It's a simple ink drawing of a monk with his arms folded together, and I've had it for many years. My kids call it "Tom." I first encountered Merton as a newly married undergraduate student in my early twenties. I was an Evangelical Protestant at the time, still part of the tradition in which I had been raised. After getting married in July 1998, my wife and I moved from Calgary, Alberta, to Waterloo, Ontario, so that I could pursue a second undergraduate degree at the University of Waterloo, my first being from an Evangelical Bible college. We had very little money, we were lonely, and I wasn't enjoying my studies as much as I thought I would. While I had dreamed since high school of becoming an academic, I was suddenly confronted with the possibility that perhaps I wasn't going to pursue this dream. I found myself in a vocational crisis, unsure of what direction my life was going to take.

1

Looking for something to read over the Christmas break after my first semester at the University of Waterloo, I looked on my shelf and noticed I had a copy of Thomas Merton's 1948 autobiography, *The Seven Storey Mountain*. I knew little about Merton, and don't remember exactly how I came to be in possession of the book, but I decided to read it. As he himself acknowledged later in his life, there are issues with *The Seven Storey Mountain*. Merton's youthfulness and exuberance are too frequently on display, and it has some stylistic issues that don't feature as prominently in his later writings. However, despite its shortcomings, *The Seven Storey Mountain* hit me squarely between the eyes. In the book, Merton recounted an unusual childhood that involved extensive travel, little in the way of religious instruction or observance, and the loss of both of his parents. He also described his wrestling with religious faith, his conversion to Catholicism, and his eventual decision to become a monk at the Abbey of Gethsemani in Kentucky. The book was for me the story of a man finding meaning and a vocation in life, and as someone in the midst of a vocational crisis, it was a godsend.

After what he later described as a "year of riotous living" during which he was rumored to have fathered a child, Merton lost his scholarship from Cambridge University and resumed his studies at Columbia University in New York (Liv, 286: May 1967). It was at Columbia that Merton began to explore Catholicism, influenced by friends, teachers, and by his reading, and in November 1938 he became a Catholic. Not long after his conversion, Merton felt a call to the priesthood, and particularly to become a Franciscan. However, although he was initially accepted to become a novice with the Franciscans, he was soon rejected by them, in large part because he was a recent convert and there was an impediment to anyone entering the Franciscans who hadn't been a practicing Catholic for three years. Immediately after this rejection, he spoke with a particularly bad confessor who, annoyed by Merton's tears, informed him that he most definitely did not have a calling to the priesthood or to religious life. This led him to conclude that his calling was to be a teacher and writer, and he started teaching English composition and literature at St. Bonaventure College (now University) in upstate New York. But his sense of calling to the priesthood, and particularly to a contemplative life of prayer and silence, nagged at him, even tortured him. He was in the grip of a crisis of vocation, but when a Franciscan finally assured him that he did indeed have a vocation to the priesthood and religious life, Merton left for the Abbey of Gethsemani, a Trappist monastery in Kentucky.

Although our circumstances were very different, I saw myself in Merton's vocational struggles. My heart raced as I read his description of travelling down the road toward the monastery, of seeing the spire of the Abbey church. And when he entered the monastery and was enclosed in what he described as "the four walls of my new freedom," I experienced both relief in knowing that this man's crisis of vocation had been resolved, as well as hope that perhaps my own crisis would find resolution too (SSM, 372).

When I finished *The Seven Storey Mountain*, I started reading everything I could by Merton, particularly his private journals. These journals, published twenty-five years after his death, reveal him at his most candid and revealing. Even though he knew that they would be published at some point, Merton held little back in his journals. He described various conflicts he was having—including conflicts with his abbot, Dom James Fox—and expounded upon his own theological and spiritual struggles. I devoured these journals, not simply because I learned more about Merton, but because, in reading the journals of this monk, I somehow learned more about myself and about the complexities of the spiritual life. Moreover, in reading these journals and then his other works, I came to understand the depth of Merton's Catholicism, and his life and witness played a significant role in my decision to be received into the Roman Catholic Church. When I was received into the church, I took the name "Benedict" as my confirmation name as a conscious remembrance of the saint whose monastic rule Merton lived under during his life as a monk. It was during this time that I received the tattoo of the Merton drawing. While youthful exuberance is perhaps to blame for this tattoo, I don't regret it. Each day it reminds me of the role Merton has played in shaping me as a Christian and, specifically, as a Catholic.

I graduated from the University of Waterloo, and started graduate school at McMaster University focusing my studies on early Christian theology. As I immersed myself in the world of patristic theology, I drifted away from Merton for lack of time. But he was never far from my thoughts, and as I neared completion of my doctorate and a position opened up at Bellarmine University, the home of the Thomas Merton Center (the official repository for Merton's literary estate), I jumped at the opportunity to apply. My office is now located in a building next to the library where the Thomas Merton Center resides, and I live only an hour's drive from the monastery where Merton lived. I write about Merton, teach a class on Merton, and am fortunate to be a regular visitor to the Abbey of Gethsemani as well as the hermitage where Merton spent the last three years of his life. I can't believe my luck.

The Development of Merton's Thought

Of course, the Merton I've experienced isn't necessarily the same Merton others have experienced. People encounter him in different ways, and this is due not only to the diversity of people and their contexts, but also to the fact that he was someone whose interests evolved throughout his life. Moreover, he wrote voluminously, and because of the sheer volume of his writings and the plethora of topics on which he wrote, as well as his willingness to share so openly in his autobiographical works, private journals, and letters, we are able to trace the development of his thinking and of his self-understanding.

I would suggest that Merton's life and thought can be split into two periods. The first period began in 1941 when Merton entered the monastery and goes roughly to the late 1950s. During this period, Merton's writings focused primarily on autobiography as well as on prayer and contemplation, and in these writings Merton's focus tended to be more insular. He often characterized monastic life and life in the world as diametrically opposed, and tended to describe his entry into the monastery as entering a refuge from the pernicious influences of the world. He obviously understood that monastic life had something worthwhile to contribute to the world, and as such, he wrote works about the spiritual life intended for a lay audience. But he did not concern himself overmuch with other facets of life in the world during this period.

His focus, however, began to shift in the late 1950s. His private journals during this time reveal that he was turning his gaze in a more sustained way toward the world as well as to other ways of thinking, including to non-Catholic Christian traditions as well as non-Christian religions. He had a profound experience on the corner of Fourth Street and Walnut Street in Louisville on March 18, 1958, during which he "suddenly realized that [he] loved all the people and that none of them were, or, could be totally alien to [him]," and this experience exemplified a change in perspective whereby he came to recognize that he was fundamentally united with, rather than separated from, the rest of humanity in the world (Jiii, 181-182; March 19, 1958). I will have occasion to write about this experience later, but it is enough to say here that his epiphany at the corner of Fourth and Walnut illustrates a change in perspective that is characteristic of the second period of his life. While he did not stop writing about prayer and contemplation, his writings during this second period also focused on social issues such as the threat of nuclear war and the rise of the civil rights movement. He also devoted significant attention to ecumenical and interreligious dialogue. Indeed, he died in 1968 during a trip to Asia where he was engaged in interreligious dialogue.

How Catholic Was Thomas Merton?

Thomas Merton's life and writings remain well known more than fifty years after his death, but in 2015 he received an added boost from none other than Pope Francis. It was in that year that, during his visit to the United States, Pope Francis surprised many by singling out Thomas Merton during his speech to Congress as one of four great Americans worthy of particular attention. After referring to Abraham Lincoln, Martin Luther King Jr., and Dorothy Day, Pope Francis said the following about Merton:

A century ago, at the beginning of the Great War, which Pope
Benedict XV termed a "pointless slaughter," another notable
American was born: the Cistercian monk Thomas Merton. He
remains a source of spiritual inspiration and a guide for many
people. In his autobiography he wrote: "I came into the world.
Free by nature, in the image of God, I was nevertheless the
prisoner of my own violence and my own selfishness, in the
image of the world into which I was born. That world was the
picture of Hell, full of men like myself, loving God, and yet
hating him; born to love him, living instead in fear of hopeless
self-contradictory hungers." Merton was above all a man of
prayer, a thinker who challenged the certitudes of his time and
opened new horizons for souls and for the Church. He was
also a man of dialogue, a promoter of peace between peoples
and religions.[1]

This was not the first time Merton's name had resounded throughout the House of Representatives; a prayer he wrote for peace was
read in the House by a congressman in 1962. But apart from a brief
reference to Merton by Pope St. John Paul II in a 1990 address to
commemorate the 25th anniversary of *Nostra Aetate*,[2] this was the
first time a pope publicly spoke so highly of the Cistercian monk.

What made Pope Francis's comments particularly significant is
that his references to Merton occurred in the United States, where
official recognition of Merton by the American church has been
muted, to say the least. In 2006 the US Conference of Catholic
Bishops (USCCB) published the *United States Catholic Catechism
for Adults*, a book that was intended to provide an exploration of the
faith for young adults. Each of the chapters of the catechism opens

1. Visit to the Joint Session of the United States Congress: Address of the Holy
Father, Vatican website, September 24, 2015, http://w2.vatican.va/content/francesco
/en/speeches/2015/september/documents/papa-francesco_20150924_usa-us
-congress.html.

2. Address of His Holiness John Paul II for the 25th Anniversary Celebration of
the Declaration "*Nostra Aetate*," Vatican website, December 6, 1990, http://www
.vatican.va/content/john-paul-ii/en/speeches/1990/december/documents/hf_jp-ii
_spe_19901206_xxv-nostra-aetate.html.

with a brief story about a prominent Catholic, many of whom are American. While the catechism includes a vignette on Dorothy Day, to whom Pope Francis also referred in his address, there are no references to Thomas Merton. This was a deliberate choice by the editorial board, chaired by then Bishop Donald Wuerl. Merton was originally to be included among those honored in the catechism, but was deleted for two reasons. First, the committee felt that young adults, for whom the book was targeted, had no idea who Thomas Merton was, and second, in the words of Bishop Wuerl, "we don't know all the details of the searching at the end of his life."[3] In other words, Merton's exploration of Eastern religions and his time in Asia spooked them.

Even before the catechism was published without the deleted Merton biography, there were those who criticized the committee for even thinking about having someone like Merton included in a book designed to teach the faith. Msgr. Michael J. Wrenn and Kenneth D. Whitehead, two catechetical translators, wrote a scathing critique of the first draft of the catechism, with much of their fury focused on the inclusion of a story about Merton as an exemplary Catholic. While acknowledging that Merton was a "gifted writer," they described him as a "lapsed monk . . . a one-time professed Catholic religious, who later left his monastery, and, at the end of his life, was actually off wandering in the East, seeking the consolations, apparently, of non-Christian, Eastern spirituality." They determined that Merton "can scarcely be considered an 'exemplary Catholic,'" and that the very fact that the editors included Merton in the very first chapter of the catechism "casts doubt on their understanding of Catholic teaching and practice."[4]

3. "Catholic Bishops Approve National Adult Catechism," *Pittsburgh Post-Gazette*, November 19, 2004, http://old.post-gazette.com/pg/04324/414174.stm.

4. Msgr. Michael J. Wrenn and Kenneth D. Whitehead, "The New National Adult Catechism Revisited," *Catholic World News*, November 1, 2003, https://www.catholicculture.org/news/features/index.cfm?recnum=26361&repos=4&subrepos=1&searchid=2035765.

A few others have communicated similar concerns about Merton's Catholic identity. Fr. John Hardon, SJ (1914–2000), a priest and theologian who spent about six months with Merton at Gethsemani at the request of his superior, called into question Merton's orthodoxy. In a recording available on YouTube, Fr. Hardon stated that, in his judgment, "Thomas Merton was not fully converted, intellectually, to the Catholic faith." According to Fr. Hardon, Merton had "so deeply imbibed non-Christian, Oriental mysticism that his concept of God was at best vague, and at worst pantheist." He went on in the recording to argue that Merton was to blame for the rise of the New Age movement.[5] Anthony E. Clark, associate professor of history at Whitworth University, echoed the concerns of Fr. Hardon when he wrote that Merton's "commitment to orthodox Catholicism appears suspiciously attenuated by the end of his life."[6] "I think Merton's toying with Asian thought and religion supplanted his Catholic orthodoxy," Clark said in a 2015 interview. Furthermore, he continued, "Merton was a man always in the Church, but one who wrote in his personal journals that he didn't want to be. He seemed to stay in monastic life by default, rather than by commitment."[7]

Merton's reputation has perhaps not been helped by some of his interpreters. For example, Ed Rice, one of Merton's friends from his time at Columbia University, wrote what can best be described as a fanciful and strange book shortly after Merton's death in which he argued that Merton happily left the monastery in 1968 fully in-

---

5. "Fr. John Hardon On: Thomas Merton," *YouTube*, https://youtube /1UGyIRE5H68. Fr. Hardon spoke similarly elsewhere, as evidenced by the transcript of another talk in which he said that Merton "organized a campaign for the movement of what we now call the New Age movement." See "New Age Movement—Q & A Session," *Fr. John A. Hardon, S.J. Archives*, http://www.therealpresence .org/archives/Heresies_Heretics/Heresies_Heretics_004.htm.

6. "Can You Trust Thomas Merton?," *Catholic Answers*, May 1, 2008, https:// www.catholic.com/magazine/print-edition/can-you-trust-thomas-merton.

7. Jim Graves, "The Complex Spirituality of Thomas Merton," *Our Sunday Visitor*, May 27, 2015, https://osvnews.com/2015/05/27/the-complex-spirituality -of-thomas-merton/.

tending never to return, and that he became a Buddhist before his untimely death.[8] Rice based his conclusions primarily on mediums who claimed to have conversations with the deceased Merton. That said, there are plenty of people, Catholic or otherwise, who would agree with Joan Baez's assessment of Merton that he was "a rebel as a Church person,"[9] particularly for his engagement with other Christian and non-Christian traditions. While some, particularly Catholics of a more traditionalist bent, dismiss Merton for this apparent rebelliousness, there are many, particularly non-Catholics who dislike or are indifferent to Catholicism, who embrace Merton for this.

However, depicting Merton as a rebel monk who went against his Catholicism is lamentably inaccurate. Those with a limited conception of Catholicism or only a passing familiarity with Merton's writings may perhaps be excused for thinking that the monk was rebelling against his Catholicism when he turned his attention to social issues like the problems of war and racism, as well as when he engaged in study of and dialogue with practitioners of non-Catholic Christian traditions as well as of non-Christian religions. That Merton got in trouble with Catholics in the United States, particularly for his anti-war writings, is a reality. But the Merton whose books were being burned by American Catholics (who were, in reality, more American than Catholic in their proclivities) in Louisville is the same Merton who received the gift of a papal stole from Pope St. John XXIII as what can be best described as an act of papal solidarity with Merton's anti-war, ecumenical, and interreligious impulses. Moreover, the Merton whose Catholicism continues to be questioned is the same Merton whose grave is venerated by pilgrims from around the world, many of whom leave prayers, sobriety medals, rosaries, and other tokens in recognition for what he has meant to them and what he continues to mean to them.

8. Edward Rice, *The Man in the Sycamore Tree: The Good Times and Hard Life of Thomas Merton* (Garden City, NY: Doubleday, 1970).

9. "Joan Baez," *Merton By Those Who Knew Him Best*, ed. Paul Wilkes (San Francisco: Harper & Row, 1984), 43.

Merton the Catholic

My contention is that we misunderstand Thomas Merton if we see him as someone who felt he had to venture away from his Catholicism in order to speak to issues that became important to him, or as someone who negated or watered down his own Catholicism in order to engage in dialogue with non-Catholic traditions. This book is my attempt to address the question of Merton's Catholicism, to delve into his understanding of himself as a Catholic and his perception of himself within the Roman Catholic Church. I argue that, in order to understand Merton, we need to understand more thoroughly how his thought was intertwined with his identity as a Catholic priest and emerged out of a thorough immersion in the church's liturgical, theological, and spiritual tradition. We shall see that his vision of a church characterized by genuine encounter and dialogue, a church that actively works for justice and peace, is one that developed in conversation with the church's tradition, not against it. Merton did not think he was articulating anything new or revolutionary when he engaged in ecumenical and interreligious dialogue, nor when he spoke out for racial justice and against the threat of nuclear war. He studied his own tradition voraciously and taught that tradition to other monks at the monastery as the Abbey's novice master. And he drew upon that tradition when he advocated for dialogue, peace, and when he spoke out against racism. When he travelled to Asia in 1968, he did not do so as a wayward figure looking to jettison his Christianity to adopt Buddhism. He travelled to Asia as a Catholic Christian devoted to the tradition that had molded him, and he was recognized as such by those he encountered.

To make my case about Merton's Catholicism, this book takes the reader through Merton's life and thought, from his path to conversion prior to entering the monastery to his final trip to Asia where he died. While I draw on a number of books he published during his lifetime, I focus most attention on his private journals and his letters to various friends and acquaintances. Merton's private journals, which he stipulated could only be published twenty-five years after his death, show Merton at his most honest and forthright, and they also reveal the depth of his Catholic formation and identity. His personal letters likewise give us valuable windows into his thinking as he articulated his ideas and perspectives to a wide range of people. In addition to his journals and letters, I focus attention on the conference notes he prepared as a teacher for the novices at the monastery. These notes not only reveal to us what Merton considered most essential for new monks at the monastery to know theologically and spiritually, but they show how deeply knowledgeable and well-read Merton was in the Catholic tradition.

In my exploration of Merton's Catholic identity, I guide the reader chronologically through his life and thought. If you are new to Merton, you will receive a comprehensive overview of his life and thought that will introduce you to who he was as a monk and writer, and also help you understand the dominant theological influences that shaped his identity and thought. If you are already familiar with Merton, my hope is that this book will deconstruct any misconceptions that may have developed over the years about him, and will foster greater understanding of how thoroughly he was shaped by his adopted Catholic tradition.

I have organized my study of Merton's Catholicism as follows. The first chapter, "Merton the Convert," examines Merton's conversion to Catholicism and his decision to become a Trappist monk at the Abbey of Gethsemani in Kentucky. My focus in the chapter will be on the theological and liturgical influences that compelled him not only to become a Roman Catholic but also to enter into one of the most austere religious orders within Catholicism. I will draw particular attention to the depth of Merton's eucharistic devotion, a devotion that would remain with him throughout his entire life.

The second chapter, "Merton the Priest," focuses on Merton's identity as a Roman Catholic priest. I will examine Merton's ordination to the priesthood, and explore the ways in which his identity as a priest shaped his understanding of his role in the church and in the world. We shall see that his daily celebration of the Mass was central to his life and his identity. His life and spirituality revolved around the Eucharist. As part of my examination of Merton's priesthood, I will also look at his opinions regarding the liturgy, particularly his frustration with the liturgical changes that took place after the Second Vatican Council. I do this in part to illustrate how seriously he took his identity as a priest but also to illustrate how difficult it can be to label Merton.

In "Merton the Novice Master," I delve into Merton's role as teacher and spiritual director to Gethsemani's novices, monks learning about monasticism and discerning their vocation as they prepared to take vows to stay at the monastery. In addition to hundreds of hours of audio recordings we possess of Merton's conferences (classes) to the novices, nine volumes of his extensive conference notes have been published, with three more volumes scheduled for publication. Merton's extensive historical and theological knowledge is on full display in these sources, as is his concern for the spiritual well-being of his fellow monks. Moreover, through his conference notes we get a clear understanding of the theological and spiritual priorities he wanted to communicate to the fledgling monks.

A central theme in Merton's conferences to the novices was devotion to Mary, the Blessed Mother. In the fourth chapter, "Merton the Devoted Son of Mary," I explore Merton's Marian devotion, illustrating how important this devotion was throughout his life. Here I will draw on his conferences to the novices, his private journals and letters, *New Seeds of Contemplation*, as well as his poetry.

In the fifth chapter, "Merton the Advocate for Peace," I turn my attention to Merton's anti-war writings of the 1960s. My primary purpose in this chapter will be to explore the theological foundations of his arguments against war and for nonviolence. Merton did not turn to the problem of war to be "with it" or relevant, but did so because, in addition to the fact that humanity was on the verge of self-destruction through a nuclear holocaust, he understood there were pivotal theological principles at stake that other Catholics were lamentably ignoring.

"Merton the Opponent of Racism" follows, and in this chapter I examine his too often neglected writings against racism, exploring how Merton understood racism to affect both society and the church, as well as how he addressed the problem of racism theologically.

I move in a slightly different direction in the seventh chapter, "Merton the Lovestruck." There is no small amount of controversy about Merton's clandestine relationship with a woman over the summer of 1966. My goal in this chapter will not be to defend this relationship, something Merton also refused to do. My focus, rather, will be on giving some context to this relationship, and particularly to look at his own assessment of this affair in the two years following. Merton is too often summarily dismissed on the basis of this relationship, but an examination of the context will hopefully assist readers to understand more thoroughly what took place.

The eighth and ninth chapters focus specifically on Merton's understanding of ecumenical and interreligious dialogue. In the eighth chapter, "Merton the Dialogist," I argue that Merton's clarion call to dialogue emerged out of his profound and deeply Catholic eucharistic theology. I will therefore delve into Merton's eucharistic theology to illustrate that Merton advocated for dialogue not in order to water down the Catholic faith, but because he understood that dialogue is the culmination and consequence of a deeply Catholic understanding of the Eucharist.

In the ninth and final chapter, "Merton the Pilgrim to the East," I examine Merton's engagement in interreligious dialogue in the last decade of his life, with particular focus on the last few months of his life in Asia before his untimely death. As noted above, some critics accuse Merton of watering down his Catholicism and compromising his orthodoxy through his interest in other religions and his dialogue with adherents of these religions. Moreover, some raise concerns that Merton was planning to abandon Catholicism for Buddhism during the final months of his life, pointing both to his interreligious dialogue and the complaints he expressed about the church in his journals. I will address these accusations in the final chapter by examining what Merton hoped to gain through interreligious dialogue, by looking at his critical comments about Catholicism, as well as by focusing on what he had to say about his own identity as a Catholic and a monk in his letters and journals during the last few years of his life.

My hope is that this book will help readers understand that, at the heart of everything Merton did and wrote, he was fundamentally shaped by his identity as a Catholic monk and priest. Far from abandoning his tradition, Merton drew upon that tradition as he called upon the church to be characterized above all by generous love in imitation of Jesus Christ. He was, as Pope Francis noted, a "man of prayer" who, in Merton's own words, endeavored throughout his life "to do God's will . . . offering myself with Christ to the Father" (Jvi, 4: January 3, 1966).

CHAPTER 1

MERTON THE CONVERT

*And my First Communion began to come towards me, down the
steps. I was the only one at the altar rail. Heaven was entirely
mine—that Heaven in which sharing makes no division or dimi-
nution. But this solitariness was a kind of reminder of the singleness with which this Christ, hidden in the small Host, was giving
Himself for me, and to me, and with Himself, the entire Godhead
and Trinity—a great new increase of the power and grasp of their
indwelling that had begun only a few minutes before at the font.*

—Thomas Merton, The Seven Storey Mountain

Introduction

The story of Thomas Merton's conversion to Roman Catholicism and his entry into the Abbey of Gethsemani is one of the most
famous in the history of Christianity. His autobiography, *The Seven
Storey Mountain*, was a surprise bestseller and quickly gained recognition as a classic of Christian spirituality. However, as early as 1950,
just two years after the book was published, Merton was already
distancing himself from his autobiography, writing in his journal
that "*The Seven Storey Mountain* is the work of a man I never even
heard of" (Jii, 458: June 13, 1950). Later in a 1967 mock curricu-
lum vitae written to go with a Festschrift to which he contributed,
Merton humorously referred to his autobiography as creating "a
general hallucination" that was "followed by too many pious books"

(Liv, 286: May 1967). In many ways, the later Merton came to see *The Seven Storey Mountain* as the reflection of a young monk who occasionally allowed the enthusiasm of a convert to cloud his better theological judgement. At the same time, Merton did not disown the book; indeed, there's evidence that he continued to recognize the value of *The Seven Storey Mountain*. Early in 1967, Merton sat down to rank all of his books systematically, graphing them along a spectrum from "awful" to "best." Merton gave none of his books the highest ranking of "best," but he did rank a number of them as "better," a step lower than "best" and a step higher than "good." In this category, alongside *Disputed Questions*, *New Seeds of Contemplation*, and *Conjectures of a Guilty Bystander*, Merton ranked *The Seven Storey Mountain* as among the best books he wrote.[1] Merton evidently understood in 1967 that *The Seven Storey Mountain* still had something to say that continued to reflect his understanding of the Catholic Church and his place in it.

In what follows, I'm going to trace out Merton's description of his path into the Catholic Church, looking at the predominant literary, theological, and liturgical influences that shaped his decision to become a Roman Catholic. I will follow that by exploring Merton's account of his early life as a Catholic, paying particular attention to the eucharistic devotion he cultivated in the years between his conversion to Catholicism and his entry into the Abbey of Gethsemani. My main purpose in doing so is to set the groundwork for demonstrating that the prominent Catholic influences on the early Merton, as well as the early Merton's understanding of Catholicism and Catholic theology, remained consistent throughout Merton's life right up until his death in 1968. And, indeed, I will argue later in the book that Merton's ecumenical and interreligious work, as well as his efforts against war, were the natural flowering of the deeply Catholic influences that shaped Merton as a young Catholic.

---

1. A reproduction of Merton's graph can be found in Thomas Merton, *"Honorable Reader": Reflections on My Work*, ed. Robert E. Daggy (New York: Crossroad, 1989), 151–52.

Merton's Path to Roman Catholicism

By Merton's own account, his childhood exposure to institutional religion was limited. As a child in France, he received some religious instruction from a Protestant minister, and years later at Oakham— a public school in England—he attended the Sunday Church of England liturgy; neither experience impressed him. Shortly after graduating from Oakham, Merton travelled to Rome where he was confronted by the beauty of frescoes and mosaics in churches, and so experienced for the first time an appreciation for Christianity. But it was only when he began his studies at Columbia University that he was seriously influenced by Catholic thought.

There was a confluence of people, books, and events during Merton's time at Columbia University that led to his eventual conversion to Roman Catholicism. The first person who, from Merton's perspective, pointed him in the direction of Rome was actually not Catholic: Mark Van Doren, a poet, literary critic, and renowned teacher at Columbia. Merton was in Van Doren's class on eighteenth-century English literature. It was not the subject that impacted Merton, but the way in which Van Doren taught it. As Merton looked back on the influence of Van Doren on his life, he wrote that Van Doren's impact was subtle but important: "As far as I can see, the influence of Mark's sober and sincere intellect, and his manner of dealing with his subject with perfect honesty and objectivity and without evasions, was remotely preparing my mind to receive the good seed of scholastic philosophy" (SSM, 140). The scholastic philosophy to which Merton referred here is the philosophy of the medieval Catholic theologians, such as St. Anselm of Canterbury and St. Thomas Aquinas, and Merton's point was that he understood Van Doren to have a Catholic approach to study, one that approximated the approach of the medieval scholastics, theologians, and philosophers who delved deeply and seriously into a plethora of philosophical and theological questions, drawing on Christian tradition but also upon ancient philosophers like Aristotle. Merton saw beauty and profundity in Van Doren's approach to literature, and he would encounter such beauty and profundity again when he came into direct contact with scholastic theology and philosophy.

This he did in February 1937 when he picked up a book by a prominent twentieth-century Catholic scholar of medieval theology. Merton was in a course on French medieval literature and was inspired by the course to delve more deeply into medieval thought. While walking past Scribner's bookstore with some money burning a hole in his pocket, he saw in the display window a copy of Étienne Gilson's *The Spirit of Medieval Philosophy*. Gilson (1884–1978) was one of the foremost Catholic intellectuals of the twentieth century. At the time Merton picked up his book, Gilson was Chair of Medieval Philosophy at the Collège de France, a position he held until his retirement, and was already renowned internationally. Merton had no idea who Gilson was, but the table of contents interested him enough to purchase the book. It was on the train ride home that Merton opened the book only to discover the words that signified that it had gone through the official process of review in the Catholic Church, a process that did not imply endorsement by the church, but demonstrated that the book was considered by the church to be free of doctrinal error: *Nihil obstat* and *Imprimatur*. Merton's discovery that he had purchased a Catholic book elicited a "feeling of disgust and deception" within him, and his feelings were rooted in his perception of the Catholic Church (SSM, 171). "While I admired Catholic *culture*," he wrote, "I had always been afraid of the Catholic Church." He had little respect for Catholic dogma, which he understood to be a "fearsome and mysterious thing" and not something that merited serious consideration (SSM, 172). Merton understood religious people to have a conception of God that was laughable: "I had simply taken it for granted that the God in Whom religious people believed, and to Whom they attributed the creation and government of all things, was a noisy and dramatic and passionate character, a vague, jealous, hidden being, the objectification of all their own desires and strivings and subjective ideals" (SSM, 174). This was a God unworthy of belief, but it was the God Merton believed Catholics to worship.

Étienne Gilson's book taught him otherwise. Despite his misgivings, Merton actually read it, and what he read transformed his understanding of Catholic theology. He learned from Gilson about the concept of *aseitas* (aseity in English), a technical term in scholastic theology that describes something essential about God's nature. It "simply means the power of a being to exist absolutely in virtue of itself, not as caused by itself," Merton wrote, "but as requiring no cause, no other justification for its existence except that its very nature is to exist" (SSM, 172–73). This one word helped Merton understand "that the belief of Catholics was by no means the vague and rather superstitious hangover from an unscientific age" (SSM, 172).

What was it about aseity that revolutionized his understanding of Catholicism? Simply put, the concept of aseity stipulates that God is completely other—completely different in being—than the created order in that God exists without cause. Existing as completely other than us, God transcends all our conceptions, all our ways of describing who God is. God is not an object within the universe. God transcends the universe as one without cause who gives existence to that which exists. Merton immediately understood from this concept that everything he thought Catholics believed about God was untrue because the God he thought Catholics worshiped is a being that simply cannot exist. God cannot be "infinite and yet finite; perfect and imperfect; eternal and yet changing—subject to all the variations of emotion, love, sorrow, hate, revenge, that men are prey to" (SSM, 174). God did not create the world because God was forced to do so (there is nothing like God but God, and therefore nothing that could force God's hand), or because God was incomplete in some way without the created order (God is completely self-sufficient and needs nothing outside of himself to be God), or because God wanted to create something to control (such a notion of God would be incongruous with the idea of aseity). Merton realized that his conception of an angry and arbitrary deity bore no resemblance at all to the Catholic understanding of God. Reading the work of an important Catholic philosopher, Merton recognized in Catholicism a seriousness of theological inquiry and thought that he had hitherto not known.

Merton's encounter with *The Spirit of Medieval Philosophy* had an immediate impact on him. He acquired "an immense respect for Catholic philosophy and for the Catholic faith." Moreover, shortly after he finished reading it, the book started to have an effect on him: "I began to have a desire to go to church—and a desire more sincere and mature and more deep-seated than I had ever had before" (SSM, 175). In the chapter immediately before the one recounting his reading of Gilson, Merton described how his life was dominated by fear and concerns as he attempted and failed to find happiness in the pleasures and joys of a worldly experience. Gilson came as something of a lifeline. Whereas he had previously dismissed Christianity as intellectually puerile and so had rejected it as offering anything that could raise him out of his misery, *The Spirit of Medieval Philosophy* demonstrated to him that there was an intellectual vibrancy to Catholic theology that could not be so easily dismissed, and caused him to think more seriously about Catholicism as a possible way forward out of his misery.

While Gilson opened Merton's eyes to the profundity of Catholic theology, another writer, Aldous Huxley (1894–1963), exposed him to the notion of asceticism, a central component of Catholicism that Merton had never considered previously. Huxley was not a Catholic, but he was interested in mystical literature, both the mystical literature that emerged out of Christianity and that which emerged out of Asian religions. On the recommendation of his friend, Bob Lax, Merton purchased Huxley's *Ends and Means*, a book of essays in which he explored various issues facing humanity. What struck Merton particularly about this book was Huxley's insistence that humanity too often catered to what was most base and animalistic, and that this was the cause of much of human strife and war. Huxley argued that to overcome these instincts, humanity needed to practice asceticism, the discipline of self-denial and prayer to attain to deeper spiritual understanding.

Asceticism was not an idea to which Merton had given any attention previously. He had lived his life thus far trying to attain happiness through physical gratification, and while he recognized that he was miserable, he had not conceived of a path to happiness apart from catering to physical pleasure. Huxley, immersed as he was in the ascetic traditions of both east and west, argued that humans were capable of transcending their basest instincts by detaching themselves from all that bound them to worldly things and led them to conflict. He made his case by pointing primarily to Buddhist writings and teachings, but he also quoted important Catholic mystical writers such as St. John of the Cross and St. Teresa of Avila, as well as Meister Eckhart; all of these writers would become important to Merton's later formation as a Catholic and as a monk.

Merton wrote that Huxley's introduction to prayer and asceticism brought "a complete revolution in my mind" (SSM, 185). *Ends and Means* convinced Merton of his "need for a spiritual life, an interior life, including some kind of mortification" (SSM, 187). He soon found himself checking out books on mysticism from the university library. Of course, as Merton admitted, he did not become an ascetic immediately after reading *Ends and Means*, but the book opened Merton up to the possibilities of searching for meaning interiorly.

Another, perhaps even more unlikely, source nudged Merton even further in the direction of Catholicism. Bramachari, a Hindu monk, is one of the most fascinating characters in Merton's autobiography. Bramachari was sent to the United States from India by his abbot who wanted him to attend the 1933 World's Fair in Chicago where there would be a World Congress of Religions. He was sent without money, but still managed to get to Chicago, albeit after the World Congress of Religions ended. By the time Merton met him, Bramachari had been in the country for five years and had managed even to acquire a PhD in Hindu theology from the University of Chicago.

This man made a huge impact on Merton's life. Bramachari recognized in Merton someone on a quest for meaning, and he took it upon himself to provide to Merton some direction. Merton noted that Bramachari never once explained his own religion or religious beliefs; he was apparently uninterested in converting Merton. He instead talked to Merton about the shape of American society and the religious beliefs he had encountered over the past five years. His critiques were those of an ascetic. He expressed amazement that people could live the way they did in America, perpetually busy and bombarded by noise, but as Merton wrote, he "was never sarcastic, never ironical or unkind in his criticisms" (SSM, 196).

Bramachari was critical of religious practice in America, particularly of Protestantism and what he perceived to be an absence of asceticism within Protestant religious observance. However, Bramachari was less critical of Roman Catholicism, and this made an impression on Merton:

> He had gone into a few Catholic churches out of curiosity. He told me that these were the only ones in which he really felt that people were praying. It was only there that religion seemed to have achieved any degree of vitality, among us, as far as he could see. It was only to Catholics that the love of God seemed to be a matter of real concern, something that struck deep in their natures, not merely pious speculation and sentiment. (SSM, 197)

Whether Bramachari was fair in his assessment of Protestantism and Catholicism, the point is that his words made an impact on Merton, as did his reading recommendations. Bramachari told Merton that there were a great many good books of spirituality in the Christian tradition, and that he should read two in particular—St. Augustine's *Confessions* and Thomas à Kempis's *The Imitation of Christ*, both classics of Christian spirituality. In retelling this story, Merton argued that Bramachari's recommendations were providential, and indeed that "one of the reasons why God had brought him all the way from India" was to tell him to read these books (SSM, 198). The ground for Merton's religious quest had been prepared by Gilson and Huxley; Bramachari planted a seed in that ground by pointing Merton in the direction of Roman Catholicism.

There is one more figure who exposed Merton more thoroughly to the Catholic tradition. As part of the research he was doing for his graduate thesis on William Blake, Merton read Jacque Maritain's *Art and Scholasticism*. Like Gilson, Jacques Maritain (1882–1973) was one of the twentieth century's most important Catholic theologians, and through *Art and Scholasticism* Merton learned about the nature of Christian virtue. He wrote that he had previously associated the idea of virtue with a kind of puritanism from which he recoiled. Maritain opened Merton's eyes to the idea that the virtues are the means by which we attain happiness and joy, "the habits which coordinate and canalize our natural energies and direct them to the harmony and perfection and balance, the unity of our nature with itself and with God, which must, in the end, constitute our everlasting peace" (SSM, 204). He learned that, far from being limitations on happiness, the virtues held the key to the kind of eternal happiness that can only occur through union with God.

All of these influences—Gilson, Huxley, Bramachari, and Maritain—provided the intellectual foundation for Merton to seriously explore Roman Catholicism in the late summer of 1938. It was a relatively quick change in religious perspective: "It had taken little more than a year and a half, counting from the time I read Gilson's *The Spirit of Medieval Philosophy* to bring me up from an 'atheist'— as I considered myself—to one who accepted all the full range and possibilities of religious experience right up to the highest degree of glory." Merton was not as yet ready to embrace Roman Catholicism fully, but he was at the point where he respected it intellectually and even "began to desire it" (SSM, 204).

He decided to go to church. Instead of spending the Sunday as he usually did on Long Island with a girl he'd been seeing, he decided to stay in Manhattan to attend a Catholic Mass for the first time. The parish he went to was the Church of Corpus Christi on 121st Street, and the experience there not only moved him closer to conversion, but (as we shall see) it also remained with him throughout his life and shaped his understanding of the importance of good liturgy. While he was suitably impressed by the architecture and art, the "richness and fullness of the atmosphere of Catholicism" of the place, he was especially moved by the people. The first thing he noticed was that the church was full and diverse. He expected the congregation to be comprised primarily of senior citizens, but this was not the case: "It was full not only of old ladies and broken-down gentlemen with one foot in the grave, but of men and women and children young and old—especially young: people of all classes, and all ranks on a solid foundation of workingmen and -women and their families" (SSM,

207). He was particularly taken with the piety of a teenage girl who knelt to pray, not in a way that was intended to impress others, but in a way that simply demonstrated a genuine desire to pray. Merton was struck by this vision of people at prayer, who appeared to have a conception of and relationship with the divine so *real* that they were "more conscious of God than of one another" (SSM, 208). Merton's portrayal is idealistic, but it's clear that he looked upon the faith of these people with both admiration and envy, desiring to have what they had.

As the liturgy progressed, Merton was impressed by the priest's homily. He found that the priest preached the theology Merton was studying, and he did so learnedly yet accessibly. The priest expounded on Christology, focusing on who precisely Christ was and is—fully human and fully God—and did so by drawing on both Scripture and tradition. Merton found the experience exhilarating: "How clear and solid the doctrine was: for behind those words you felt the full force not only of Scripture but of centuries of a unified and continuous and consistent tradition" (SSM, 208–9). The priest was not making up the theology or developing insights on the fly. Rather, the priest knew the tradition well and knew how to talk about theological matters in conversation with that tradition.

Merton was floundering spiritually, and with each new discovery—Gilson, Huxley, Bramachari, and Maritain—he came to stand on what he considered more solid ground, slowly coming to find his own identity in the theology and practice of the Catholic Church. But it was only at Corpus Christi parish that he saw others who not only believed the theology he was reading but lived it out:

> These words, this terminology, this doctrine, and these convictions fell from the lips of the young priest as something that were most intimately part of his own life. What was more, I sensed that the people were familiar with it all, and that it was also, in due proportion, part of their life also: it was just as much integrated into their spiritual organism as the air they breathed or the food they ate worked in to their blood and flesh. (SSM, 209)

Merton saw in the priest and the congregation something he desperately wanted for himself. He was already attracted to the theology, but he wanted the theology to become meaningful for his own life concretely.

Merton didn't stay for the entire Mass; when the bells rang for the consecration of the host, he hurried out of the church. But he left Corpus Christi transformed, at peace and happy. "All I know," he wrote, "is that I walked in a new world." As a result, his reading became more thoroughly Catholic. Interestingly, Merton did not mean that he immersed himself in works of Catholic theology. Rather, he started reading works of Catholic literature, broadly speaking. Merton was already an admirer of James Joyce (1882–1941), the renowned Irish novelist. In what is surely one of the most impressive statements in *The Seven Storey Mountain*, Merton wrote that, by the age of 23, he had already read Joyce's notoriously complex and large novel *Ulysses* at least twice, and possibly three times. However, although he had tried reading *A Portrait of the Artist as a Young Man* years before, Merton could never get through it, always stopping at the part that recounts the narrator's spiritual crisis. At around the time he went to Corpus Christi, Merton picked up the novel again, and this time he was impressed by it, particularly with the infamous sermon on hell. Although Joyce intended the priest's sermon on hell to repulse the reader, Merton loved it. He enjoyed the style of it, and as was the case when he heard the homily at Corpus Christi, he loved the foundation of tradition that undergirded Catholic teaching: "There was something eminently satisfying in the thought that these Catholics knew what they believed, and knew what to teach, and all taught the same thing, and taught it with coordination and purpose and great effect" (SSM, 211). Joyce left the church and had little sympathy with it, but his novels are filled with Catholic imagery and depictions of Catholic life, and Merton was utterly taken with the depiction of Catholicism in Joyce's novels. Although Joyce wasn't solely focused on the church in his novels, "in the background was the Church, and its priests, and its devotions, and the Catholic life in all its gradations, from the Jesuits down to those who barely clung to the hem of the Church's garments" (SSM, 212).

Merton Becomes a Catholic

But while Joyce's Catholic imagination intrigued Merton, the writings and biography of Gerard Manley Hopkins (1844–1889), the English poet and convert to Catholicism, proved to be the catalyst that finally pushed Merton to conversion. Merton was taken both with Hopkins's poetry and notebooks and with his life as a convert to Catholicism and later as a Jesuit. Indeed, it was in the context of reading a biography of Hopkins that he finally made the decision to become a Catholic. Prior to reading this biography, Merton remained indecisive about converting. Something was holding him back from taking the final step, even though he had come to recognize in Catholicism something beautiful, good, and true. But as he sat with this biography of Hopkins, something happened. It was near the end of the summer of 1938 and the news was not good. Germany had invaded Czechoslovakia and war was on the horizon. One rainy day, Merton borrowed G. F. Leahy's biography of Hopkins from the library. Just after lunch, he returned to his room and started reading. He read about Hopkins at Balliol College at Oxford, about Hopkins's desire to become Catholic, and about his letters to John Henry Newman—the English convert to Catholicism canonized in 2019—about becoming Catholic.

What happened next merits full quotation:

> All of a sudden, something began to stir within me, something began to push me, to prompt me. It was a movement that spoke like a voice.
>
> "What are you waiting for?" it said. "Why are you sitting here? Why do you still hesitate? You know what you ought to do? Why don't you do it?"
>
> I stirred in the chair, I lit a cigarette, looked out the window at the rain, tried to shut the voice up. "Don't act on impulses," I thought. "This is crazy. This is not rational. Read your book."
>
> Hopkins was writing to Newman, in Birmingham, about his indecision.

"What are you waiting for?" said the voice within me again. "Why are you sitting there? It is useless to hesitate any longer. Why don't you get up and go?"

I got up and walked restlessly around the room. "It's absurd," I thought. "Anyway, Father Ford would not be there at this time of day. I would only be wasting time."

Suddenly, I could bear it no longer. I put down the book, and got into my raincoat, and started down the stairs. I went out into the street. I crossed over, and walked along by the grey wooden fence, towards Broadway, in the light rain.

And then everything inside me began to sing—to sing with peace, to sing with strength, and to sing with conviction.

I had nine blocks to walk. Then I turned the corner of 121st Street, and the brick church and presbytery were before me. I stood in the doorway and rang the bell and waited.

When the maid opened the door, I said:

"May I see Father Ford, please?"

"But Father Ford is out."

I thought: well, it is not a waste of time, anyway. And I asked when she expected him back. I would come back later, I thought.

The maid closed the door. I stepped back into the street. And then I saw Father Ford coming around the corner from Broadway. He approached, with his head down, in a rapid, thoughtful walk. I went to meet him and said:

"Father, may I speak to you about something?"

"Yes," he said, looking up, surprised. "Yes, sure, come into the house."

We sat in the little parlor by the door. And I said: "Father, I want to become a Catholic." (SSM, 215–16)

Confronted with the story of Hopkins's desire and willingness to become a Catholic, Merton experienced internal conflict about his own hesitancy to take a step that he clearly wanted to take. There was a battle of wills within him, a battle between the part of him that took comfort in delaying having to make a decision and the part of him that desired to embrace Catholicism.

While there is no reason to doubt the veracity of Merton's account above, it is worth noting that Merton seems to have consciously modeled the narrative of his conversion on the famous conversion scene found in book VIII of St. Augustine's *Confessions*,[2] thereby illustrating the influence of Augustine (354–430) on the young monk. Leading up to his conversion, Augustine experienced internal calamity as he struggled with both wanting and not wanting to enter the church. This internal struggle finally reached a breaking point when, while in Milan, he heard two stories of prominent figures converting. As was the case for Merton's reading about Hopkins's conversion, Augustine heard stories of conversion and started immediately to ask why it was that he was delaying what he actually wanted to do. In crisis, Augustine left the house for a garden. In crisis, Merton left his apartment to walk toward Broadway. When Augustine finally resolved to convert, he wrote that he experienced joy and certainty: "The light of certainty flooded my heart and all dark shades of doubt fled away."[3] When Merton resolved to do the same, he wrote something similar: "And then everything inside me began to sing—to sing with peace, to sing with strength and to sing with conviction" (SSM, 216). The moment-of-conversion stories told by Augustine and Merton are not identical. Augustine's took place in a fourth-century house and garden in Milan, while Merton's took place in the bustle of New York City in the twentieth century. At the same time, there's a remarkable similarity between them in terms of the structure and dramatic tenor that illustrates

---

2. Augustine's narrative of his conversion can be found in Saint Augustine, *Confessions*, trans. Maria Boulding (Hyde Park, NY: New City Press, 1997), 137–57.

3. *Confessions*, 157.

both Merton's familiarity with Augustine's autobiography and his conscious desire to model his recounting on the narrative found in *the* classic Catholic autobiography, *Confessions*. While Merton did not appear to have any inkling that his own autobiography would join the ranks of Augustine's *Confessions* as a classic of Catholic spirituality and autobiography, the influence of Augustine's story on the young monk writing about his own conversion is clearly on display.

The New Catholic

Merton received instruction from one of the priests at Corpus Christi parish, and on November 16, 1939, he was conditionally baptized (it was common practice at this time to baptize those who had been already baptized in other Christian traditions if there was any doubt that the original baptism was not validly celebrated) and received his First Communion. While I will write more in a later chapter about Merton's eucharistic theology, it is important to highlight the way in which he wrote about receiving the Eucharist for the first time. The numerous references to the Eucharist throughout the first half of *The Seven Storey Mountain* indicate that Merton's conversion revolved in no small part around his understanding of the significance of the Eucharist, and that this eucharistic devotion continued to be important for the young monk writing the book in the mid-1940s. His words about his First Communion merit full quotation, and they begin with Merton kneeling at the altar rail during the Mass:

> When the little bells were rung I knew what was happening. And I saw the raised Host—the silence and simplicity with which Christ once again triumphed, raised up, drawing all things to Himself—drawing me to Himself . . .
>
> And my First Communion began to come towards me, down the steps. I was the only one at the altar rail. Heaven was entirely mine—that Heaven in which sharing makes no division or diminution. But this solitariness was a kind of reminder of

the singleness with which this Christ, hidden in the small Host, was giving Himself for me, and to me, and with Himself, the entire Godhead and Trinity—a great new increase of the power and grasp of their indwelling that had begun only a few minutes before at the font.

I left the altar rail and went back to the pew where the others were kneeling like four shadows, four unrealities, and I hid my face in my hands.

In the Temple of God that I had just become, the One Eternal and Pure Sacrifice was offered up to the God dwelling in me: the sacrifice of God to God, and me sacrificed together with God, incorporated in His incarnation. Christ born in me, a new Bethlehem, and sacrificed in me, His new Calvary, and risen in me: offering me to the Father, in Himself, asking the Father, my Father and His, to receive me into His infinite and special love—not the love He has for all things that exist—for mere existence is a token of God's love, but the love of those creatures who are drawn to Him in and with the power of His own love for Himself.

For now I had entered into the everlasting movement of that gravitation which is the very life and spirit of God: God's own gravitation towards the depths of His own infinite nature, His goodness without end. And God, that center Who is everywhere, and whose circumference is nowhere, finding me, through incorporation with Christ, incorporated into this immense and tremendous gravitational movement which is love, which is the Holy Spirit, loved me.

And He called out to me from His own immense depths. (SSM, 224–25)

Looking back on this moment, Merton the monk wanted his readers to understand that it was not for him a mere ritual, but a moment of profound significance. Moreover, this passage illustrates the centrality of the Eucharist for the young Merton, a centrality that, as we shall see, never waned. Merton wrote beautifully and poetically—albeit somewhat loquaciously—about the humility of God, a God who is willing to give himself to us hidden in a small host, a God who desires to become one with us through the Eucharist, a God who incorporates us into the divine self out of love. From the perspective of the man writing his autobiography seven years later, this was a moment of tremendous significance, a moment when everything changed for him, when he became one with the God he now called his Father.

It should be noted that it was just before his First Communion that Merton came into contact with a Catholic philosopher who would go on to have an immense influence on his life, even after he entered the monastery—Daniel Walsh (1907–1975). Merton had heard of Walsh through friends, and decided to enroll in his course on St. Thomas Aquinas (1225–1274) for the fall semester. Merton didn't need this course for his MA; in fact, the course took time away from the studies he needed to do for his MA exams in January. But his curiosity, once peaked, could not be contained. He registered for the course and wrote, "Dan Walsh turned out to be another one of those destined in a providential way to shape and direct my vocation."

There were a number of things that impressed Merton about Walsh. He was, to Merton's mind, a superb teacher who endeavored simply to allow the brilliance of St. Thomas's theology to shine through his lectures without inserting himself in the mix. He spoke about the *Summa Theologica* with "childlike delight and cherubic simplicity," and reacted with pure joy when he saw that his students understood the material (SSM, 219). However, what impressed Merton most was the way Walsh understood the Catholic theological enterprise as a whole. Walsh was, according to Merton, "a true Catholic philosopher" who refused to align himself with a particular theological school of thought, who rose above the theological silos by which Catholic theology divides itself, and instead saw "Catholic philosophy in its wholeness, in its variegated unity, and in its true Catholicity." He was quite content to study St. Thomas alongside other scholastic theologians like St. Bonaventure (1221–1274) and Duns Scotus (1266–1308), not as if they were theological enemies proposing radically different conceptions of the Divine. Rather, he saw "them as complementing and reinforcing one another, as throwing diverse and individual light on the same truths from different points of view, and thus he avoided the evil of narrowing and restricting Catholic philosophy and theology to a single school, to a single attitude, a single system" (SSM, 220).

Given the way in which Merton tended throughout his life as a Trappist monk to refuse to situate himself in any particular camp, we cannot underestimate the influence that Walsh had on the young Merton in terms of exposing him to a Catholic way of doing theology. Prior to the Second Vatican Council, when "school theology" was prominent and various theologians situated themselves in one school or the other, Merton consistently articulated a theology that was broad in scope, encompassing the entire tradition, rather than simply the dominant Thomistic tradition. That said, as we will see throughout this book, Merton was deeply influenced by Thomistic theology, both through his own reading of Thomas and through his reading of neo-Thomist theologians like Gilson, Maritain, and Josef Pieper (1904–1997). However, due perhaps to the theological training he received from Walsh, Merton appeared allergic to the idea of subscribing exclusively to one or another camp. This approach to theology became more pronounced with the Second Vatican Council. During the council, and in its wake, Catholicism saw the church split into two camps, which Merton identified as "conservatives" and "progressive." Again, as we shall see, Merton refused to side with one or the other, and indeed sharply criticized both for deficiencies in their approach to ecclesial renewal. Merton's ability to see beyond theological division and to view Catholic theology in its wholeness and catholicity began early in his Catholic journey under the tutelage of Dan Walsh.

However, apart from the influence of Walsh, Merton's first year as a Catholic was not characterized by religious fervor. "I should have begun to pray, really pray," he wrote, but he did not know how to do so, he did not have a spiritual director, nor did he cultivate a devotion to Mary apart from occasionally saying a rosary. Without these things, Merton "simply slipped into the ranks of the millions of tepid and dull and sluggish and indifferent Christians who live a life that is still half animal" (SSM, 229).

A conversation with his friend, Bob Lax, changed this situation. Merton and Lax met while working together on a magazine called *The Jester* during their time at Columbia University. They quickly became close friends and remained so right to the end of Merton's life (Lax lived until September 2000).[4] While Lax would eventually follow Merton into the Catholic Church, he was not yet Catholic when he and Merton had a conversation while walking down Sixth Avenue one evening. At the end of the conversation, Lax turned to Merton and asked pointedly, "What do you want to be, anyway?" Merton was taken aback by the question and didn't quite know how to answer. What he wanted to say was that he hoped to be a famous writer and a noted professor, but he knew that this was not the answer he should give as a Catholic. "I don't know," he said, "I guess what I want is to be a good Catholic." Lax would have none of this answer, asking him to clarify what exactly he meant by "good Catholic." And after hearing Merton's response, Lax very matter-of-factly told Merton how he should have answered:

"What you should say"—he told me—"what you should say is that you want to be a saint."

A saint! The thought struck me as a little weird. I said:

"How do you expect me to become a saint?"

"By wanting to," said Lax, simply.

"I can't be a saint," I said, "I can't be a saint." And my mind darkened with a confusion of realities and unrealities: the knowledge of my own sins, and the false humility which makes men say that they cannot do the things that they *must* do, cannot reach the level that they *must* reach: the cowardice that says: "I am satisfied to save my soul, to keep out of mortal sin,"

---

4. For an excellent overview of Lax's life see Michael N. McGregor, *Pure Act: The Uncommon Life of Robert Lax* (New York: Fordham University Press, 2015).

but which means, by those words: "I do not want to give up my sins and my attachments."

But Lax said: "No. All that is necessary to be a saint is to want to be one. Don't you believe that God will make you what He created you to be, if you will consent to let Him do it? All you have to do is desire it." (SSM, 237–38)

Lax's statements hit Merton hard, and when he confirmed with Mark Van Doren that Lax's understanding of Christianity was, to his mind, the correct understanding, Merton was convicted.

He soon bought an expensive copy of the first volume of the collected works of St. John of the Cross (1542–1591), reading and underlining the first few pages. While St. John of the Cross did not make an immediate impact—Merton wrote that he understood the words on the page to be significant but that they "were all too simple for me to understand" (SSM, 238)—it is noteworthy that, after his convicting conversation with Lax, he turned to the mystics and specifically to one of the most important mystical theologians in Western Christianity, one recognized as a Doctor of the Church. Even though Merton didn't really understand what he was reading, this initial exposure to John of the Cross obviously made an impact insofar as it nudged him, however imperceptibly, that much further toward a contemplative vocation. Moreover, St. John of the Cross came to play a huge role in Merton's understanding of the contemplative life. One of his early books, *The Ascent to Truth* (1951), is essentially an in-depth exploration of St. John of the Cross's mystical theology, and his interest in the Spanish mystic continued throughout his life. The notes Merton wrote for his course for novices at the monastery on Christian mysticism contain an extended section on John, and the last book he submitted for publication before his death, *The Climate of Monastic Prayer*, also contain numerous references to him.[5]

---

5. Thomas Merton, *The Climate of Monastic Prayer* (Collegeville, MN: Liturgical Press, 2018).

Merton spent the summer after this conversation writing alongside close friends from Columbia at a cottage owned by Lax's brother-in-law near St. Bonaventure College in upstate New York. He described the summer as being idyllic yet filled with conflict as he struggled with trying to put into practice what he knew he needed to do—strive for sanctity—after his conversation with Lax. Returning to New York City in August, Merton returned to a world teetering on the brink of war, and when war was finally declared after the bombing of Warsaw, he experienced the kind of crisis that often accompanies events that make one confront suffering and mortality. Merton heard about the bombing on his way to High Mass, and so went to the liturgy conscious of the tenuousness of the world around him. In the midst of the chaos of a world at war, Merton was struck by the solidity, the permanence of the church, and the eternality of God's love: "[The Church] was thanking Him *in* the war, *in* her suffering: not for the war and for the suffering, but for His love which she knew was protecting her, and us, in this new crisis. And raising up her eyes to Him, she saw the eternal God alone through all these things, was interested in His action alone, not in the bungling cruelty of secondary causes, but only in His love, His Wisdom" (SSM, 250). The liturgy clearly made an impact on Merton that day, and as he received the Eucharist, he was conscious both of his own sin and of the eternality and love of God even in the midst of war.

Calling to the Priesthood

It was shortly after this Mass that Merton suddenly came to a conclusion about his vocation. A group of friends had stayed long into the night at Merton's apartment, and they all eventually fell asleep. They woke late in the morning, and by early afternoon they were ready for breakfast, which Merton procured from a local restaurant. As they sat eating and listening to records, the idea that he should become a priest and enter a monastery suddenly came to him and he casually mentioned this to his friends, none of whom took him seriously. But after they left, Merton felt compelled to leave his apartment and make his way to St. Francis Xavier parish on Sixteenth Street. He had never visited this church and didn't know why he wanted to go there, but instinct told him to enter. When he arrived, the church looked empty and the doors were locked. However, he noticed a basement door hidden under the main stairway that led up to the main doors. There was nothing noteworthy about the door; indeed, Merton says that under normal circumstances he would not have noticed it at all, but that, having seen it, something within him prompted him to go in. He entered and realized he was in the lower church where people had gathered for Eucharistic Adoration. As he sat down, the people began singing the *Tantum Ergo*, the penultimate verse of St. Thomas Aquinas's hymn to the Blessed Sacrament.

And as he gazed upon the monstrance containing the consecrated host, Merton realized that he was faced with a choice, that he had been called into that parish to answer a question posed to him by God: "Do you really want to be a priest? If you do, say so." The hymn ended, the priest lifted the monstrance to bless the people, and it was at that moment that Merton answered the call to the priesthood:

> I looked straight at the Host, and I knew, now, Who it was that I was looking at, and I said:
>
> "Yes, I want to be a priest, with all my heart I want it. If it is Your will, make me a priest—make me a priest."
>
> When I had said them, I realized in some measure what I had done with those last four words, what power I had put into motion on my behalf, and what a union had been sealed between me and that power by my decision. (SSM, 255)

Months earlier, walking down the street with his friend, Merton struggled to find a response when told by Lax that, as a Catholic, he should want to become a saint. He was filled with ambition to become a great writer and an accomplished professor. A life devoted to God, a life lived in obedience to the will of God, was far from his mind. But that conversation with Lax convicted Merton, led him to realize that he needed to give the totality of himself to God, and in the basement of St. Francis Xavier church, gazing upon Christ made humbly present in the eucharistic bread, Merton chose to set aside his worldly ambitions in order to strive to become the saint Lax told him he needed to become. For Merton, this meant accepting a calling from God to the priesthood, a calling he now pursued unreservedly.

It is significant that Merton's decision to become a priest occurred in a eucharistic context, for reasons that will become more clear when I look at Merton's understanding of himself as a priest and his eucharistic theology. I have already referred to Merton's effusive description of his First Communion. This description contained, of course, the monk's thoughts while reflecting back on his experience, but it indicates the degree to which Merton's Catholic identity revolved around his understanding of the centrality and profundity of the Eucharist. Merton's decision to become a priest, his willingness to say yes to what he perceived to be God's calling, was the most important decision of his life as a Catholic. Everything hung upon it. And it was a decision Merton made in the midst of eucharistic adoration, while gazing upon Christ in the monstrance. This would not be the last time that something of significance happened to Merton in the context of the Eucharist, nor will it be the last time we get a glimpse of the depth of Merton's eucharistic theology and piety.

As classes began again, Merton turned to Dan Walsh, the theologian whose teaching and theology so impressed him. They met in a bar, and as Merton wrote, through Walsh "Christ impressed the first definite form and direction about my vocation" (SSM, 260). Walsh told Merton that he was not surprised by this calling to the priesthood, and mentioned that he thought he had such a vocation from the moment the two met. Walsh proceeded to tell Merton about the plethora of religious orders within Roman Catholicism, from the Jesuits through to the Benedictines. It was clear to both Walsh and Merton that the diocesan priesthood was not in the cards, most likely because both realized that Merton was called to solitude of some sort, both to pray as well as to write. Walsh was most enthusiastic about the Trappists and had spent the previous summer on retreat at Our Lady of Gethsemani in Kentucky. But when he suggested the

Trappists to Merton, Merton would have none of it, arguing that he was capable only of living out a religious rule that was less stringent than that followed by the Cistercians of the Strict Observance. Far from being attracted to the Trappist life, Merton was initially terrified of it. However, when Walsh mentioned the Franciscans, Merton expressed more enthusiasm. He saw in the Franciscans an authentic Christian spirituality rooted in the life and teachings of St. Francis, a saint who would always maintain an important place in Merton's devotion. He had already visited a Franciscan college with Lax, St. Bonaventure College (now St. Bonaventure University) in upstate New York, and he was impressed by the simplicity and peace that permeated the atmosphere there. It was this simplicity and peace that attracted him to the Franciscans, not the "tremendous and heroic poverty" that is central to the Franciscan charism (SSM, 261). As he admitted, one of the things that attracted him to the Franciscans was his mistaken perception that their Rule seemed rather easy, as he felt he was incapable of following any religious rule that was too stringent and demanding. Convinced that the Franciscans were the right fit for him, Merton received from Walsh an introductory note for a Franciscan friend of his at the monastery of St. Francis of Assisi.

Merton soon met with Fr. Edmund, Walsh's friend, and arrangements were made to enter the novitiate the following August. Far from being the lackadaisical Catholic he was previously, Merton became increasingly disciplined in his spiritual life: "Now, at last, God had become the center of my existence" (SSM, 266). He began to live a far more structured spiritual life. He became a daily communicant and went frequently to confession. Moreover, while he acknowledged that he was still unpracticed in prayer, it was during this time that he attempted "mental prayer," by which Merton appears to mean prayer rooted in silent meditation. He also purchased for himself a copy of St. Ignatius of Loyola's *Spiritual Exercises* and went through them on his own, an hour a day for thirty days.[6] The

---

6. See Ji, 135 (January 13, 1940), where Merton refers to going through the *Spiritual Exercises*.

Spiritual Exercises introduced Merton to something approaching contemplative prayer, however distracted he found himself.

In the spring of that year, he left for a trip to Cuba where he decided he would go on pilgrimage to the Basilica of Our Lady of Cobre. The pilgrimage was for him transformational, and his description of it both in his personal journal as well as in *The Seven Storey Mountain* demonstrates that Merton fully immersed himself in the sacramental life while in Cuba. Living in New York, he was attending daily Mass and spending periods of time in prayer each day. But the culture of New York was not one infused with Catholic culture. However, in Cuba Merton experienced Catholic culture for the first time *as a Roman Catholic*. In *The Seven Storey Mountain* Merton described Cuba as a kind of Catholic wonderland where he could wander in and out of churches in which Mass was continually being said: "Everywhere I turned, there was someone ready to feed me with the infinite strength of the Christ Who loved me." While in New York he could make the Eucharist part of each day, in Cuba "everything lent itself to Communion" (SSM, 280).

Cuba deeply shaped Merton's eucharistic imagination, particularly his understanding of the profundity and depth of the eucharistic sacrifice, and indeed, the climax of his pilgrimage occurred at a Franciscan church in Havana where Merton appeared to have, if not a mystical experience, at the very least a profound experience of the transcendent. Merton wrote that he had already been to Mass at another church, but that he came to the Church of St. Francis to hear yet another Mass. He saw as he entered a large group of children seated in rows at the front of the church though he didn't know why they were there. The priest consecrated the bread and the wine, and after he placed the chalice back on the altar after raising it aloft, the children began loudly to recite the creed in Spanish: "Creo en Diós. . . ." It was at that moment that, as Merton wrote in his journal, "something went off inside me like a thunderclap" (Ji, 218: April 29, 1940). Merton described the experience in his autobiography:

As sudden as the shout and as definite, and a thousand times more bright, there formed in my mind an awareness, an understanding, a realization of what had just taken place on the altar, at the Consecration: a realization of God made present by the words of Consecration in a way that made Him belong to me.

But what a thing it was, this awareness: it was so intangible, and yet it struck me like a thunderclap. It was a light that was so bright that it had no relation to any visible light and so profound and so intimate that it seemed like a neutralization of every lesser experience.

And yet the thing that struck me most of all was that this light was in a certain sense "ordinary"—it was a light (and this most of all was what took my breath away) that was offered to all, to everybody, and there was nothing fancy or strange about it. It was the light of faith deepened and reduced to an extreme and sudden obviousness.

It was as if I had been suddenly illuminated by being blinded by the manifestation of God's presence . . .

This contact was not something speculative and abstract: it was concrete and experimental and belonged to the order of knowledge, yes, but more still to the order of love . . . It was love as clean and direct as vision: and it flew straight to the possession of the Truth it loved.

And the first articulate thought that came to my mind was:

"Heaven is right here in front of me: Heaven, Heaven!"

It lasted only a moment: but it left a breathless joy and a clean peace and happiness that stayed for hours and it was something I have never forgotten. (SSM, 284–85)

Merton's description of this experience in his private journal is similarly effusive: "The unshakeable certainty, the clear and immediate knowledge that heaven was right in front of me, struck me like a thunderbolt and went through me like a flash of lightning and seemed to lift me clean up off the earth" (Ji, 218: April 29, 1940).

It was not often that Merton wrote this way about an experience. To my mind, there are only three other places in his writings in which he described having a transformative experience of something that seems to defy adequate description—an experience in Rome in which he sensed the presence of his father, his awakening at the corner of Fourth and Walnut in Louisville on March 18, 1958, and his encounter with the transcendent before the statues of the Buddha at Polonnaruwa in Sri Lanka during his final trip to Asia in 1968; the latter two I will discuss in further detail later in the book. In the case of his experience in Havana at the Church of St. Francis, what we see here is a deeply Catholic awakening to the mystery and profundity of the Eucharist. As already noted, Merton had been attending daily Mass in New York, and it was during Adoration of the Blessed Sacrament at St. Francis Xavier church that he came to the decision that he was called to the priesthood. It's clear, therefore, that the Eucharist had come to play a central role in Merton's early life as a Catholic. However, his experience in Havana brought him to another level of comprehension of the Eucharist, one rooted in the experience of the Eucharist in terms of divine love. While he previously understood what the Eucharist was about in terms of Christ's Real Presence in the bread and in the wine, Merton was overwhelmed by an experience of the Eucharist as a manifestation of God's love, a love that went beyond intellectual knowledge:

> It ignored all sense experience in order to strike directly at the heart of truth, as if a sudden and immediate contact had been established between my intellect and the Truth Who was now physically really and substantially before me on the altar. But this contact was not something speculative and abstract: it was concrete and experimental and belonged to the order of knowledge, yes, but more still to the order of love. Another thing about it was that this light was something far above and beyond the level of any desire or any appetite I had ever yet been aware of. It was purified of all emotion and cleansed of everything that savored of sensible yearnings. It was love as clean and direct as vision: and it flew straight to the possession of the Truth it loved. (SSM, 285)

In his 2005 encyclical, *Deus Caritas Est* (God Is Love), Pope Benedict XVI described the Eucharist primarily as an encounter with divine love:

> The ancient world had dimly perceived that man's real food—what truly nourishes him as man—is ultimately the *Logos*, eternal wisdom: this same *Logos* now truly becomes food for us—as love. The Eucharist draws us into Jesus' act of self-oblation. More than just statically receiving the incarnate *Logos*, we enter into the very dynamic of his self-giving. The imagery of marriage between God and Israel is now realized in a way previously inconceivable: it had meant standing in God's presence, but now it becomes union with God through sharing in Jesus' self-gift, sharing in his body and blood. The sacramental "mysticism," grounded in God's condescension towards us, operates at a radically different level and lifts us to far greater heights than anything that any human mystical elevation could ever accomplish.[7]

Pope Benedict went on in the following paragraph to write that such an encounter with divine love, if truly experienced and understood, cannot but transform us individually and communally to love God and others. While the pope did not suggest that one needs to have a transcendent experience like the one Merton had in Havana, it seems clear that what Merton experienced was an overwhelming sense of the kind of divine love Benedict described above. The sheer depth of God's love, manifested in the humility of his condescension to become one with us in the Eucharist, became completely present to Merton. As will be seen when we examine Merton's eucharistic theology, he never lost his sense of the profundity of divine love manifested in the Eucharist. This experience "was something I have never forgotten," and it seems that it lived with Merton throughout his life (SSM, 285).

7. Pope Benedict XVI, *Deus Caritas Est* 13, Vatican website, December 25, 2005, http://w2.vatican.va/content/benedict-xvi/en/encyclicals/documents/hf_ben-xvi _enc_20051225_deus-caritas-est.html.

A Crisis of Vocation

Merton returned home from Cuba full of peace, enthusiastic about joining the Franciscans. However, while out at the cottage in upstate New York, he began to have some doubts about his vocation. All kinds of questions about his vocation began to whirl about his mind to the point that he woke up one morning and the peace he had enjoyed for the previous six months was gone. These doubts seemed to come out of nowhere: "the blow fell suddenly" (SSM, 294). His desire to become a Franciscan and a priest still remained, but his certainty that this was the life to which he was called by God was replaced by an agonizing doubt that left him with the sense that everything he thought was certain about his future and his identity was now up in the air. His doubts were rooted in no small part in the fact that he had not revealed everything about his former life before his conversion to Catholicism to Dan Walsh or to Fr. Edmund, the Franciscan who accepted him. The Franciscans had agreed to accept him into the novitiate, but they had done so without actually knowing who he really was. Merton thus felt compelled to disclose his former life to Fr. Edmund. Precisely what he said to Fr. Edmund is unclear, but what is clear is that Merton's comments, as well as his status as a new convert, gave the Franciscan pause. He asked Merton to return the next day, and when he did, Fr. Edmund informed him that he should withdraw his application to the novitiate. Merton was devastated. He left the Franciscan friary and went into a parish belonging to the Capuchins to think things over. He went into the confessional and broke down, unable to speak through his tears. The priest was evidently unimpressed with Merton's behavior and told him, in no uncertain terms, that he most definitely did not have a vocation to the priesthood. Merton left with the tortured belief that he did not have a vocation to the one thing that he longed for above everything else—the monastic life and the priesthood.

Interestingly, faced with this supposed realization that he was not called to religious life, Merton didn't slip back into a lackadaisical practice of his faith, which would perhaps have been an understandable reaction. Rather, he decided that, even if he wasn't called to the monastic life, he was going to live out the monastic life as fully as he could while living in the world. He purchased four breviaries in order to pray the daily offices of prayer, offices then generally only prayed by priests and religious. Merton wrote that this decision to pray the offices was transformational for him, particularly as these prayers directed him more fully to center his life around the Eucharist given that the entire liturgy, including the offices of prayer, centered around the Mass. Moreover, Merton noted that it did not take long before he began to realize that God was transforming him through his prayer:

> I would be able, after not so many months, to realize what was there, in the peace and the strength that were growing in me through my constant immersion in this tremendous, unending cycle of prayer, ever renewing its vitality, its inexhaustible, sweet energies, from hour to hour, from season to season in its returning round. And I, drawn into that atmosphere, into that deep, vast universal movement of vitalizing prayer, which is Christ praying in men to His Father, could not help but begin at last to live, and to know that I was alive. (SSM, 302)

He was immersing himself more fully in the liturgy of the church, devoting himself as fully as possible to a prayer-filled life in the world.

He also made the decision to become a Third Order Franciscan, which for him meant being able to keep to a particular religious rule even without wearing a monastic habit. Merton soon sought out a job teaching at a Catholic college, and his decision to do so was tied as much, if not more, to his Eucharistic devotion as it was to his desire for employment. He wanted to teach, but more than that, he wanted to "live under the same roof as the Blessed Sacrament" (SSM, 300). In short, Merton chose to live the life of a lay-contemplative, someone called to a life of prayer even if not called to formal religious life. His hope? "All I knew was that I wanted grace, and that I needed prayer, and that I was helpless without God, and that I wanted to do everything that people did to keep close to Him" (SSM, 301).

Merton soon got a job teaching English at St. Bonaventure College. He lived in a small room near where the friars also lived. He adopted a semi-monastic life, spending long periods of time in solitude and in prayer, and in yet another display of eucharistic piety, he attributed his spiritual growth during this time to "the God Who lived under that same roof with me, hidden in His Sacrament, the heart of the house, diffusing His life through it from the chapel Tabernacle" (SSM, 304–5). Lest one perhaps think this eucharistic piety reflects the spirituality of a young monk, it is worth noting that Merton expressed himself similarly in a 1966 letter to Anthony L. Bannon, an editor of the diocesan newspaper for Buffalo, in response to the latter's request for some reflections on his time at St. Bonaventure. Merton told Bannon that his time at St. Bonaventure was one of the happiest periods of his life, and that, although it was a transitional period in his life, his time there was absolutely pivotal in leading him finally to the Abbey of Gethsemani: "Living there in that quiet atmosphere, *under the same roof with the Blessed Sacrament,* I was able to cut out drinking and smoking and with my head clear I was discovering a lot of new things about life: namely, that it could be pretty good if you gave it half a chance" (Lv, 163; TM to Anthony L. Bannon: February 12, 1966, emphasis added). It is noteworthy that, twenty-five years after leaving St. Bonaventure, and eighteen years after publishing *The Seven Storey Mountain*, Merton continued to emphasize that the highlight of teaching there was living close to the tabernacle where Christ was present.

Becoming a Trappist

During Holy Week of 1941, Merton went on retreat at the Trappist Abbey of Gethsemani in Kentucky. Although he reacted with horror when Dan Walsh mentioned the Trappists to him when he was contemplating a vocation to the religious life, something opened up in him while at St. Bonaventure, "something that required, demanded at least a week in that silence, in that austerity, praying together with the monks in their cold choir" (SSM, 310). In preparation for his retreat, he went to the library and read entries in the *Catholic Ency-clopedia* about the Cistercians. In the process, he came across entries for the Carthusians and the Camaldolese, two other contemplative orders that placed even more emphasis on silence and solitude than the Cistercians. Merton was taken with the descriptions of silence and solitude, but tortured by his belief that he did not have a voca-tion to monastic life.

His retreat to the Abbey of Gethsemani was a remarkable ex-perience for him, and his recounting of this retreat, both in *The Seven Storey Mountain* and in his personal journal, is replete with eucharistic references that demonstrate the degree to which his eu-charistic understanding was central to his understanding and practice of the Catholic faith, as well as to his calling to become a Trappist at Gethsemani.

The opening lines of his first journal entry at Gethsemani illustrate how immediately taken he was with the place: "I should tear out all the other pages of this book and all the other pages of everything else I ever wrote, and begin here. This is the center of America. I had wondered what was holding this country together, what has been keeping the universe from cracking in pieces and falling apart. It is this monastery if only this one" (Ji, 333: April 7, 1941). On Wednesday of Holy Week, Merton reflected in his journal about the structure of life at the monastery, and particularly about the significance of structuring the day, and indeed the whole of existence, around the Eucharist. It's clear from his entry that he found a life centered around the Eucharist deeply attractive. He thought the other offices of the day at the monastery were beautiful, and he singled out Compline and the *Salve Regina* at the end of the day as being particularly moving. But Merton was struck by how everything at Gethsemani culminated in the Mass. The Eucharist was not something that was part of each day, or simply another thing to do. It was the very purpose of monastic existence. When Merton compared this existence to his own in his personal journal, he was struck by the sharp contrast:

> And for me, what has Mass been? Something that begins the
> day. But the important work of the day has been teaching and

writing, and this is all wrong. I can say it, now, because I see it confusedly. How long is it going to take me to live this truth, and find this true balance in my life? Through how many tribulations? How will I find all the pieces of this truth, that tells me I must belong to God, not to myself: and so far all I have thought about has been myself, even kneeling before God in His tabernacles, even at Mass, asking Him to give and give me more, never thanking Him for anything, praising myself for everything He gave me. (Ji, 341: April 9, 1941)

In this journal entry, he acknowledged that his attraction to the liturgy was partly an aesthetic one, and that while the aesthetic element was important, the liturgy is about so much more:

To love the Liturgy merely because it is the greatest art the world has ever seen or dreamed of is to crucify Christ all over again. To make His passion nothing but a drama that stimulates our emotions like any other good drama is to be Pilate and Caiaphas and all His executioners in one—it is to be Judas. That is to take Christ's passion, in the Holy Mass, for ourselves, as a luxurious enjoyment to our senses and our minds. Because the Drama of the Liturgy is not there to please us but to *kill* us: in that Drama we must die, or we are Judases, betrayers. (Ji, 342)

The Eucharist is intended to take us out of ourselves, away from our selfishness and toward others. "Charity begins in the love of God," he wrote in the same entry, "and that centers in Mass" (Ji, 341). To make the Mass about one's own personal satisfaction is so selfish as to be, in Merton's words, "satanic" (Ji, 342). Rather, a life centered around the Eucharist, around the liturgy that manifests that generous love of God, is a life that takes one out of one's self in generous love toward others. It is, in other words, a life dominated by love.

When Merton looked at the monks at the Abbey of Gethsemani, this life of love was precisely what he saw. In *The Seven Storey Mountain*, Merton recounted how profoundly moved he was by the first Mass he attended at the abbey, putting into the mouth of Christ what he felt during the liturgy:

"Do you know what Love is? You have never known the meaning of Love, never, you who have always drawn all things to
the center of your own nothingness. Here is Love in this chalice
full of Blood, Sacrifice, mactation. Do you not know that to
love means to be killed for the glory of the Beloved? And where
is your love? Where is now your Cross, if you say you want to
follow Me, if you pretend to love Me? . . . But these men are
dying for Me. These monks are killing themselves for Me: and
for you, for the world, for the people who do not know Me,
for the millions that will never know them on this earth."
(SSM, 324)

Merton was overwhelmed by what he perceived to be an existence
not only temporally structured around the Mass, but existentially
structured around it so as to live out the love experienced in the
Eucharist.

"After Communion," he wrote, "I thought my heart was going
to explode" (SSM, 324). Why? Because he believed that he was
not called to this life centered around the Eucharist, even though
he desperately wanted this life. He made the Stations of the Cross
in the abbey church on Easter Sunday before leaving, all the while
grieving that this life was forever barred to him. He found himself
deeply attracted to their life of solitude and prayer, a life revolving
around the Eucharist, but he was "tortured" with the realization
that such a life could never be his (SSM, 328). While this vocational
crisis would soon get resolved, the point I want to draw out is that
Merton's attraction to the Cistercians was rooted not simply in an
attraction to solitude and contemplation, but was primarily rooted
in the deep devotion to the Eucharist that had become central to
his identity as a Roman Catholic. It was one thing for him to live
under the same roof as the Blessed Sacrament and to participate daily
in Mass, both of which marked his existence at St. Bonaventure. It
was another thing altogether to throw oneself headlong into a life
of wholehearted and lovingly generous self-sacrifice made possible
by a eucharistically centered existence, which is what he understood
the monks at Gethsemani to be doing. Merton longed to emulate

their example. Unfortunately, after his experience in the Capuchin church and the priest who told him that he definitely had no vocation to monastic life or the priesthood, Merton believed that the life for which he longed was an impossibility for him. "I wished it was not impossible," he wrote in his journal after returning from the monastery (Ji, 356: April 18, 1941).

A few months after returning to St. Bonaventure College, Merton met the impressive figure of Baroness Catherine de Hueck who had come to the college to talk to the priests, religious, and students about the work she was doing in Harlem. Following a calling to be poor among the poor, de Hueck created Friendship House in Harlem, a place of refuge and love in the midst of poverty. Merton found her inspiring, and recognized in her life the Franciscan apostolate of poverty to which he was attracted when he initially pursued his vocation with them. He therefore asked de Hueck if he could come to Friendship House for a few weeks with the idea that perhaps this was the life to which he was called.

Without knowing it at the time, his decision to spend some time at Friendship House would finally lead him back to the Trappists. While he was inspired by his experience in Harlem, the idea of entering the Abbey of Gethsemani recurred continually. In the fall, after he had returned to St. Bonaventure, de Hueck again came to the college and asked Merton directly if he would like to return to Harlem to stay. Merton was caught off guard by the question, but he resolved at that moment to leave St. Bonaventure in January to live in Harlem at Friendship House. He immediately went to the president of the college to let him know that he would be moving to Harlem in January and that he therefore needed to find someone to take his place for the forthcoming term. While he was not convinced that he was definitely called to live out his life at Friendship House, he had come to the conclusion that he was no longer called to teach at the college. "Harlem may be a vocation," he wrote, "but Saint Bonaventure isn't. Ever since I came here I have not regarded the place as anything permanent for myself" (Ji, 449–50: November 4, 1941). While he enjoyed being at the college, he was left with the sense that he was still in full possession of his will there. He did not have to give up anything to be at the school. "It demanded nothing of me," he wrote in *The Seven Storey Mountain*. "It had no particular cross. It left me to myself, belonging to myself, in full possession of my own will" (SSM, 359). Perhaps going to Harlem would provide the cross that he felt he needed to have.

At the same time, the thought of joining the Trappists kept nagging him. Things came to a head during a conversation with his former professor, Mark Van Doren. It was the day after Thanksgiving, and Merton joined Van Doren in New York for lunch at the Columbia Faculty Club. Almost immediately Van Doren asked Merton about his vocation to the priesthood, wondering if he was just going to let the matter drop or whether he was going to pursue this calling despite what the Capuchin priest had said to him. When Merton shrugged off the question, Van Doren replied with a comment that struck Merton deeply: "I talked about that to someone who knows what it is all about, and he said that the fact you had let it all drop, when you were told you had no vocation, might really be a sign that you had none." What seemed to bother Merton most about this statement was his realization that, deep down, he *knew* he had a vocation to the priesthood. "The spontaneous rebellion against the mere thought that I might definitely *not* be called to the monastic life," he wrote, "that it might certainly be out of the question, once and for all—the rebellion against such an idea was so strong in me that it told me all I needed to know" (SSM, 362). Rather than simply take the Capuchin priest's comment as the final word on his vocation, Merton realized that he needed to test his vocation, to find out whether or not he could actually be called to the monastic life for which he longed.

He returned to St. Bonaventure College. A few days went by, but on Thursday of that week, Merton became convinced that he needed finally to find out whether he could and should become a Trappist. The pages in which Merton described what happens next are beautifully written and dramatic, and, as was the case when he described his conversion to Catholicism, there is much here that is reminiscent of Augustine's conversion scene. When Augustine was in the throes of inner turmoil, wondering whether he should finally commit to becoming a Catholic or whether he would acquiesce to the passions that kept him from definitively taking the leap, his turmoil took place in a garden. Merton's moment of "conversion"—this one to the monastic life—similarly took place in a garden, specifically a grove to which he frequently went at St. Bonaventure where there was a grotto to Our Lady of Lourdes and a shrine to the Little Flower, St. Thérèse of Lisieux. He knew that he should simply go to the room of Fr. Philotheus, one of the friars who was something of a spiritual director for him, to seek his guidance about his vocation. But instead of doing this, he left the building and went into the grove, begging for assistance from the Little Flower. He finally resolved to go back to the building to speak to Fr. Philotheus, "but when I got within about six feet of his door it was almost as if someone had stopped me and held me where I was with physical hands. Something jammed in my will." He ran back to the grove. What Merton most feared was that Fr. Philotheus would confirm that he did not have a vocation to monastic life, and while the uncertainty of not knowing whether or not he had a vocation was torture, the thought of finding out definitively filled him with terror.

Merton wrote that there had never been a time in his life when he felt "so special an anguish" (SSM, 364). He began praying to St. Thérèse of Lisieux, begging her to give him some guidance, and promising to her that, if he got into the monastery, he would be her monk, devoted to her. In his personal journal, Merton recounted that things suddenly became very clear to him after making this prayer:

> While I am praying to her the question becomes clear: all I want to know is, do I have a chance to be a priest after all. I don't want [Fr. Philotheus] to argue for or against the Trappists. I *know* I want to be a Trappist. I remember the terrific sense of holiness and peace I got when I first stepped inside Gethsemani, something more certain and more terrific than ever hit me anywhere else—and which stayed with me until I got all mixed up about the vocation, the end of the week, in that terrible impasse: I want to be a priest—but I am told there is an impediment. (Ji, 457–58: November 28, 1941)

And then suddenly, as if in answer to his prayer to the Little Flower, Merton felt that he could hear the bells of Gethsemani ringing, and while he knew it was only in his imagination, the impression of hearing the bells ringing for the end of Compline seemed so real that he was overcome. And to his mind, "the bell seemed to be telling me where I belonged—as if it were calling me home" (SSM, 365).

Whereas an almost physical force tried to keep him from approaching Fr. Philotheus earlier, this sign filled him with the confidence finally to ask the priest for guidance. Merton found him and told him of all his hesitations and concerns, and immediately Fr. Philotheus told him that he saw no impediment to keep him from the monastery and from the priesthood. The relief and certainty Merton experienced at that moment was profound:

> It may seem irrational, but at that moment, it was as if scales fell off my own eyes, and looking back on all my worries and questions, I could see clearly how empty and futile they had been. Yes, it was obvious that I was called to the monastic life: and all my doubts about it had been mostly shadows. Where had they gained such a deceptive appearance of substance and reality? Accident and circumstances had all contributed to exaggerate and distort things in my mind. But now everything was straight again. And already I was full of peace and assurance—the consciousness that everything was right, and that a straight road had opened out, clear and smooth, ahead of me. (SSM, 365)

At this point things progressed quickly. Merton immediately wrote to the abbot at Gethsemani, asking for permission to present himself as a postulant at Christmas. He received a positive reply. However, he soon also received another letter, this one from the draft board. Whereas Merton had previously been deemed unfit for combat due primarily to the state of his teeth, the board was revisiting previous judgments given the increased certainty that the United States was about to enter the war. Merton wrote the draft board, asking for time given that he was entering a monastery. Things became more uncertain when, shortly after sending this letter, Japan attacked Pearl Harbor and the United States officially entered the war. Nevertheless, the day after Pearl Harbor, the feast of the Immaculate Conception, Merton received another letter from the draft board granting him a one-month reprieve to discern his vocation.

Merton immediately went to the president of the college, Fr. Thomas, to ask permission to leave immediately even though the term had not yet been completed. His colleagues in the English department met to determine who would share out the remainder of his classes, and Merton packed up his things to catch a train that evening. He arrived at the gates of the Abbey of Gethsemani on December 10, 1941. The gatekeeper remembered him from his retreat in the spring. "This time have you come to stay?" he asked.

> "Yes, Brother, if you'll pray for me," I said.
> Brother nodded, and raised his hand to close the window.
> "That's what I've been doing," he said, "praying for you." (SSM, 371)

And with that, "Brother Matthew locked the gate behind me and I was enclosed in the four walls of my new freedom" (SSM, 372).

Conclusion

In August 1963, Merton wrote a preface for a new Japanese translation of *The Seven Storey Mountain*. He took the opportunity to reflect on the book and to assess who he was then and who he had become, fifteen years after the book was published. Merton occasionally lamented aspects of *The Seven Storey Mountain* in his journals and in his correspondence, most frequently expressing dismay at the young Merton's naivete and youthful judgmentalism, particularly toward non-Catholic Christian traditions.[8] And in his 1963 preface for the

---

8. See, for example, his 1965 letter to Mrs. Mycock in which he criticized the lack of charity he showed toward Anglicans and the Anglican tradition in *The Seven Storey Mountain*. "My thought at the time of writing was hardly matured and I just said what came to mind, as people so often do, and more often did in those days" (Liv, 319; TM to Mrs. Mycock: April 2, 1965).

Japanese edition of the book, Merton expressed similar reservations about his autobiography, particularly the negative way in which he characterized the world in it. However, Merton acknowledged that the book has a life of its own apart from him, and he couldn't simply go back and change it. "The story no longer belongs to me," he wrote, "and I have no right to tell it in a different way, or to imagine that it should have been seen through wiser eyes." He also made clear in his preface that under no circumstances did he regret or question his conversion, his decision to enter the Abbey of Gethsemani, or his ordination as a priest: "Certainly I have never for a moment thought of changing the definitive decisions taken in the course of my life: to be a Christian, to be a monk, to be a priest" (HR, 63). In other words, what Merton would change about his biography was not the way in which he described the distinctly Catholic influences that compelled him to become Catholic, to become a monk, and to be ordained a priest. He would change his assessment of the world and of other non-Catholic traditions, but not his assessment of the significance of those things that influenced him to make the decisions he made, particularly his deep devotion to the Eucharist and the continued influence of the great mystics and theologians he read then and continued to read throughout his life.

CHAPTER 2

MERTON THE PRIEST

There is only one thing—and that is better than anything else I have done in my life. For six months I have been saying Mass.

—*Journal entry, December 30, 1949*

Introduction

Alone in his hermitage on September 22, 1967, a little over one year before his untimely death, Thomas Merton made a recording. Because severe dermatitis in his hands hampered his ability to write, he often used a tape recorder to dictate various things for a monk down at the monastery to type. On occasion, however, he used the recorder for his own purposes, and on that day Merton recorded himself chanting the entirety of the Cistercian Mass in Latin for the seventeenth Sunday after Pentecost. His journal entry for the day gives no clue as to why he did this, nor does he explain himself on the tape. But as one listens to Merton chant a liturgy with which he was deeply familiar after more than twenty-five years as a monk of the Abbey of Gethsemani, one hears his love for the liturgy, both in the brief explanations he provided about certain parts of the liturgy as well as in the passion with which he chanted it.

Central to the narrative of *The Seven Storey Mountain* is the tension between Merton's desire to become a priest and his belief that he had no such calling. When Fr. Philotheus at St. Bonaventure

College finally told him that he saw no canonical impediment preventing him from becoming a monk and a priest, Merton found his true calling. Merton did not enter the Abbey of Gethsemani on December 10, 1941, only to become a monk in a contemplative order. He entered also to become a priest, to offer daily the sacrifice of the Mass for himself, his community, and for the whole world. In 1953, describing the journal entries from *The Sign of Jonas* that covered the period of his ordination, Merton wrote that he understood ordination to the priesthood to be "the one great secret for which I had been born" and that it was for him "a matter of life or death, heaven or hell" (SJ, 181).

From the day he was ordained a priest until his death, the celebration of the Mass was central to Merton's daily existence. Indeed, the last entry in his personal journal—dated December 8, 1968—ends with a reference to where he was going to say Mass that day: "Today is the Feast of the Immaculate Conception. In a little while I leave the hotel. I'm going to say Mass at St. Louis Church, have lunch at the Apostolic Delegation, and then on to the Red Cross place this afternoon" (Jvii, 239: December 8, 1968). In this chapter, I'm going to examine Merton's identity as a Roman Catholic priest, focusing on his understanding of what the priesthood meant for him personally, as well as what it meant for how he viewed his role in the church and the world. As part of this examination, I'm going to explore Merton's relationship to the liturgy, focusing particular attention on his assessment of the liturgical changes that took place in the wake of the Second Vatican Council.

Merton's Ordination to the Priesthood

On May 26, 1949, seven years after entering the monastery and a year after publishing *The Seven Storey Mountain*, Merton was ordained a priest. This was a moment for which he had been waiting years, and the culmination of the calling he described so vividly in his autobiography. In late December, Merton was ordained to the subdiaconate and at the Christmas Midnight Mass he performed the duties of this office for the first time.[1] His physical proximity to the altar, plus his new role in the liturgy itself left an impression: "For now I am much more a *part of the Mass* than ever before. I am much more closely identified with the Host Who is broken on the altar. I am a member, that is an instrument, a limb He uses in explicit reference to His Mass and His worship of the Father" (Jii, 257–58: December 25, 1948). In March he was ordained as deacon, and in the lead-up to his ordination he thought about the significance of this moment: "The first thing about the diaconate is that it is *big*. The more I think about it the more I realize that it is a *major* Order. You are supposed to be the strength of the Church. You receive the Holy Spirit *ad robur* [for strength], not only for yourself, but to support the whole Church" (Jii, 290: March 15, 1949). And when he was ordained on March 19, he wrote the following in his journal about the experience: "I don't think I have ever seen a day like yesterday, and I am still dazzled by a dazzle that comes at me from all sides and from a source that I am not used to and which I can't spot at all" (Jii, 294: March 20, 1949).

But it was the priesthood that consumed Merton's thoughts, and in the weeks leading up to his ordination on the feast of the Ascension in May, his journal demonstrates just how thoroughly he longed to be ordained: "It seems to me impossible that I should live the next two and a half weeks without keeling over, dying of heart failure, or having the house come down on top of my head. How can I possibly achieve such a wonder as the priesthood? To do the one thing that saves the world and brings health to it and makes you capable of being happy!" (Jii, 309–10: May 8, 1949). Three days before his ordination, Merton's excitement was palpable: "I keep thinking: 'I shall say Mass—I shall say Mass'" (Jii, 314: May 23, 1949). And the day before his ordination, he contemplated his own unworthiness

---

1. The subdiaconate was the lowest of the major orders and it largely disappeared after the Second Vatican Council. The subdeacon was permitted to carry the chalice with the wine, to set the altar for the celebration of the Eucharist, and to read the Epistle at Mass.

in the face of the profound weight of responsibility that would rest on his shoulders as a priest:

> How could I dare to go to the altar and say Mass after the way I have treated my other obligations, at least interiorly, in the past two or three years?[. . .]And yet I can go to the altar with confidence and great joy and know that my Mass is going to make a tremendous difference to the happiness and salvation of the world, not only *in spite* of the fact that it is my Mass, but even *because* it is my Mass, that is, because of the special mercy of Christ to those who have nothing of their own to offer, nothing except weakness and misery and sin. (Jii, 316–17: May 25, 1949)

This quotation illustrates the degree to which Merton understood the transformative effects of the Eucharist and the immensity of the Mass—of *his* Mass as priest—for the transformation of the world. In the face of this profundity, Merton felt overwhelmed by his unworthiness, yet he could not ignore the reality of the calling he received.

The day for his ordination finally arrived, and while ordinations were commonplace at the Abbey of Gethsemani, Merton's was unique insofar as the Associated Press sent a photographer to document the affair. His editors and friends, James Laughlin and Robert Giroux, came as did his friends from Columbia University, Bob Lax, Ed Rice, and Sy Freedgood. Dan Walsh, the professor who was so influential on his early theological and spiritual life, was also there.[2]

In the days following his ordination, Merton recorded his thoughts in his journal about the days of celebration. There's a breathlessness to his account that shows how deeply the experience of the previous days transformed him:

> I could not begin to write about the ordination, about saying Mass, about the *Agape* [love banquet] that lasted three days

2. To read more details regarding Merton's ordination, see Michael Mott, *The Seven Mountains of Thomas Merton* (Boston: Houghton Mifflin, 1984), 251–54.

with all those who came down . . . A sense of the absolutely tremendous work that has been done in me and through me in the last three days, each day bringing its own growth. Ordination, anointing, ordination Mass—then the first low Mass and what followed, finally the Solemn Mass yesterday and the talking in the afternoon out under the trees of the avenue. I am left with the feeling not only that I have been transformed, but that a new world has somehow been brought into being through the labor and happiness of these three most exhausting days, full of sublimity and of things that none of us will understand for a year or two to come. (Jii, 317: May 29, 1949)

This was the culmination of a journey that began back in the basement of St. Francis Xavier parish when, in the presence of the Blessed Sacrament, Merton accepted a call to the priesthood. While he would, as we saw in the previous chapter, come to question the reality of his vocation, the confirmation of this calling in the grove at St. Bonaventure College in 1941 finally reached fruition in 1949.

The depth of Merton's eucharistic piety, a piety already seen in the previous chapter, is on full display in the journal entries written in the two weeks following his ordination. Calling his first three Masses "my three greatest graces" (Jii, 317: May 29, 1949), he wrote that the "Mass is the most wonderful thing that has ever entered into my life" (Jii, 319: June 4, 1949). On June 10, two weeks after his ordination, Merton's joy and wonder continue:

> The Mass becomes more wonderful every day. When I get to the altar it seems as if nothing in the world could possibly trouble me and I sail through everything in a glow of intense peace in which I can grasp nothing particular of the great thing that is going on, but in which I am simply possessed by the action of which I am the dazzled instrument . . . The big thing in my day used to be Communion: now it is rather the *action* of the Mass, the Sacrifice of which Communion is only a part. The center of balance of my spiritual life has shifted from the half hour when I kneel in the dark by Our Lady of Victories to the ten or fifteen minutes in which the Body and

Blood of Christ are on the altar before me and I stand with
my hands sketching that cramped little gesture of supplication
that we have instead of the wide-flung arms of the *Orantes*.
(Jii, 321: June 10, 1949)

In the weeks leading up to his ordination, Merton wondered about
the ways in which becoming a priest would change him spiritually.
It is clear from the quotation above that it was having a definite effect. The Mass itself had become a central aspect of his spirituality
because he had gone from being a participant of Communion to a
celebrant of the sacred mysteries themselves.

In an entry written a few days before this one, Merton described
the great mystery of the Eucharist and what it meant for him to be
part of this mystery: "About the lucidity and peace of this perfect
sacrifice I have nothing coherent to say. But I am very aware of the
most special atmosphere of grace in which the priest moves and
breathes at that moment—and all day long." But, Merton went on,
this was not a grace meant for him alone as the priest. It has social
implications insofar as the priest at the altar becomes the means by
which God manifests love to all: "This grace is something private
and inalienable, but it springs also from the social nature of the
Mass. The greatest personal gift that can come to anyone is to share
in the infinite act by which God's love is poured out upon all men"
(Jii, 319: June 4, 1949).

Comments like this were not reserved only to his private journals.
In a letter to his abbot when the latter was at another monastery on
visitation, Merton wrote euphorically about what celebrating the
Mass meant to him spiritually: "Rev. Father, I wish I could explain
to you what gets into my heart and simply carries me away. The
Mass has done it more than anything else." He continued by telling
Dom James Fox that the Mass was teaching him about his unity
with Christ through the Eucharist, and consequently, his union with
others: "All of a sudden I have seen what it *means* to be a member of
Christ, and have developed a sense of what we are all made for and
heading for, that wonderful union in Him, 'that they may be one as

Thou Father and I are one, that they may be one in us . . . Thou in me and I in them'" (Liii, 17: TM to Dom James Fox; October 1, 1949). In a November 1949 letter, Merton told his friend Bob Lax that he was teaching a class on mystical theology to the novices, and that the entire course was designed to help them more thoroughly to understand the depth of the Mass: "The Mass is the center of everything and in so far as it is Calvary it is the center of Scripture and the key to everything—history, everything."[3] In another letter to a religious sister he wrote, "I wish I could stand all day at the altar and be, most fully, Christ" (Lii, 193: TM to Sr. Therese Lentfoehr: June 2, 1949). Merton summed up the transformative power of his daily Mass in a 1950 autobiographical essay called "The White Pebble":

> Morning after morning you go to the dim altar weaker and more lowly than you have ever been before, and leave it lost in a more incomprehensible greatness than you have ever known before. A few months of the Mass have emptied me more and filled me more than seven years of monastic asceticism. (TMSE, 12)

Merton the Priest

From the day he was ordained until the last day of his life, with only a few exceptions, Merton celebrated the Mass daily, and his private journals and letters reveal how important this was to him. In a December 30, 1949, journal entry, reflecting on the year that had passed, he referred with joy to his ordination: "There is only one thing—and that is better than anything else I have done in my life. For six months I have been saying Mass. That one fact is teaching me to live in such a way that I do not care whether I live or die" (Jii, 389: December 30, 1949). Early the next year, Merton wrote about the way in which the Mass he celebrated brought him to an

---

3. *When Prophecy Still Had a Voice: The Letters of Thomas Merton and Robert Lax*, ed. Arthur W. Biddle (Lexington: University Press of Kentucky, 2001), 110. TM to Robert Lax (November 27, 1949).

understanding of the relationship between solitude and community that existed in tension within a contemplative monastery like Gethsemani: "The solution is in the Mass where all these things are found and where we are all close together and proclaim God together and are offered to God together and all the rough ways are made plain and the crooked ways are straightened and the hills are leveled and the valleys filled" (Jii, 397: January 9, 1950). Merton recognized that, far from being an exercise in solitude whereby the individual is raised to union with God through Christ without regard for others, the Eucharist brings us into relationship with one another even in the midst of physical solitude. He made this point powerfully in the aforementioned autobiographical essay, "The White Pebble," in which he described the way the Mass pulled him out of himself: "If you are afraid of love, never become a priest, never say Mass. The Mass will draw down upon your soul a torrent of interior suffering which has only one function—to break you wide open and let everybody in the world into your heart. If you are afraid of people, never say Mass!" (TMSE, 13).

Merton understood his daily celebration of the Mass to bring him into closer contact with others in the world, even though he was separated from them by the walls of the monastery. Shortly after his ordination, Merton wrote that "the greatest personal gift that can come to anyone is to share in the infinite act by which God's love is poured out upon all [people]" (Jii, 321: June 10, 1949). Throughout his life, he took this idea seriously, offering his Masses for his friends and for the wellbeing of the world.

Two months after his ordination, at the end of a letter to the famous French Catholic philosopher and theologian Jacques Maritain, Merton wrote that the Mass was his "greatest joy" and that he would be sure to remember Maritain at Mass. Indeed, he continued, when he arrived at the memento of the living, during which he remembered all the people for whom he is praying in his Mass, "the names of so many, many dear souls come to me on the tide of God's love from the depths of my heart" that a liturgist would undoubtedly take issue with how much time he spent on that part of the Mass.

But as a priest, he recognized that his friends were in need and "that they depend in large measure upon that Mass" (Liii, 25–26: TM to Jacques Maritain; July 9, 1949).

Merton's letters are filled with promises to his correspondents that he would remember them at Mass, a fact that demonstrates just how thoroughly he understood the Mass to be the primary means by which he united his prayers with those in the world. Indeed, he promised to say Mass for so many of his correspondents that it would be unwieldy to list all the examples here. However, a few references will illustrate the seriousness with which he took his role as a priest. First, his letters are filled with assurances to those who lost someone that he would say Mass for the dead. For example, he wrote to Ethel Kennedy to tell her that he would say Mass for President John F. Kennedy in 1963, and again for Robert Kennedy in 1968 after he learned of their tragic deaths.[4] He didn't just offer this to his Catholic correspondents, however. The day after the assassination of Martin Luther King Jr., Merton sent a telegram to Coretta Scott King, promising her that his morning's Mass was going to be offered for him and for her.[5] And in a letter to the Zen Buddhist, D. T. Suzuki, Merton wrote that he constantly remembered the victims of Hiroshima and Nagasaki when he said Mass, and that he felt their intercession for him (Li, 566: TM to Daistetz T. Suzuki; April 11, 1959).

But Merton didn't reserve his Masses only for the dead. Indeed, many of his letters to both Catholic and non-Catholic correspondents end with assurances that he would remember them or people close to them in his Mass, and it is clear that he understood this remembrance of them to be a profound gesture of friendship and unity. In a letter to the Chinese Catholic scholar John Wu, whom he befriended and met a number of times, Merton told him that he was going to say Mass for him and his family. He underlined the

4. Li, 447. TM to Ethel Kennedy (November 23, 1963); Li, 449. TM to Ethel Kennedy (June 22, 1968).

5. Li, 451. TM to Coretta Scott King (April 5, 1968). See also Li, 645. TM to June Youngblut (April 9, 1968).

significance of this act for himself as a priest when he wrote that it "will be a joy to stand in the presence of the heavenly Father, in Christ, and speak of you and all whom you love and of China" (Li, 621: TM to John C. H. Wu; June 7, 1962).

While his Catholic correspondents undoubtedly understood the meaning of this gesture, Merton felt compelled to explain to his non-Catholic correspondents why it was that he was saying Mass for them even though they were part of another religious tradition. In 1961, Merton wrote a beautiful and intimate letter to Dona Luisa Coomaraswamy, a scholar who was Jewish by birth and who worked for interfaith unity. She had learned that Merton was planning to write something about her husband, and so sent him a letter along with some books to assist him in this task. Merton was overwhelmed by her generosity, but even more impressed by her expressed desire to engage in dialogue with him. Merton replied enthusiastically to her, and at the end of his letter, he told her that he would express his friendship to her through his Mass: "The best my friendship can offer you is prayer, during the psalms at night, in my Mass at dawn. (I have a rare privilege . . . of saying Mass just at sunrise, when the light of the sun falls on the altar, and powerfully lights up the mystery of the divine presence)" (Li, 127: TM to Dona Luisa Coomaraswamy; January 13, 1961). Merton wrote similarly to his Muslim correspondent in Pakistan, Abdul Aziz. The two struck up a correspondence through a mutual friend—the Melkite priest and Islamic scholar, Louis Massignon—and the letters Merton wrote Aziz are among some his most moving. In his January 30, 1961, letter to Aziz, Merton thanked Aziz for the prayers the latter offered for Merton at dawn. He wrote that he had actually been praying for Aziz at that same time when he said Mass. Realizing that Aziz may not understand the meaning of this, Merton explained to him that the Mass is "the moment of the nearest presence of God in our lives" as Catholics, and as such, "I wish then to share this bounty with you" (Li, 46: TM to Abdul Aziz; January 30, 1961).

Merton's daily Mass, by which he united himself through his priestly ministry to those in the world, was a central, perhaps the central, part of his day. Merton's journals and correspondence in the 1950s and 60s demonstrate how fundamental his priesthood was to his self-identity and how pivotal his daily Mass was for him personally. The 1950s was a difficult decade for Merton as he struggled with the question of whether he should remain a monk at Gethsemani or whether he was called to a Catholic religious order, such as the Carthusians or Camaldolese, that was more focused on solitude and silence. While the possibility of leaving for one of these orders was closed to him in 1956, another opportunity emerged in 1957 when he was invited by Dom Gregory Lemercier's Benedictine Monastery of the Resurrection in Cuernavaca, Mexico, to live a life of solitude and prayer.[6] In response to this invitation, and unbeknownst to his own abbot, Dom James Fox, Merton petitioned Rome for exclaustration (canonical approval to transfer to another monastery within another order). Merton later somewhat lamented this decade of vocational restlessness, but at the time he experienced tremendous emotional and spiritual turmoil as he struggled to come to terms with his own calling.

But even in the midst of this misery, Merton wrote frequently that he found solace and moments of clarity in the Mass. While he wanted to leave Gethsemani, he found that saying Mass led him to become more open to God's will. He experienced similar moments of clarity and openness during eucharistic adoration. When, after months of anxious waiting, a letter from Rome arrived in response to his request for exclaustration, Merton did not open it immediately but took the letter to the novitiate chapel, knelt down before the Blessed Sacrament, and opened it. He evidently felt that his vocational crisis should find its resolution in the presence of Christ in the Eucharist. The answer from Rome was no, and Merton was surprised that he "felt no anger or resistance," only peace and joy that God's will had been revealed to him so clearly. Later that night, while praying again before the

6. For a detailed account of this period of Merton's life, see Donald Grayston, *Thomas Merton and the Noonday Demon: The Camaldoli Correspondence* (Eugene, OR: Cascade Books, 2015).

tabernacle, Merton continued to experience peace: "Empty, silent, free, opening, into nothing—a little point of nothing that alone is real. What do you ask? Nothing. What do you want? Nothing. Very quiet and dark. The Father. The Father" (Jiii, 359: December 17, 1959).

In the midst of his most tumultuous period at Gethsemani, it is noteworthy that he found solace in his daily Mass and in eucharistic adoration. Even when he was questioning who he was as a monk and whether he was called to become a monk elsewhere, Merton never questioned his own identity as a priest. He instead found his identity in his priesthood, experiencing peace and clarity when saying the Mass and when praying before the tabernacle.

Merton expressed similar sentiments regarding his experiences of saying the Mass throughout the 1960s. Indeed, while some Catholics view Merton's ventures into ecumenical and interreligious waters during the 1960s with suspicion, it is worth noting that his private journal entries during this decade are replete with references to his daily celebration of the Mass. Often he wrote about having a change in perspective after his Mass, though he usually didn't explain what changed. "Saying my Mass after Chapter," he wrote in one entry. "This morning, clear sun, quiet chapel, and a whole new outlook. Happy!" (Jiv, 55: October 2, 1960). In another entry, he recorded being conflicted about who he was as a writer, wondering whether he should continue writing, and wrote that he received clarity after his Mass: "It all cleared up after High Mass when I saw my only solution is to do what I have always wanted to do, always known I should do, always been called to do: follow the way of emptiness and nothingness" (Jiv, 135: June 29, 1961).

Sometimes Merton simply noted in his journal something about the beauty of the Mass he celebrated, and these entries demonstrate further how central the Mass was to his daily existence. In one entry, he described his morning Mass as follows: "At Mass, which was all before sunrise and without lights, the quality, the 'spirituality' of the pre-dawn light on the altar was extraordinary. Silence in the chapel and that pure, pearl light! What could be a more beautiful liturgical sign than to have such light as witness of the Mystery?" (Jiv, 268: November 24, 1962). Sometimes his entries included detailed references to the things he noticed while saying Mass: "Rain this morning during my early Mass, Mass of Our Lady. At the last Gospel I could see the blue vineyard knob in the grey west with a scapular of mist on it, and then during thanksgiving those other knobs, the pointed one, the woods, of which I never tire" (Jv, 109: June 13, 1964).

When he was given permission in August 1965 to move out to a hermitage approximately one mile from the monastery, Merton walked to the monastery each day to say Mass. He would usually celebrate the Mass alone, but he also participated in the new practice of concelebration that had been introduced to Gethsemani as part of the post-Vatican II liturgical reforms. For reasons he did not explain, Merton told one of his correspondents in 1966 that his appreciation for the Mass had grown since becoming a hermit: "I have a deeper and deeper sense of the great importance of the Mass, as you too intimate in your letter. There is no question of it" (Li, 528: TM to Linda (Parsons) Sabbath; March 19, 1966).

Almost two years after moving to the hermitage, Merton received permission to say Mass alone at the hermitage. He ordered an altar from a local woodworker, and set it up in the hermitage with icons above it. He at first said Mass in the front sitting room of the hermitage, with the altar next to the fireplace. In the spring of 1968, an attached chapel was built onto the hermitage for Merton to say Mass. He said his first Mass at the hermitage on July 16, 1967, and his description of this first Mass shows how meaningful the experience was for him: "Mass about 4:30 or 4:45. Said it slowly, even sang some parts (of Gregorian Kyrie, Gloria, Preface, and other bits). It was a beautiful Mass and I now see that having the altar there is a *great* step forward and a huge help." Being able to say Mass at the hermitage, he wrote, "changes the shape of the day" (Jvi, 265: July 16, 1967). In a letter to a friend, Merton described the way in which he went about saying Mass at the hermitage: "I say Mass very quietly now by myself, early in the morning, finishing about dawn sometimes: after the preface I turn out the light and have nothing but the two candles shining on the ikons" (Lii, 258: TM to Sr. Therese Lentfoehr; September 5, 1967). The Mass was already a central part of his day, but at the hermitage, all alone, the Mass became part of his meditation each morning, with his liturgy punctuated by long periods of silence.

In addition to writing about the Masses he said in solitude, he also described Masses he celebrated with others at the hermitage. When Merton hosted a group of contemplative nuns in December 1967, they celebrated Mass together at the hermitage. "Mass at the hermitage today was unutterably good," he wrote, "something I simply can't articulate" (Jvii, 20: December 7, 1967). Merton also said Mass when the son of John Wu and his wife visited in the summer of 1968. Merton collaborated with John Wu, a Chinese Catholic, in the writing of *The Way of Chuang Tzu*, Merton's book exploring Chinese religion, and when his son came to visit while on a honeymoon with his new wife, Merton celebrated Mass with them. And the day before he left for his trip to Asia, he celebrated Mass at the hermitage one last time, this time with Br. Maurice Flood, Br. Patrick Hart, and Phil Stark, SJ.

The journal entries he wrote during this final trip—a trip that included stops in New Mexico, Alaska, and California, before finally crossing the Pacific—include numerous references to the Masses he celebrated in various locations.[7] At one point, Merton wrote in his journal about needing to make plans to say Mass each day while in California, demonstrating that this was a primary concern of his during the trip.[8] While in Asia, Merton's days were shaped by his

7. In New Mexico, see Jvii, 178 (September 16, 1968). In Alaska, see Jvii, 194–95 (September 29, 1968). In California, see Jvii, 199–200 (October 8, 1968); 200 (October 11, 1968); 201 (October 13, 1968).

8. Jvii, 200 (October 8, 1968). "I decided the best thing would be to come to the monastery and say Mass in the evening (as I could not contact the pastor in Mendocino about saying Mass in his church)."

daily celebration of the Mass, and his journal entries often contain references to these celebrations. For example, two days after engaging in dialogue with a Jain laywoman from Bombay, Merton described the Mass he celebrated with the nuns at Loreto House: "After Mass I am surrounded on all sides, praised, questioned, admired, revered— so much so that I can hardly eat breakfast" (Jvii, 222: October 26, 1968). In another entry, Merton recorded his experience of dialogue at an Islamic college in Calcutta (present-day Kolkata) before describing the Mass he said at a Catholic hospital with the Canadian High Commissioner and others. Near the middle of November, Merton concelebrated Mass with a Nepalese priest. The liturgy included Nepalese music and drums. He found the experience "very moving" (Jvii, 280: November 17, 1968).

Journal entries from the days leading up to the conference in Bangkok contain numerous references to the Masses he said as well as to making arrangements for saying Mass.[9] A highlight of his trip was being able to say Mass at St. Thomas Mount in Madras, India. St. Thomas was and is widely revered in India as an apostle to the subcontinent, and St. Thomas Mount is a shrine built on the place traditionally understood to be the place where he died. The experience of saying Mass there moved him. The day after his famous entry describing his experience seeing the statues of the Buddha at Polonnaruwa, about which I will write in a later chapter, Merton wrote about saying Mass in the home of a Catholic professor of philosophy, Lee Beng Tjie, when he travelled back to Singapore. And, as I mentioned at the beginning of this chapter, Merton's very last journal entry concludes on a eucharistic note as he talked about his plans for that day. Merton died tragically two days later, and given the way in which, throughout his life, his identity as a priest profoundly shaped his self-understanding, it is fitting that the last words he would write in his private journal would be about the Mass he was about to say in a church that was named after St. Louis, Merton's monastic name.

9. For example, see Jvii, 297 (November 24, 1968).

These snapshots from Merton's private journals and letters demonstrate that his identity as a priest was not simply part of his identity as a contemplative and as a monk. His priesthood defined who he was as a contemplative and as a monk, and his days were punctuated by the daily celebration of the Mass, either alone or in community, from the day he was ordained in 1949 to his death in 1968. The seriousness with which Merton took his priesthood is further illustrated by his references to the liturgy and to the post-Vatican II liturgical reforms.

Merton's Understanding of the Liturgy

The latter years of Merton's life coincided with the liturgical reforms initiated by the Second Vatican Council's constitution on the liturgy, *Sacrosanctum Concilium*, and he commented often on the reforms happening in the monastery and throughout the world. Merton's initial enthusiasm for the constitution was tempered by the shape the liturgical reforms came to take, but despite his misgivings about the reforms, misgivings that I will outline in more detail below, he advocated for an openness to both progressives and conservatives, arguing that a liturgical renewal rooted in an ecclesiology of communion necessitated, above all, love for the other.

Only a few days after the promulgation of *Sacrosanctum Concilium*, Merton wrote in his journal that he'd had an opportunity to read through the constitution, and was deeply impressed. As novice master, Merton devoted three sessions to the constitution in the days following its release, all of which were recorded. He had a complete copy of the constitution because it had been published in its entirety in the *New York Times*, which James Laughlin sent to him. His enthusiasm for the document is palpable from the recordings. The promulgation of *Sacrosanctum Concilium*, he said, "is a great event in the church," "the biggest thing that's happened in liturgy in sixteen hundred years." There have been liturgical reforms previously, but they were "small potatoes" compared to the "real revolution in the liturgy" brought about by *Sacrosanctum Concilium*. This constitution, he exclaimed, "is God giving to his church, through his church, the theology of the liturgy."[10] And in a letter written at this time to Dom Aelred Graham, an English Benedictine, Merton wrote:

> The new Constitution on Liturgy from the Council is most exciting and very rich, it seems to me. I am going through it with the novices. There is great work ahead. This is the first real liturgical reform in 1600 years, and if it is properly under-stood and implemented, it will amount to a revolution in the sense of a metanoia for the whole Church. I know that there will be some false starts and some blunders, but the Holy Spirit will take care of us. (Liii, 188: TM to Dom Aelred Graham; December 16, 1963)

As the final sentence indicates, Merton knew that liturgical reform was risky, and in a letter to Dom Denys Rackley, a Carthusian at La Grande Chartreuse written five days after the constitution's promulgation, he expressed some reservations about the liturgical doors opened by the council:

> Our great danger is to throw away things that are excellent, which we do not understand, and replace them with mediocre forms which seem to us to be more meaningful and which in fact are only trite. I am very much afraid that when all the dust clears we will be left with no better than we deserve, a rather silly, flashy, seemingly up-to-date series of liturgical forms that have lost the dignity and the meaning of the old ones. (Liii, 187: TM to Dom Denys Rackley, OCART; December 9, 1963)

However, despite his concerns about where the liturgical reform might lead, Merton was convinced of the need for renewal on ecclesiological grounds, as he made clear in his talks to the novices on *Sacrosanctum Concilium*. Telling the novices that the liturgy is

---

10. Thomas Merton, *Liturgical Schema of the Council* (December 16, 1963, 089 TR-3), audio tape, *Thomas Merton Center*, Bellarmine University.

"theology-lived," he argued that the liturgy is supposed to manifest the "true nature of the church" both to those within and those outside the church. This does not always happen, however: "Does it manifest the true nature of the church if you have one guy in a corner mumbling, and an altar boy kidding around with another altar boy and there's a bunch of nonsense going on, and nobody knows what's happening, and there's just a bunch of mumbo-jumbo going on in the corner?" According to Merton, the laity were in some cases little more than spectators, detached from the liturgy and detached from one another, and because of this, the Eucharist as a sacrament of unity rooted in communion was lost. Hence Merton's enthusiasm for the emphasis in *Sacrosanctum Concilium* on greater participation of laity in the liturgy: "The nature of the liturgy is such that if you don't have everyone fully participating in it, you don't have fully liturgical worship."[11] Reform of the liturgy necessitates the full, conscious, and active participation of the laity, for it is only through this that the true nature of the church is manifested. Whereas the Council of Trent emphasized Christ's presence in the Eucharist and in the priest, Merton argued that *Sacrosanctum Concilium* completed the picture by emphasizing Christ's presence in the communion of the faithful, a communion manifested in the union of all in the work of prayer and worship.

In a 1964 essay titled "Liturgical Renewal: The Open Approach," Merton went into more detail about what needed to be reformed and how such reform might be accomplished. He characterized the old spirit of the liturgy as being one that was the "psychological residue" of years of praying the liturgy in a way that was cold, formal, and lacked what Merton referred to as "personal communication" (SCel, 234). The priest and the people have ceased communicating with one another to such a degree that the whole thing has become impersonal: "All that matters is that the sacraments be valid, the formulas correct, and the gestures rubrically exact" (SCel, 235). This attitude—which Merton described as a "I am the priest, you are the laity, and this is strictly a business deal" mentality—led to liturgical

---

11. Thomas Merton, "Liturgical Schema of the Council" (December 16, 1963, 089 TR-3), audio tape, *Thomas Merton Center*, Bellarmine University.

experiences that were dead and cold, and to an understanding of the liturgy that was individualistic since worshippers practiced their own interior worship while waiting for the priest to finish up his business (SCel, 234).

What concerned Merton most was not the style of pre-Vatican II worship; as we shall see, he valued much in the Latin liturgy. Rather, Merton complained that pre-Vatican II worship was plagued by a spirit characterized by "validism" and "officialism" that had translated into a liturgy in which the people do not participate and through which the church was not truly manifest (SCel, 235). Therefore the liturgy needed to be reformed. However, Merton was clear that "it is not the old forms that must go so much as the old spirit," and he argued that the old spirit needs to be replaced by a spirit of openness, which he understood to be the goal of the reform initiated by *Sacrosanctum Concilium* (SCel, 234). By openness, Merton did not intend a freewheeling experimentation with the tradition. Rather, he understood this spirit of openness to mean a fundamental shift in celebrating the liturgy such that "a new sense of sacred space, of community, of oneness in the Spirit" would be discovered "as a result of communication on a deep level." And this communication was made possible by the liturgy itself, which is, by its very nature, designed to "open the mind and heart of the participant to this experience of oneness in Christ" (SCel, 236).

Interestingly, when Merton described concretely what this kind of liturgy might look like, he appealed not to the new but to the old, pointing specifically to his experience of the liturgy at Corpus Christi parish in New York City in 1938, which he described in *The Seven Storey Mountain* and to which I referred in the previous chapter. Here in this essay on liturgical reform, Merton wrote that it was in no small part because of the liturgy at Corpus Christi that he became a Catholic, a monk, and a priest. He described it as follows:

> Corpus Christi had the same Roman liturgy as everyone else in 1938. It was just the familiar Mass that is now being radically reformed. There was nothing new or revolutionary about it; only that everything was well done, not out of aestheticism

or rubrical obsessiveness, but out of love for God and His truth. It would certainly be ingratitude of me if I did not remember the atmosphere of joy, light, and at least relative openness and spontaneity that filled Corpus Christi at solemn High Mass. (SCel, 237)

Merton here tried to steer a middle course between those calling for total reform with little regard for the tradition and those refusing to countenance reform of the old. There was, Merton wrote, nothing of the new in the traditional Latin High Mass Merton experienced at Corpus Christi, but neither was the liturgy celebrated in order to be beautiful or out of slavish adherence to the rubrics. It was open, spontaneous, and beautiful because it was performed out of love. The lesson Merton derived from the liturgy at Corpus Christi was that "it is not the style that matters but the spirit," and he illustrated the difference between the old spirit and the new with a series of dichotomies: "Is Christian worship to be communion in correctness or communion in love? Oneness in Law or oneness in Christ? Sharing in valid sacraments or in the Spirit of life that is in the Risen Savior?" While the laws of the church are important, we must "learn to participate in a free, open, joyous communion of love and praise" (SCel, 238–39).

Although he was cautiously open to "sober and reasonable experimentation," the essay reads like an appeal to liturgical progressives not to forget tradition (SCel, 233–34). He argued that reform of the liturgy should not necessitate a jettison of the old. Merton wrote this essay one year after the introduction of the "new Mass," and his assessment of this Mass was that the reform was moving in the right direction. There were now real opportunities for participation. Particularly with the altar now facing the people, communication between priest and people was established, and both were now more aware "that they are together *celebrating* the mystery of our Redemption in the Eucharistic Sacrifice and the Lord's Supper" (SCel, 232). He also wrote positively about concelebration and communion under both species as being "among the most impressive and praiseworthy additions of the new Liturgy." At the same time, while he wrote that liturgical renewal should involve the vernacular, he recommended caution. Perhaps betraying his own love for the Latin liturgy, Merton argued that Latin liturgies should still be preserved in some monasteries. Moreover, he expressed reservations about the translation currently in use. "A certain sacred and timeless seriousness is required in our vernacular liturgical texts," he wrote, "or they will rapidly become unbearably trite" (SCel, 233).

As with everything pertaining to Merton, we make a mistake if we try to pin him down and label him regarding liturgical reform, and "Liturgical Renewal: The Open Approach" indicates why. On the one hand he could speak enthusiastically about reform and even encourage liturgical experimentation. On the other, he held up as a standard for the liturgical movement the traditional liturgy he experienced at Corpus Christi. Merton's willingness to embrace the new coupled with reservations about rejecting the old played out repeatedly in the years following *Sacrosanctum Concilium* up to his death in 1968. There were times when he spoke positively about the liturgical changes taking place. For example, when in 1966 Dan Berrigan visited the Abbey of Gethsemani, bringing with him a new English liturgy that they used in their concelebration, Merton described the liturgy as "very open, simple, even casual, but very moving and real" (Jvi, 149: October 13, 1966). And in an April 1968 letter, he wrote positively about the possibilities offered by the folk Mass in answer to a question from a high school junior who wrote to him: "Good folk music at Mass can be a big help, but bad singing and trifling hymns are not much help. But so is bad Gregorian an obstacle rather than a help. I think what counts is life and fervor in the celebration of the liturgy, and whatever helps that in the right way is good" (Lii, 366: TM to Philip J. Cascia; April 10, 1968).

But Merton also frequently expressed frustration with the willingness with which progressives were willing to rid the liturgy of that which had timeless value. Merton's frustrations come through in a 1965 letter to an Anglican: "As I tell all my Anglican friends, 'I hope you will have the sense to maintain traditions that we are now eagerly throwing overboard'" (Liv, 279: TM to Mother Mary Margaret; April 29, 1965). He was particularly concerned about the ease with which Latin and Gregorian chant were being abandoned, even in the monastery: "The monks cannot understand the treasure they possess, and they throw it out to look for something else, when seculars, who for the most part are not even Christians, are able to love this incomparable art" (Liv, 236: TM to Dom Ignace Gillet; September 11, 1964). And yet, the Merton who complained often about the loss of the Latin, is the same Merton who experimented with small group liturgies with nuns at his hermitage in 1967, describing one of these liturgies as "really groovy" (Lii, 139: TM to John Howard Griffin; December 8, 1967).

Merton's example of liturgical openness rooted in tradition and an ecclesiology of communion is as relevant today as it was in the years following *Sacrosanctum Concilium*. As he wrote in a 1965 letter, he was "deeply attracted" to "austere, traditional Latin liturgy" (Lv, 324: TM to Rita; November 14, 1965), and his journals and letters from 1963 to his death are replete with laments about the shape of the liturgical reforms, and particularly the loss of Latin and Gregorian chant. He worried about what he saw as the rush to experimentation that could lead to the loss of that which is important and valuable: "One fears that in the reforms and renovation that are now under way, there may be no end of hasty, ill-considered and sweeping changes in which a lot that is profoundly significant and alive will be discarded thoughtlessly, simply because those making the changes have no way of realizing that they are throwing out something of permanent and timeless value." The point was not to change simply for the sake of change. Liturgical reform should mean only "eliminating what is peripheral, excessive, meaningless, confusing and even absurd" so as to arrive at a liturgical simplicity and nobility that will communicate precisely what it is that the church is.[12] Merton had a love for the traditional liturgy, and clearly wanted to preserve as much of that liturgy as possible, provided that it opened up opportunities for lay participation and that it eliminated that which had compromised its simplicity and beauty.

12. Thomas Merton, letter to the editor, *Commonweal* (February 7, 1964): 574.

But his love for the traditional liturgy did not blind him to the problematic ecclesiology often associated with it, and it was for this reason that Merton advocated for liturgical reforms focused on greater lay participation that would enact a new spirit more in line with an ecclesiology of communion. Merton's commitment to a new spirit allowed him to hold in tension a love of tradition alongside a recognition for the need to reform, and even experiment with, the liturgy, and so allowed him to steer a middle course between two extremes. The new spirit for which Merton called was incompatible with conservative unwillingness to change anything, but was likewise incompatible with progressive attempts to bulldoze conservatives with reforms that paid little heed to the tradition and that ended up replacing "one kind of constraint by the other" (SCel, 243). A liturgical reform that is centered on a communion of love must have at its heart an openness to others, and so an openness to a diversity of views. To close oneself off to the other is immediately to live into the old spirit of the liturgy, and Merton was convinced that this old spirit could and would continue alive and well in the new forms as long as those committed to the reforms remained allergic to that which was timeless and valuable in the tradition and to those who value that tradition. Merton's exhortation to love and, even more importantly, his example of liturgical openness to others rooted in an ecclesiology of communion, remain important today as we continue to squabble about the liturgy and about a myriad of other issues: "Let us frankly realize that our task is precisely this: to demonstrate our elementary charity and unselfishness—indeed our Christian maturity—by setting aside our own preferences (whether progressive or conservative) in order to arrive at some working formula by which we can all continue to worship as one in Christ" (SCel, 244).

Conclusion

When people think about Thomas Merton, they usually think about his writings on prayer and contemplation, about his essays against war and racism, and perhaps about his understanding of interreligious dialogue. He's seen primarily as a contemplative, a monk, and a social activist. However, we do Merton a disservice if we do not also pay attention to his identity as a priest in the Roman Catholic Church. This was a calling about which he wrote in great detail in *The Seven Storey Mountain* and in *The Sign of Jonas*, and it remained central to his identity throughout his life at the Abbey of Gethsemani. The Mass was pivotal to the structure of his days. In celebrating it, Merton frequently experienced moments of theological and spiritual clarity, as well as moments of consolation. Moreover, he understood it to be one of the primary ways in which he manifested his friendship with the many people with whom he corresponded. And his passion about the liturgy and about the liturgical changes that came in the wake of the Second Vatican Council indicates just how thoroughly the Mass came to sink deeply into the very fiber of his being. We will see in a later chapter just how much Merton's eucharistic theology came to affect other facets of his thought, particularly his conception of dialogue.

CHAPTER 3

MERTON THE NOVICE MASTER

It has been a great life. I can see the grace of God all through it. It is the best job in the monastery, master of novices, from every point of view.

—*Thomas Merton, August 20, 1965*
(in his last talk to the novices as their novice master)

Introduction

The process of becoming a monk at the Abbey of Gethsemani in the 1950s and 60s involved a man spending approximately one month as a postulant, after which time he spent two years as a novice under the direction of a novice master who gave regular classes (referred to as conferences) on theology, church history, monasticism, as well as on numerous other topics. The novice master also met individually with each novice to provide spiritual direction as the new monk oriented his life to the monastic schedule and discerned whether he was called to be a monk. Given that he shaped the future of the monastery through his teaching and direction of incoming monks, the novice master was, behind the abbot, the most important position in the monastery.

In 1955, Dom James Fox asked Thomas Merton to be Gethsemani's novice master, a position Merton held until 1965 when he moved permanently to the hermitage. In his final conference (class) as novice master on August 20, 1965, Merton remarked humorously on his long tenure as a teacher within the monastery; before he was master of novices he had been master of scholastics (in charge of training monks for ordination to the priesthood):

> Well, I have spent exactly half my monastic life in the novitiate: two years as novice and ten as novice-master. And the rest of the time, practically, I was with the students [monks training to become priests], because I was either a student or the master of students. So all my life I've been in the novitiate or the ju-niorate—I've never graduated![1]

He said all of this without regret, for, as he continued, the position "is the best job in the monastery, master of novices, from every point of view." One of the reasons he enjoyed being novice master was that it enabled him "to be continually learning, because you learn by teaching" ("A Life Free from Care," 218).

Merton took his role as novice master seriously. Over the ten years he held this position, he wrote voluminously, both for publication as well as in the form of letters to his many correspondents. Yet despite his prodigious output, he still did manual labor with the novices once or twice each week, and met regularly with each of them for spiritual direction.[2] Even more impressive was the extensive preparation Merton put into his conferences for the novices, evidence for which can be found in the eleven substantial volumes of his lecture notes that have been published thus far; another one is scheduled for publication. The published volumes contain Merton's extensive notes on monastic history and theology, mystical theology, the meaning of monastic vows, the minutiae of monastic life, as well as on Scripture. The forthcoming volume contains the notes for his classes on various liturgical feasts. However, these notes are not the only sources we have for exploring

---

1. Thomas Merton, "A Life Free from Care," *Cistercian Studies Quarterly* 5.3 (1970): 218.

2. May 20, 2020, email correspondence with Br. Paul Quenon, OCSO.

Merton's teaching role as novice master. In 1962 his novitiate conferences began to be recorded, and the Thomas Merton Center at Bellarmine University possesses hundreds of his talks to the novices on a
wide range of topics ranging from those listed above to the examination
of various patristic authors, Mariology, Thomistic theology, Celtic art,
poetry, and a myriad of other topics.[3]

In this chapter, I'm going to explore Merton as novice master, the
one charged with the theological and spiritual formation of incoming
monks. An examination of Merton's role as novice master will give
a sense of the seriousness with which he took his role, as well as of
his devotion both to the novices and to the monastery as a whole.
Moreover, an exploration of his conferences will demonstrate his
extensive historical and theological knowledge—most of which was
self-taught—and will illustrate what theological and spiritual topics
he understood to be most vital for new Trappist monks to explore.

How Merton Became the Novice Master

In 1951, Dom James Fox appointed Merton as Master of Scholastics, a new position at the monastery. The Master of Scholastics
was in charge of educating monks in the choir who were no longer
in the novitiate but who required further formation as they prepared
for the priesthood. Merton had already given occasional lectures to
the novices, and Dom James evidently felt that he was well-suited to
the task of teaching and directing the scholastics. His appointment
as Master of Scholastics came at a time when he was struggling with
his vocation as a Cistercian monk, a struggle that he experienced
regularly. In the late 1940s, he questioned whether he should leave
the Abbey of Gethsemani for a more contemplative monastic setting,

---

3. For a list of the recordings housed at the Thomas Merton Center, see "Novitiate Conferences," *Thomas Merton Center*, n.d., http://merton.org/Research/AV
/novitiate.aspx. The titles given to the tapes were assigned by the monks who recorded the conferences and do not always reflect the range of topics that Merton
addressed in each particular conference.

preferably the Carthusians, a monastic order Merton understood to be more focused on solitude and contemplation than the Trappists. His vocational crisis abated in the wake of his ordination to the priesthood, but it continued to bubble under the surface. Dom James perhaps felt that giving Merton charge over the scholastics would calm his restlessness, and this does appear to be the case in the immediate days following his appointment. "The fact that I have suddenly ended up in this position [as Master of Scholastics] clarifies all the foolish pages of this journal I have written about my own problems as a scholastic," he wrote. "For now I know that the reason why I had to resist the temptation to become a Carthusian was in order to learn how to help all the other ones who would be one way or another tempted to leave the monastery." He concluded this entry by writing that he could no longer devote any attention to his vocational crisis: "For now I am a grown-up monk and have no time for anything but the essentials" (Jii, 459, 460: June 13, 1951).

Six months after his appointment as Master of Scholastics, Merton wrote that this position actually gave to him the solitude for which he longed when he was tempted by the Carthusians:

> It is a strange thing, now that I have twenty-five scholastics to look after, I am more alone that [*sic*] I ever was before. When I am alone, I really am alone. When I am with them, I am also with God, which is the same as solitude—a deep and rich solitude. The more I get to know my scholastics the more reverence I have for their individuality and the more I meet them in my own solitude. The best of them, and the ones to whom I feel closest, are also the most solitary and at the same time the most charitable. All this experience replaces my theories of solitude. I do not need a hermitage, because I have found one where I least expected it. (Jii, 466: January 10, 1952)

However, another vocational crisis soon hit as Merton was tempted to join the Camaldolese order in Italy, an order that focused more attention on the eremitical (solitary) than the cenobitic (communal) monasticism. While Merton didn't keep a private journal from 1953 to 1956, we do possess correspondence from this time, including Merton's letters to and from Camaldoli.[4] It is unnecessary to delve into this particular crisis. It suffices to say that Merton again felt his desire for contemplation suffocated by the monastic life as practiced at Gethsemani and hoped that greater solitude could be found at Camaldoli where monks live as hermits. Note that Merton was not tempted to leave monasticism or the Catholic Church, but, as was the case with his yearning for the Carthusians, he desired what he perceived to be a deeper, more eremitic, form of Catholic monasticism.

However, despite his vocational issues, Merton evidently took seriously the task of educating and forming the scholastics under his charge as Master of Scholastics. Fr. John Eudes Bamberger (1926–2020) was a scholastic under Merton's direction, and recalled what he was like as a teacher in a 1991 interview. Describing Merton as "very conscientious, very approachable," Bamberger talked about his ability to communicate in class: "He was a communicator. So that when he spoke about things, he spoke in a concrete way and you felt you were talking to somebody who wasn't just repeating something he had read. Also he spoke with warmth and conviction, and even enthusiasm, and finally with a certain sense of intimacy that you felt as you read his books."[5] In addition to going out regularly with the scholastics to do manual labor—Bamberger says that Merton "was a very hard worker, physically, did that with as much energy as he taught"—Merton was also "an excellent spiritual director" who was considerate and accessible (interview with John Eudes Bamberger, 24, 31). Fr. Flavian Burns, who was abbot of Gethsemani when

---

4. For these letters and for a detailed analysis of this correspondence, see Donald Grayston, *Thomas Merton and the Noonday Demon: The Camaldoli Correspondence* (Eugene, OR: Cascade, 2015).

5. Victor A. Kramer, "Merton's Vocation as Monastic and Writer: An Interview with John Eudes Bamberger, O.C.S.O," *The Merton Annual* 4 (1991): 24, 33. In another place in the interview, he says the following about Merton as a teacher: "He had a very agile mind, and a very energetic delivery, very personal, and he was quite enthusiastic. He was always enthusiastic as a speaker, almost always, and in particular when he spoke about prayer and the monastic life, he exuded energy and enthusiasm" (23).

Merton died in 1968, similarly remembered Merton's abilities as a spiritual director, recalling that he met with all of his students once a week for direction. Burns noted that he himself profited immensely from this relationship with Merton: "I owe him more than I owe any other human being, I think for what I really treasure in my life."[6]

Merton remained the Master of Scholastics until 1955. It was during the summer of this year that he made his most energetic attempt to become a hermit at Camaldoli in Italy, putting immense pressure on his abbot and the abbot general of the order, Dom Gabriel Sortais, to accede to his desire to leave. The situation became so difficult that Giovanni Battista Montini, who was then Archbishop of Milan and was later elected Pope Paul VI in 1963, became involved. Anselmo Giabbani, prior of Camaldoli, to whom Merton had written about joining Camaldoli, was friends with Archbishop Montini, and as the tension over the situation rose, Giabbani showed Montini Merton's letters to get guidance and feedback. Both Merton and Dom James were open to Montini's thoughts, and in a lengthy and pastoral letter written to Merton, Archbishop Montini advised Merton that his place was at Gethsemani.

It was Merton's vocational crisis during these summer months that paved the way to him becoming the novice master at Gethsemani. Faced with Merton's continued requests for a transfer (*transitus*) to Camaldoli, Dom James travelled to Europe to speak with Dom Gabriel Sortais regarding what to do about the situation with his Master of Scholastics. Neither of them felt that it was in Merton's best interest, nor frankly in the interest of the order, to have him leave for Camaldoli, but they also recognized that Merton seemed to have a genuine calling to greater solitude than he had experienced so far. They therefore decided that he could become a hermit at Gethsemani by moving into the newly built fire tower, and Dom James proposed this to Merton immediately upon his return to the

6. Victor A. Kramer, "Merton's Contributions as Teacher, Writer and Community Member: An Interview with Flavian Burns, O.C.S.O.," *The Merton Annual* 3 (1990): 82.

monastery with the understanding that he was to test his vocation to solitude fully by becoming "a real hermit one hundred percent. Not just half a hermit."[7] According to Fox, Merton expressed initial interest in this proposal, but for reasons that aren't entirely clear, he proposed something different. In a letter to Dom Gabriel Sortais written shortly after his meeting with the abbot, Merton explained what happened as follows:

> You have told Dom James that I could be allowed to make the trial of the solitary life here. I thought at first that God wanted this trial of me, and I was going to ask to do it, knowing that Dom James would probably give me permission. Now, at the same time, one of our officers [the novice master, Fr. Walter Helmstetter] has been elected Abbot of the Genesee, which is very inconvenient for Dom James, since if I were to leave for the woods, he will have to replace two of his Father Masters at one time. So I thought I must, before God, leave myself entirely in the hands of Dom James, and *he* has decided to give me the office of Father Master of the Choir Novices to replace Father Walter (the new Abbot of the foundation). You see how poor we are in personnel when it is I, the *only one* that Dom James can entrust with the novices without having to seek a dispensation.[8]

Merton wrote that Dom James appointed him novice master in large part because the abbot was left with no alternatives given the regulations of the Trappists that the novice master must be a priest who is over thirty-five and has been in the order for at least ten years. There was another priest Dom James could have appointed to this post, but he was only thirty-one and had not been in the order for ten years. To appoint the younger priest would have necessitated a dispensation from

7. James Fox to Giovanni Battista Montini (October 20, 1955) in Grayston, *Thomas Merton and the Noonday Demon*, 158.

8. TM to Gabriel Sortais (October 18, 1955) in Grayston, *Thomas Merton and the Noonday Demon*, 154–55.

the abbot general, and Merton suggested that Dom James appoint him
novice master to avoid having to do this. Dom James, however, had
a different recollection of events. In a letter he wrote to Archbishop
Montini, the abbot wrote that, when presented with the possibility
of becoming a full-time hermit, Merton got cold feet. According to
Dom James, "it was evident that [Merton] began to be afraid of his
proposal to be a hermit."[9] In a letter recounting these events to Gabriel
Sortais, Dom James noted that, the day after he told Merton about
the possibility of him testing his vocation to greater solitude, Merton
wrote a note to Dom James offering himself to become the novice
master. Dom James "concluded that the sudden proposal of being a
hermit one hundred percent immediately unnerved him, and that he
was . . . looking for an honorable way out of the hermitage dream."[10]
In other words, the idea for being appointed as novice master came
from Merton himself, which Dom James interpreted as the result,
not of selflessness and self-sacrifice on Merton's part—which is how
Merton understood what he was doing—but of Merton recognizing
his lack of readiness to become an actual hermit.

It is worth noting that, regardless of which version is closest to
the truth, the fact remains that, despite Merton's protestations about
monastic life at Gethsemani not affording him enough time for
solitude, by offering himself as novice master, he demonstrated that
his ultimate allegiance was to his brothers at Gethsemani. And while
Dom James took Merton's volunteering for the position to mean that
he developed cold feet about becoming a hermit, the fact remains
that the abbot had no qualms about appointing Merton to one of
the most important offices in the monastery. "I believe," Fox wrote
to Montini, "he will make an excellent Master of Novices."[11] This was

9. Fox to Montini (October 20, 1955) in Grayston, *Thomas Merton and the
Noonday Demon*, 158.

10. As quoted by Grayston in *Thomas Merton and the Noonday Demon*, 200. See
Fox to Sortais (October 18, 1955), unpublished letter, *Thomas Merton Center*, Bellarmine University.

11. Fox to Montini (October 20, 1955) in Grayston, *Thomas Merton and the
Noonday Demon*, 158.

not a flippant decision on the part of Fox, made simply to appease a restless monk. As Fox himself noted in a reflection on Merton written after his death, the position of novice master "is a supremely important position in the Community. The future of the Community depends on the right training of the novices." And in that reflection, as he assessed Merton's role as novice master, Fox concluded that his initial instinct was correct. Merton was indeed "an excellent" novice master who "put his whole heart and soul into his work."[12]

For Merton's part, his letters at this time indicate that he was enthusiastic about becoming novice master. One of his most intimate correspondents was Jean Leclercq, a monk and distinguished scholar at the Abbey of Clervaux in Luxembourg. Leclercq was well aware of Merton's vocational issues through the letters Merton sent him. In a letter to Leclercq written less than two months after his appointment as novice master, Merton expressed equanimity and even contentment with his situation, suggesting that, paradoxically, his new position actually brought with it greater solitude than he had previously. "I have found a surprising amount of interior solitude among my novices," he wrote, "and even a certain exterior solitude which I had not expected. This [the novitiate] is, after all, the quietest and most secluded corner of the monastery. So I am grateful to God for fulfilling many of my desires when seeming to deny them."[13] Two years later, in a letter to Jacques Maritain, Merton referred again to the "unexpected solitude" he discovered in the novitiate, but more importantly, he described what his novices meant to him and particularly his love for them: "Love is no distraction. If I didn't love these little ones, they could distract me. They would be an obstacle. But if I didn't love them I wouldn't love God either" (Li, 27; TM to Jacques Maritain: October 9, 1958).

12. James Fox, "The Spiritual Son," in *Thomas Merton, Monk: A Monastic Tribute*, ed. Patrick Hart (New York: Sheed & Ward, 1974), 151.

13. TM to Jean Leclercq (December 3, 1955) in *Survival or Prophecy: The Letters of Thomas Merton and Jean Leclercq*, ed. Patrick Hart (New York: Farrar, Straus and Giroux, 2002), 72.

Merton as Novice Master

In his lecture notes for the novices about the *Constitutions* of the Cistercians of the Strict Observance, the regulations that govern all facets of Trappist life, Merton outlined the role and importance of the novice master. Describing the appointment of a capable novice master as "one of the most grave obligations" of the abbot, Merton first outlined to the novices the basic requirements for the position, explaining that, according to the constitutions and canon law, the novice master must be at least thirty-five, a priest, and have been professed as a monk for at least ten years. The novice master should be a monk known for "his prudence, charity, piety and observance of the rule," someone who has "distinguished himself by an exemplary life" and who is deeply prayerful. "In other words," Merton continued, "the novice master must be deeply imbued in the Spirit of the Order and must be able to impart that spirit to others, not only by words but above all by example. [This is] a terrible responsibility." The novice master's role in the formation of novices is, as Merton noted, absolutely vital—"The future of the Order depends on the right formation of novices"—and that formation occurred through both individual spiritual direction and detailed instruction (Cvii, 166, 167, 169–70). I will address the former before focusing on the latter.

Merton as Spiritual Director

When one looks not only at the scheduled amount of time he spent teaching the novices—he held two thirty-minute conferences and one forty-five-minute conference each week—but also, as shall be seen below, the time and energy he put into preparation for these conferences, it is extraordinary that he had time for much else. Yet, in addition to continuing his writing, Merton also met with every novice for spiritual direction once every other week for thirty minutes, though he would often meet with novices for an hour depending on the situation.[14] This is impressive given that there were as many as forty novices at times.

14. May 20, 2020, email correspondence with Br. Paul Quenon, OCSO.

In 1959, four years after becoming novice master, Merton published a booklet on spiritual direction. If we are to understand Merton's role as spiritual director, it is worthwhile to look briefly at his theology of spiritual direction as articulated in this booklet before looking at the testimonies of those who received spiritual direction from him at the monastery.

The emphasis in Merton's booklet on spiritual direction is on the importance of establishing a personal relationship between the director and the one being directed. Spiritual direction is, Merton wrote, "a continuous process of formation and guidance, in which a Christian is led and encouraged *in his special vocation*, so that by faithful correspondence to the graces of the Holy Spirit, he may attain to the particular end of his vocation and to union with God."[15] Thus, "a spiritual director is . . . one who helps another to recognize and to follow the inspirations of grace in his life, in order to arrive at the end to which God is leading him" (*Spiritual Direction*, 9). In order for the director to be able to provide this kind of guidance, there must exist a genuine human relationship. "Direction is, by its very nature," Merton wrote, "something *personal*" (*Spiritual Direction*, 22). The one receiving direction has to be completely open with the director, willing to speak truthfully and humbly, and the director has to be able to provide clear guidance without fear of offending the one being directed. Moreover, the one receiving direction has to allow the director to see his true self, apart from all the illusions and masks that blind us from seeing who we really are. But for that to occur, the director has to foster "an atmosphere of confidence and friendliness in which the penitent can say anything that is on his mind with the assurance that it will be dealt with *frankly and honestly*" (*Spiritual Direction*, 29–30). Merton insisted that there has to be personal intimacy, even friendship, in this relationship. Moreover, the director should always have in mind the worth and value of the one seeking direction. "A true director can never get over the awe he feels in the presence of a person," he wrote, "an immortal soul, loved

---

15. Thomas Merton, *Spiritual Direction and Meditation* (Collegeville, MN: Liturgical Press, 1960), 5.

by Christ, washed in His most Precious Blood, and nourished by the sacrament of His Love" (*Spiritual Direction*, 25–26).

Testimonials from his former students indicate that Merton's style of direction mirrored what he wrote in his pamphlet, particularly in terms of treating each person with respect and fostering an atmosphere that was friendly and therefore conducive to personal transformation. James Conner, OCSO, described the first time he went to receive spiritual direction, noting the difference in Merton's style of direction in comparison to his predecessors:

> The very first time I went in for direction, after giving the blessing he said, "sit down." That was a revolutionary thing at that time, you never sat down with the abbot, the prior or the novice master, you always knelt at the side of their desk. I always sensed this was part of his real respect for each person, making sure he was dealing with them on an equal basis.[16]

Other former students commented on the way in which Merton was completely present to them during direction. For example, the psychologist and author James Finley, who spent time as a novice under Merton, described Merton's style of direction as follows: "The thing about him is that he seemed so transparently present. He was authentically present."[17] Timothy Kelly, OCSO, a novice under Merton who later served as abbot of Gethsemani from 1973–2000, said something similar: "He was always really present. If you were speaking with him, he was very present to you."[18] Br. Columban Weber described his individual meetings as follows:

16. Paul M. Pearson, "'A Dedication to Prayer and a Dedication to Humanity': An Interview about Thomas Merton with James Conner, OCSO," *The Merton Annual* 23 (2010): 214.

17. Glenn Crider, "Interview with James Finley: Cultivating a Contemplative Lifestyle," *The Merton Annual* 19 (2006): 358.

18. George A. Kilcourse Jr., "'The Great Honesty': Remembering Thomas Merton—An Interview with Abbot Timothy Kelly, O.C.S.O.," *The Merton Annual* 9 (1996): 200.

On a one-to-one he was marvelous. He reminds me a lot of
the great communicators of our time—John Paul II, Mother
Teresa of Calcutta, Matthew Fox, etc. These people are great
actors, and are able to attune themselves to the particular audience at hand. You feel as if you are the only person in the world
and that for them, you are.[19]

While Merton did not appreciate being interrupted during periods
of time when he was writing—as Matthew Kelty, OCSO, put it,
"Once the man was at his work, you left him alone"[20]—the time he
devoted to direction was time given over completely to the novices,
and this willingness to be utterly present to his students was borne
out of his recognition of their dignity and worth.

Merton's respect for his students also manifested itself in the manner in which he would give direction. Many made note of Merton's
unwillingness to take a one-size-fits-all approach to directing, an
unwillingness born out of his understanding that each novice was
unique and his path to the contemplative life was not going to be
identical with other paths. In his pamphlet on spiritual direction,
Merton wrote that the role of the director is to help those under his
care understand who they really are in God's eyes and so to obey
their "real Director—the Holy Spirit, hidden in the depths of our
soul" (*Spiritual Direction*, 30). For Merton this meant helping those
under his direction in their discernment of the Spirit's working in
their lives without dictating his own preconceived notions of who
and what they were supposed to be.

Fr. James Conner told a story that illustrates this approach beautifully. Conner's previous director gave very specific guidance about
how to pray, modeled on an Ignatian style of meditation, a style
that did not accord with Conner's way of praying. Conner remem-
bers that, after he made profession to become a monk, he came to

19. Gloria Kitto Lewis, "Learning to Live: Merton's Students Remember His
Teaching," *The Merton Annual* 8 (1995): 97.

20. Matthew Kelty, OCSO, "Looking Back to Merton: Memories and Impressions—An Interview," *The Merton Annual* 1 (1988): 58.

Merton for guidance, telling him that he didn't really know how to meditate because he found himself unable to pray in the manner he was taught. He was worried that perhaps Merton would judge him, but what he received was affirmation that he found freeing:

> He just looked at me really quietly and said, "Well, it sounds like the Spirit is working in you." It was such a freeing thing for me; it just freed me to be myself and to discover how I could find God in prayer. It didn't tie me down to something that seemed impossible. Merton left it up to me to find what suited me best. I think I just gradually discovered myself, how to pray in a way that suited me, fitted me. (Interview with James Conner, 215)

James Finley described Merton's form of directing as being similarly freeing: "He accepted me and gave me a lot of slack and kind of gave me permission to find my own way. He was honest with me, and that helped me be honest with myself" (interview with James Finley, 357). In his recent memoir, Br. Paul Quenon described Merton's style of directing this way: "As a spiritual director, Fr. Louis [Merton's monastic name] seemed to be mostly nondirective. I expected something more from him, but what I got was space to breathe, to be myself, and to develop at my own pace."[21] Merton understood that his role as director was primarily to give space for the Spirit to work, recognizing the dignity and uniqueness of each person and of the work God was going to do in them.

As novice master and spiritual director to new monks, Merton was adamant that he was uninterested in making disciples. He made this point in his conference notes on spiritual direction, which he wrote as part of his course on Christian mysticism. "It is especially necessary for the director to be a humble man who puts the interests of the ones directed above his own," Merton wrote, "and does not simply seek to subjugate them to his own ideas and dominate

---

21. Paul Quenon, OCSO, *In Praise of the Useless Life: A Monk's Memoir* (Notre Dame, IN: Ave Maria Press, 2018), 30.

them by his own 'spirituality.' " He continued: "He does not want to attract disciples to himself and surround himself with a coterie of dependents" (Ciii, 279). Fr. Timothy Kelly noted that he and the other novices understood this point. Merton was not under the impression that the novices needed to become little "Mertons" to succeed as Trappists at Gethsemani. Rather, he had the humility to recognize his own shortcomings as a monk, as well as the wisdom to understand that the novices under his care needed to find their own way as monks. While he could and would gently guide them in direction, his goal was to provide the space for each novice to become most fully who God wanted them to be.

Merton as Teacher

In addition to individual spiritual direction, novice masters were to provide regular instruction to the novices. By all accounts, Merton was a gifted teacher beloved by his novices. Fr. James Conner, who experienced a number of different teachers at the monastery, recalled the change that took place in the novitiate when Merton started giving regular conferences to the novices: "His whole style, his whole manner, his whole presentation, and even the material he was giving us was much more beneficial for all of us." Given their experience of other teachers at Gethsemani, Conner remarked that Merton "was a tremendous relief to all of us." Before Merton, scholastics and novices were held to strict rules of silence in the classroom, meaning that there was little to no opportunities for questions and discussions. Merton's style was different; he welcomed questions and discussion. Moreover, while previous teachers taught mainly from textbooks, Merton created his own courses and course notes and taught things "which obviously meant something to [him] and which he thought should have a meaning for" his novices (interview with James Conner, 213, 217).

The seriousness with which Merton took his task as teacher for the novices is on display in the extensive conference notes he prepared. As already noted, eleven substantial volumes of these conference notes have been published, with one more volume scheduled for publication. According to Merton's reading of the constitutions of the Order and of canon law, the novice master was entrusted with teaching novices on such matters as "the *Rule*, monastic life, [the] virtues, etc." (Cvii, 168). Merton went above and beyond with his novices. In addition to detailed and extensive instruction on the Rule of St. Benedict as well as on the history of medieval Cistercian history and theology, Merton delved into the minutiae of the *Usages* of the Cistercians of the Strict Observance that governed every aspect of Trappist life until they were revised in the wake of the Second Vatican Council; he examined the *Carta Caritatis*, the eleventh century founding document of the Cistercians, as well as the *Customs* and *Constitutions* adopted by the Trappists that provided specific guidance for how the Cistercians of the Strict Observance would follow St. Benedict's *Rule*; and he explored in detail (this volume of his conference notes contains almost 500 pages) the vows taken by Trappists. He also provided to his novices a detailed history of monasticism prior to St. Benedict's *Rule* as well as of non-Benedictine monasticism, and taught a course on the history of Christian mysticism. Moreover, he gave conferences on Scripture and scriptural interpretation, as well as on the liturgy. Amazingly, these conference notes do not encompass the totality of everything he taught. Beginning in 1962, Merton's novitiate conferences began to be recorded, and a glance at the list of titles of his conferences shows the breadth of topics he tackled. In addition to giving broad overviews of the patristic period, Merton gave classes on specific writers, including Tertullian, Clement of Alexandria, Origen, Jerome, Augustine, Pseudo-Dionysius, John Climacus, and Gregory the Great, to name just a few. He focused attention on medieval thinkers like Anselm and Thomas Aquinas, explored theological topics of importance, including trinitarian theology and Mariology, and even focused attention on certain facets of modern poetry.

Merton taught the novices three times per week, with two thirty-minute conferences and one slightly longer forty-five-minute conference. He therefore needed to do substantial preparation for teaching, but the published conference notes show that his preparation went above and beyond what was required. According to John Eudes Bamberger, "regularly he had prepared more material than he could cover in the allotted time."[22] While he never got through all of his prepared material, the novices would all receive a mimeographed copy of Merton's conference notes at the end of their course of study.

The conference notes themselves give evidence both of Merton's extensive teaching preparation and of the sheer breadth of his historical and theological knowledge, and illustrate "Merton's own deep love for and commitment to monastic tradition."[23] His notes on John Cassian (360–435) and the Fathers explore monastic spirituality from the Apostolic Fathers to the fourth century, and include extensive quotations from patristic writers taken directly from the *Patrologia Latina* and the *Patrologia Graeca*, the multi-volume collection of patristic texts in Latin and Greek collected in the nineteenth century by the French patrologist, Fr. Jacques-Paul Migne. English translations of the Fathers were not as prevalent as they are today, but Merton's proficiency with languages allowed him to introduce his novices to the original sources. Moreover, at a time when the clerical and monastic formation in Catholicism focused almost exclusively on Latin patristic and medieval sources—with a specific focus on the medieval—Merton exposed his students to the riches of the Greek patristic tradition. In so doing, as Columba Stewart notes, "Merton had the prescience even before the [Second Vatican] Council to reclaim the eastern tradition that, married with the genius of Augustine, formed the great Latin mystics from Gregory the Great onward."[24]

While there were few resources for studying the Greek Fathers, Merton dove headlong into the sources, as well as into any secondary sources he could find (which were usually in French), and his conference notes demonstrate how thoroughly acquainted he was with the material. This will come as little surprise to those who have made

---

22. John Eudes Bamberger, OCSO, "Preface," in Cvii, vii.
23. Patrick F. O'Connell, "Introduction," Ci, xvi.
24. Columba Stewart, "Preface," Ci, xii.

their way through Merton's private journals and his correspondence. In his journals, Merton regularly noted what he was reading, and the Greek Fathers appear with regularity. And as he himself noted in a 1961 letter to Dorothy Day, his own theology had been influenced by this exposure to their thought (see Li, 143; TM to Dorothy Day: December 20, 1961).

In the opening sentences of his conference notes on John Cassian and the Fathers, Merton explained to his novices why he understood the Greek writers to be important:

> If for some reason it were necessary for you to drink a pint of water taken out of the Mississippi River and you could choose where it was to be drawn out of the river—would you take a pint from the source of the river in Minnesota or from the estuary at New Orleans? This example is perhaps not perfect. Christian tradition and spirituality certainly do not become polluted with development. That is not the idea at all. Nevertheless, tradition and spirituality are all the more pure and genuine in proportion as they are in contact with the original sources and retain the same content. (Ci, 5)

This declaration regarding the importance of returning to the sources is one that gets repeated regularly by Merton throughout his novitiate conferences, illustrating the degree to which he was imbued with the spirit of important twentieth-century Catholic theologians who influenced the church up to and during the Second Vatican Council. In the run-up to this council, figures like Romano Guardini (1885–1968), Jean Danielou (1905–1974), Hans Urs von Balthasar (1905–1988), Henri de Lubac (1896–1991), Yves Congar (1904–1995), and Louis Bouyer (1913–2004) argued that the church had for too long been focused on medieval theology to the neglect of important patristic sources and ideas, and that therefore renewal of the church needed to occur through a return to the original sources.

These thinkers formed what became known as the *ressourcement* movement, and while the church did not immediately appreciate the movement—Pope Pius XII's 1950 encyclical, *Humani Generis*, was an attack against the *ressourcement* movement—they ended up playing a central role at the Second Vatican Council, which took up the mantle of renewal through a return to the sources.[25] That Merton was familiar with and influenced by these theologians is demonstrated in a 1967 letter he wrote to an Italian university student who had asked him what theologians had most influenced him. After naming important patristic and medieval thinkers—including Augustine, Gregory the Great, Thomas Aquinas, Bernard, and Duns Scotus—Merton provided a list of modern theologians that reads as a who's who of twentieth-century Catholic theology that includes a number of key figures in the *ressourcement* movement: "Hans Von Balthasar, De Lubac, Danielou, Bouyer, Dom Leclercq, K. Rahner, Romano Guardini, Jacques Maritain, E. Gilson" (Lii, 349; TM to Mario Falsina: March 25, 1967). Moreover, Maritain and Gilson were both important precursors to the *ressourcement* movement as they were read by key *ressourcement* thinkers. Merton was, however, not only familiar with the writings of these theologians, but was a correspondent with a number of them; we possess letters exchanged between Merton and Balthasar, Danielou, Leclercq, Maritain, and Gilson. Thus, Merton's call to return to the sources was rooted in the spirit of the *ressourcement* movement such that, years before the Second Vatican Council's 1965 *Perfectae Caritatis* (Decree on the Appropriate Renewal of the Religious Life) called for renewal of monasticism through "a continuous return to the sources,"[26] he was already introducing his students to these sources.

Merton's knowledge of these early Christian sources, as well as of the sources of monastic and specifically Cistercian history, is on display in his conference notes. It is worth going briefly through

25. For an account of the role the *ressourcement* theologians and movement played at the Second Vatican Council, see John O'Malley, *What Happened at Vatican II* (Cambridge, MA: Harvard University Press, 2008).

26. Decree on the Appropriate Renewal of the Religious Life: *Perfectae Caritatis* 2, Vatican website, October 28, 1965, http://www.vatican.va/archive/hist_councils /ii_vatican_council/documents/vat-ii_decree_19651028_perfectae-caritatis_en.html.

each volume of the published notes in order to get a sense both of his modus operandi as well as of the breadth of his knowledge and reading. In his survey of monastic spirituality prior to John Cassian in the fourth and fifth centuries, Merton introduced his students to writings and thinkers of the first and second centuries, including Ignatius of Antioch (died in 108), the *Didache*, and the First Epistle of Clement, both written late in the first century. He then focused attention on prominent Alexandrian theologians of the second and third centuries, Clement of Alexandria (150–215) and Origen (died in 254), quoting liberally from their writings.[27] He afterward focused extensive attention on the first Desert Fathers, paying particular attention to Antony the Great (251–356) and Pachomius (292–348), before delving into the Cappadocian Fathers—Basil of Caesarea (330–379), Gregory of Nazianzus (329–390), and Gregory of Nyssa (335–394)—and their contributions to monastic spirituality. He followed this with brief accounts of Palestinian, Mesopotamian, Syrian, and Egyptian monasticism—all of which he would focus on in greater detail in a later course—before delving into a figure Merton clearly understood to be immensely important—Evagrius Ponticus (345–399), a somewhat controversial figure, but one Merton considered to be the "greatest theologian of the desert" and "one of the fathers of Christian mystical theology" (Ci, 88).

It was at this point that Merton devoted extensive attention to John Cassian (360–435), a monk who profoundly influenced the shape of monasticism in the Western church. In his account of Cassian's life and writings, Merton provided substantial quotations from and citations to the Latin texts. According to Merton, Cassian influenced figures from Benedict to Dominic to Thomas Aquinas to the early Cistercians, and as such, Merton argued that "every monk should know him thoroughly." Cassian is, according to Merton, "*the*

27. It is worth noting that Merton's love of Clement in particular was so great that, in 1962, he published a small translation he did of selections from Clement's *Protreptikos. Clement of Alexandria: Selections from* The Protreptikos—*An Essay and Translation by Thomas Merton* (New York: New Directions, 1962).

great monastic writer—the Master of the spiritual life par excellence
for monks—the source for all in the West" (Ci, 99). He was also a
bridge between the Greek East and the Western church in that he
spent significant time with the Desert Fathers in the East, and their
influence on his monastic theology shaped his thought substantially.

This course on Cassian and the Fathers is indicative of Merton's
approach when preparing and delivering his classes. Merton's notes
are filled with references to primary and secondary source. Despite
untranslated primary sources from the patristic period, Merton exposed his novices directly to the Fathers themselves, and was as-
sisted in doing so thanks to secondary sources in French caused by
the resurgence of patristic study taking place in France in the mid-
twentieth century. As the editor of Merton's novitiate conferences
notes writes, his notes "attest to the depth of Merton's own exploration of the material."[28] The breadth of his reading of the patristic
period, including his deep familiarity with John Cassian's writings,
was impressive, and his ability to distill the theologies of numerous
authors in a way that was accessible yet thorough astounds.

Merton's breadth of knowledge and reading is on even further
display in his notes on pre-Benedictine monasticism. I've already
mentioned that Merton wasn't content simply to give to the novices
an exposure to Latin sources, but wanted them also to have a thorough immersion in the Greek sources. His classes on pre-Benedictine
monasticism demonstrate that he wanted to go even beyond the
Greek sources to look at non-Greek or Latin monasticism at a time
when knowledge of this form of monasticism was in short supply
in the West. Thus, in this course, Merton exposed the novices to
Syrian and Persian monasticism, providing them not only with a
history of monasticism in these regions, but introducing them to the
writings and thought of important figures like Theodoret of Cyrus
(393–457), whose *Historia Religiosa* provides an outline of Syrian
monastic practice and theology; Aphraat the Wise, a third and fourth
century theologian from Persia; Ephrem the Syrian (306–373), a

28. O'Connell, "Introduction," Ci, xxiv.

poet and hymnist whose influence on Syrian monasticism was immense; and Philoxenos of Mabbug (440–543), a Syrian bishop and
theologian who brought together the Syrian tradition with much
of Greek theological thought as embodied in Origen and Evagrius.

Merton was "one of the very few who were beginning to recognize the significance of Syriac texts for the development of early
Christianity,"[29] and he understood that his novices would benefit
from exposure to Syriac texts and thinkers. It is safe to say that, while
the novices may at least have known the names of the Greek Fathers
referenced by Merton, they knew less about Syrian and Persian monasticism. Merton's ability not only to read and distill monastic
thinkers in such a way as to make them accessible to new monks
impresses, but so does the scale of his research. The renowned scholar
of early Christian studies at Catholic University of America, Sydney
H. Griffith, wrote that one can only be in "awe that Merton had
time and energy enough to search out all the material he consulted,
some of it still hard to find and most of it still available only in
specialized libraries." Indeed, Griffith noted that Merton's course on
pre-Benedictine monasticism was so unique that it was very likely
"the first general survey in America of the works of the major 'monastic' thinkers among the Syriac-speaking Fathers of the Church."[30]

Merton's breadth is further demonstrated in his course on the
history and theology of Christian mysticism, a course that was intended for and given to the priests in formation at Gethsemani in
1961 to make up for a gap in their education. While this was not
a course given specifically to the novices, his notes are important
for two reasons. First, they are "a valuable witness both to Merton's
own knowledge of and interest in" the Christian mystical tradition,
and show which figures and movements most influenced him and
that he considered to be most significant for contemporary readers.[31]
These notes reveal the degree to which Merton was familiar with and

29. Patrick F. O'Connell, "Introduction," Cii, xliii.
30. Sydney H. Griffith, "Preface," Cii, viii.
31. Patrick F. O'Connell, "Introduction," in Ciii, liii.

impacted by patristic theologians and mystics like Clement of Alexandria, Gregory of Nyssa, as well as by medieval mystics like Meister Eckhart (ca. 1260–ca. 1328), and Julian of Norwich (fourteenth century). Second, in these notes, Merton articulated something of his teaching philosophy. The goal of his classes was not simply to impart information, but to form students in such a way that they came away transformed. As he wrote by way of introduction to this course, "the Christian mystical tradition is something that has been handed down not only to be talked about but to be *lived*" (Ciii, 4). There is, he argued, an intrinsic connection between theology and mysticism. "Without mysticism there is no real theology," he wrote, "and without theology there is no real mysticism." And to prove his point, he did what he did in his course on Cassian and the Fathers by emphasizing the importance of returning to the sources, particularly "a return to the patristic sources" (Ciii, 16). Why? Because the great writers of the patristic period did not make an artificial separation between theology and spirituality, between doctrine and mysticism. Pointing to the work of the great twentieth-century theologian, Hans Urs von Balthasar, Merton commented that, for the Fathers, "personal experience and dogmatic faith were a living unity" (Ciii, 36). Theology is, he continued, the outward articulation of the experience of union with God in Jesus Christ. The theology formulated by the church during the patristic period reflects the "collective memory and experience of Christ living and present within her." Therefore, the study of this theology cannot but transform, particularly in the case of contemplative monks who can and should enter into the mindset of the early church. This understanding of the transformational nature of theology, of a theology not divorced from spirituality, is rooted particularly in the Greek Fathers but also articulated through the Western mystical tradition that Merton also focused attention upon in his course on Christian mysticism. And it is this understanding of the transformational study of theology that affected the way in which he endeavored to form the novices and other students through his teaching. As he noted, the mystical and theological tradition of the church "*forms and affects the whole man*," and as such, exposure to this tradition "is not merely a matter of study and reading" (Ciii, 35). One must be immersed in the tradition, and so be shaped by it.

His course on Christian mysticism took students from the mystical theology found in the Gospel of John—Merton referred to this gospel as "the true source of all Christian mysticism" (Ciii, 38)—through Greek Fathers like Irenaeus of Lyons (d. ca. 200), Clement, Athanasius (d. 373), the Cappadocian Fathers, Evagrius, Pseudo-Dionysius (fifth–sixth centuries), Maximus the Confessor (d. 662), and up through prominent figures of fourteenth- through sixteenth-century mysticism from Meister Eckhart to Teresa of Avila (1515–1582) and John of the Cross (1542–1591).

Even in a course focusing specifically on the Rule of St. Benedict, Merton's notes reveal an "assiduous reading and digesting of primary and secondary sources,"[32] and the footnotes throughout the published edition of these notes show his thorough preparation and his understanding of the *Rule*. Moreover, his desire for the novices to understand the *Rule* less as a legal document requiring rigid observance, and more as a text that can, when followed, transform, illustrates once again that his pedagogy was rooted in the transformation of his students. The *Rule* is not just a document, but "a life that should take possession of [our] inmost hearts." It is not an end in itself, but a means to an end: "This end is union with God in love, and every line of the *Rule* indicates that its various prescriptions are given us to show us how to get rid of self-love and replace it by the love of God" (Civ, 6).

This concern for the formation of the novices continues in his course on monastic observances which focused on the *Usages* of the Trappist order, the regulations that governed various aspects of life in the monastery and gave structure to that life. These regulations included such facets of Trappist life as how the monastery building should be structured, when and how long the offices of prayer should be, what the time between the night vigils and the office of Lauds

---

32. Patrick F. O'Connell, "Introduction," Civ, xiii.

should be used for by monks, the role bells play in regulating the monastic schedule, etc. Lectures on these topics had the potential to be dry and legalistic, but as noted by one of the monks at the Abbey who studied under Merton, he sought to show "that the observations are not simply rules to be obeyed, but a way of life to be lived out."[33] Merton the novice master didn't want to tell his novices about these observances in order to instill in them a slavish adherence to the rules. Rather, he emphasized that he wanted the novices "to understand what we are doing" in order that they would more fully comprehend that the monastic observances have as their aim the fostering of a life conducive to contemplation (Cv, 5).

It is for this reason that Merton's course on the monastic observances is the most practical of his conferences, containing as it does what is "perhaps his fullest teaching on prayer" in his section describing the meditation and prayer that should occur between the night vigils and the office of Lauds.[34] One looks in vain in Merton's writings on prayer and contemplation for much in the way of specific guidance about how to pray; he preferred instead to write about the basic principles and theology undergirding the contemplative life. Merton appeared to understand that the way he prayed wasn't necessarily the way others can or should pray, and so he was reluctant to have others emulate him. As he wrote in a letter to a Muslim correspondent from Pakistan who asked him to describe his method of prayer, "I do not ordinarily write about such things" (Li, 64; TM to Abdul Aziz: January 2, 1966). While he did not describe his own method of prayer to the novices, he did provide for them guidance on meditation clearly borne out of his own experience (see Cv, 75–92). He thus delved into the purpose of meditation, focusing specifically on its role in coming to a deeper recognition of our union with God, giving practical suggestions about how to meditate, such as incorporating the repetition of a brief prayer, such as the Jesus Prayer ("Lord Jesus Christ, Son of God, have mercy on

33. James Conner, OCSO, "Preface," Cv, vii.
34. James Conner, OCSO, "Preface," Cv, viii.

me, a sinner"), in conjunction with one's breathing. He also recommended that one of the best places to meditate was in the presence of the Blessed Sacrament.

Indeed, a eucharistic theme weaves its way throughout Merton's conferences on monastic observances. He emphasized to the novices that every facet of life in the monastery centers around the Eucharist, that the various regulations and rules set out in the *Usages* have as their focus a way of life that is "above all Eucharistic" (Cv, 5). Merton thus took the opportunity when describing the regulations regarding private masses and communion to impart to his novices an in-depth eucharistic theology, telling them that all monks ought to "meditate frequently on [the Eucharist], reading about it, studying it, and making it our whole life" (Cv, 107). He also told the novices that they should make daily visits to the Blessed Sacrament in the tabernacle, recognizing that the cultivation of the contemplative life is inextricable from a pronounced eucharistic devotion. "The great source of all 'graces of prayer,'" he wrote, is "contact with Jesus in the sacrament of love" for there is a "*special grace of love* that comes from and with our visits to the Blessed Sacrament" (Cv, 146). The contemplative life, he continues, "is not seriously attained, in practice, without a fervent Eucharistic life" (Cv, 148).

The largest volume of the conferences is Merton's treatment of the vows taken by monks, and again, the focus is pastoral rather than legalistic. That said, perhaps the most interesting facet of Merton's presentation on the vows is his extensive use of Thomas Aquinas's *Summa Theologiae*. Merton regularly made reference to Thomas Aquinas throughout his conference notes on various topics, usually including a specific citation of the *Summa*. These citations illustrate Merton's familiarity with Thomas, but no set of conference notes demonstrates Merton's knowledge of the *Summa* as do these notes on monastic vows. His numerous citations of the *Summa* are not just peppered into the text for lip service. Rather, these references give "every indication of being the fruit of personal reflection and sincere conviction."[35] As O'Connell notes when commenting on

35. Augustine Roberts, OCSO, "Preface," Cvi, viii.

Merton's familiarity with Thomas Aquinas, "No text of Merton, even *The Ascent to Truth*, shows such familiarity with and reliance on the work of Thomas Aquinas—virtually every major section of the work is developed from the Thomistic framework of the *Summa*, and scholastic terminology abounds throughout."[36]

Merton's interest in Thomistic theology didn't begin at the monastery, as I already noted when looking at his early life prior to entering the monastery. His professor at Columbia, Daniel Walsh, kindled his interest in medieval theology, including Thomistic theology. That interest in Thomas Aquinas continued when he entered the monastery. One of Merton's earliest writings, *The Ascent to Truth*, is an early writing (published 1951) in which he brought Thomas Aquinas into conversation with John of the Cross. It's a technical book, not easily accessible, and not one that Merton himself ranked very highly among his writings. Nevertheless, it shows Merton's familiarity with, and interest in, Thomistic theology early in his monastic career. This interest in Thomistic theology never abated, and his journals and letters contain numerous references to prominent neo-Thomist writers such as Étienne Gilson (1884–1978), Jacques Maritain (1882–1973), and Josef Pieper (1904–1997); indeed, as noted already, he corresponded with both Gilson and Maritain, becoming particularly close with the latter. Pieper's work appears to have been particularly significant for Merton in the latter part of his life. Some of the most compelling and interesting passages of *Conjectures of a Guilty Bystander*, published in 1965, are reflections on what Thomas and his methodology have to teach Catholics about entering into dialogue with others, particularly in light of the Second Vatican Council's exhortations to dialogue, and these passages are replete with references to Pieper's work on Thomas.

As Merton's conference notes on the monastic vows illustrate, his familiarity with Thomas was not a passing or superficial one. For example, Merton began his treatment of the vows by looking at the Catholic theology of humankind, focusing specifically on what Thomas had to say in this regard. Merton thus provided a

---

36. Patrick F. O'Connell, "Introduction," Cvi, xiv.

brief but comprehensive summary of questions 1–114 of the *Prima Secundae* in Thomas's *Summa Theologiae*, in which Thomas outlines the structure of the moral life (see Cvi, 16ff.). Later in the notes, Merton drew on Thomas's theology of the religious life and of contemplation, quoting from the *Summa* at length and in Latin (see Cvi, 114ff.). While Merton drew on other sources in his treatment of the vows—there are, for example, numerous references to John Cassian, Augustine, Maximus the Confessor, Bernard of Clairvaux, Bonaventure, among others—one would be hard-pressed to find pages in the conference notes devoid of citations of Thomas.

Merton's breadth is further illustrated in his conference notes on the key documents of Cistercian life—the *Carta Caritatis*, the *Customs*, and the *Constitutions*. Here again, we see in plain view Merton's method of returning to the sources—returning to the fount—as a means of renewing the church and the order. As John Eudes Bamberger writes, "He was at pains to 'return to the sources' in order to maintain continuity with traditional monastic values while adapting them to the men and conditions of the mid-twentieth century."[37] And his adherence to this way of teaching put him fully in line with the approach Pope John XXIII urged the fathers of the Second Vatican Council to take when he referred to *aggiornamento*.[38] Thus, when teaching the novices about what the *Constitutions* have to say about the studies that monks who are priests ought to undertake after ordination, Merton argued that such study should and must involve going to the sources. Telling them to go beyond the theological manuals, Merton emphasized that the priests should study patristic theology, "especially St. Augustine or St. Gregory," Thomistic theology, and, of course, Bernard of Clairvaux and the other Cistercian fathers (Cvii, 119).

Merton's own intimate familiarity with Bernard of Clairvaux, as well as other early Cistercian fathers, is demonstrated in his courses on medieval Cistercian history and theology. Merton opened his

37. John Eudes Bamberger, OCSO, "Preface," Cvii, vii.
38. Bamberger, viii.

notes on the Cistercian fathers by writing that "to be a Cistercian is in fact to have the spirit of Bernard," and it was out of this conviction that he devoted extensive attention to Bernard's life, writings, and theology for the novices (Cviii, 1). These conference notes are evidence of Merton's sustained and thorough engagement with Bernard throughout his life, engagement that is illustrated in numerous studies published by Merton on Bernard. In addition to a 1954 book on Bernard called *The Last of the Fathers* in which he provided an account of Bernard's life and writings while also providing something of a commentary on Pope Pius XII's encyclical on Bernard (*Doctor Mellifluus*),[39] he wrote numerous articles on Bernard's thought, exploring the relationship between action and contemplation in Bernard, his understanding of interior simplicity, and his conception of transforming unity with God.[40] Merton's familiarity with Bernard was not the result only of his reading of secondary studies on the great Cistercian, but was the consequence of reading Bernard himself.

While Merton's course on the Cistercian fathers was focused largely on Bernard, he did not entirely neglect other Cistercian fathers who were influential on the formation of the Order, as well as influential on Merton himself.[41] These fathers included Aelred of Rievaulx (1110–1167), Guerric of Igny (1070–1157), Isaac of Stella (1110-1169), William of St. Thierry (1085–1148), and Adam of Perseigne (ca. 1145–ca. 1221).[42] Furthermore, in his course on medieval Cistercian history, Merton painstakingly went through the rise and decline of Cistercian monasticism from the eleventh to the

39. Thomas Merton, *The Last of the Fathers: Saint Bernard of Clairvaux and the Encyclical Letter* Doctor Mellifluus (New York: Harcourt, Brace, 1954).

40. These articles can all be found in Thomas Merton, *Thomas Merton on St. Bernard* (Kalamazoo, MI: Cistercian Publications, 1980).

41. Merton's treatment of these fathers can be found in the appendices he wrote to his course on the Cistercian fathers: Thomas Merton, Cviii, 307–95.

42. For a description of Merton's familiarity with these authors, complete with references to Merton's writings on them, see Patrick F. O'Connell, "Introduction," Cviii, xliv–lii.

fourteenth centuries, showing a comprehension of that history in a manner that is remarkable.

Merton also focused attention in his conference notes on Scripture and on the liturgy. I'll write at more length about Merton's liturgical conferences when I examine his understanding of Mary in the next chapter, particularly as these conferences focus attention on the liturgical celebrations of the Marian feasts. His conference notes on Scripture are unfortunately incomplete and somewhat fragmentary. In the first set of conference notes, he provided a detailed account of how Scripture should be interpreted, drawing on Thomas Aquinas as well as a number of important contemporary Catholic biblical scholars. After giving these lectures, Merton proceeded to delve into Genesis and Exodus in an extensive series of lectures by which he demonstrated to the novices how they should read and understand the Scriptures. These conference notes—along with writings on Scripture like *Bread in the Wilderness, Praying the Psalms,* and *Opening the Bible*—demonstrate the centrality of Scripture in Merton's thought.

In addition to the twelve volumes of conference notes we possess, we also have recordings from three years of Merton's conferences as novice master, from 1962–1965, as well as three years of recordings from the weekly conferences he gave that were open to the entire community after he moved permanently to the hermitage. While the conference notes give us a clear picture of the breadth of Merton's research and knowledge, the recordings give us insight into what he was like as a teacher. Given his extensive preparation, there was no way he was able to get through all of the material he prepared. Moreover, had Merton simply read through the prepared material verbatim, it's likely the novices would not have found him to be an engaging teacher. The recordings illustrate that Merton did not strictly adhere to the text. Rather, as one of his former students, John Eudes Bamberger, describes it, "I can still recall how he would rapidly glance at his extensive notes and, skipping over some paragraphs, spontaneously comment at length on selected passages."[43] At the end

43. Bamberger, "Preface," in Cvii, vii.

of a particular course, the novices would all receive a mimeographed copy of Merton's conference notes, so he clearly felt that he could focus on points he understood to be particularly important in class without the obligation of going through all the material.

Moreover, the recordings illustrate that class time was not taken up solely with the material he planned to cover. The conferences usually began with various announcements having to do with life at the monastery. This included mundane matters such as instructions about keeping windows open or closed, turning off lights in empty rooms, etc., but these announcements also sometimes included a reflection for a recently deceased monk whom the novices would not have known personally, or requests for prayer that Merton received from those outside the monastery. In fact, sometimes these house-keeping matters would end up getting discussed for the entire class, as occurred on May 12, 1962, when he brought up that a Quaker protester sailing a small boat into a nuclear testing site in the Pacific had asked Merton for prayer. While Merton was supposed to delve into John Cassian on that day, the entire class ended up being about the liceity of nuclear testing in general and nuclear war in particular in response to questions raised by the novices themselves. It is clear from the recording that the novices felt comfortable asking questions of their novice master, and were even willing to challenge him at times. And for his part, Merton evidently welcomed such question-ing, and responded to challenges seriously. For example, when one of the novices suggested that perhaps the protestor was simply doing this stunt to get his name in the papers, Merton gently but firmly replied: "I don't think that's correct. I don't think he wants headlines everywhere. I think he's got something else up his sleeve. There are easier ways to get your name in the paper. And furthermore, he's not going to get his name in the papers. You think this is going to make anybody's headlines? This isn't going to make anybody's headlines at all. This stuff does not get publicity."[44] And for the rest of the class, Merton focused his attention on the moral theology of

44. Thomas Merton, "Nuclear testing" (May 12, 1962, 002 TR-3), audio tape, *Thomas Merton Center*, Bellarmine University.

nuclear war, largely because his students had questions he felt he needed to address.

To get a sense of what Merton was like as a teacher, it is perhaps instructive to look briefly at the recording of Merton's very last conference to the novices as novice master just before moving to the hermitage permanently. At this point, Merton had been teaching novices for ten years, and his comfort with them as well as their comfort with him was evident. As was the case during almost all of Merton's conferences, there was abundant laughter. Instead of beginning the conference with the usual announcements, he began humorously recounting all the possibilities there were for making a big deal out of him becoming a hermit, including a description of the rites for putting away a hermit that one of the monks had found in the Coptic Rite. Merton's description of the rite doesn't strike the reader as overly funny when reading the transcript, but the recording is filled with laughter from the novices as Merton provides a detailed description of the rite, complete with the bishop praying the prayer for the dead over the prostrate hermit before he enters his hermitage. There's levity and joy in the room, and the mutual love shared between Merton and the novices is evident, a love that is also on display in other conference recordings. Merton also acknowledged all the notes he received from the novices, as well as the spiritual bouquet outlining the devotional acts that the novices promised to make as a way of praying for and supporting him as he embarked on a life of solitude.

After these introductory comments, Merton talked about his time as novice master, and his words illustrate what the position meant to him and his spiritual growth, telling them that having continually to give conferences to the novices meant a great deal of research, but also a great deal of soul-searching to make sure that he was living up to what he was teaching:

> It's the best job in the monastery, master of novices, from every point of view. Don't let anybody kid you that it is terribly hard. It is a very consoling job and it is a good job . . . Incidentally, too, you learn; you learn a great deal. It is a wonderful life to be continually learning, because you learn by teaching; and I

appreciate it more than I can say . . . The thing that is trying about giving out all the time is that you are constantly telling yourself: "These characters are looking at me and they are saying, 'Does this son of a gun practise what he preaches?'— 'What's the use of this guy sitting up here and telling us this stuff?'" It causes a lot of searching. You have to keep on your toes. And you have to try and make sure that you never say anything you don't mean. Which is a discipline. It is good training. So I'm grateful for that. ("A Life Free from Care," 218)

The purpose of Merton's final conference to the novices was to delve into the purpose of the solitary life as a way of explaining why he was becoming a hermit. It isn't necessary to go through Merton's presentation itself, though I encourage you to read it if you have not done so. Rather, I want to draw attention to Merton's teaching style. While he spent the first five or so minutes in lighthearted banter with the novices, there comes a distinct point when Merton the teacher turned on, as it were. I play the recording of this conference regularly for my undergraduate students, and each time I play it, I'm struck by the way in which Merton suddenly shifts in tone and demeanor. The shift is subtle, but definitely perceptible. There's a passion and directness that causes the listener to sit up and take notice, and it's something my students always perceive. While precisely what it is about Merton's presentation that makes it so effective is difficult to describe or pinpoint, the recording illustrates just how gifted he was as a teacher and communicator, and why he was so beloved as a novice master.

Conclusion

While Merton became novice master in the aftermath of a vocational crisis, and although he taught during another vocational crisis during the late 1950s, the conference notes he prepared as a teacher, the recordings we possess of his teaching, as well as the testimonials we have of his style of spiritual direction demonstrate that Merton took his role as novice master with profound seriousness, recognizing that he needed to do what he could to form his students spiritually and theologically both for their own good as well as the good of the community. In his private journals, as well as in his discussions with friends and the abbot, he often complained about monasticism as it was lived at the Abbey of Gethsemani, and he was not shy about telling the novices about his frequent temptations to leave Gethsemani to become a hermit. At the same time, as John Eudes Bamberger wrote, "the chief impression that Father Louis made on his fellow monks was that he was a true brother."[45] And Merton's private journals also contain numerous comments about how much he loved Gethsemani and his fellow monks. I would argue that Merton's conference notes are further evidence of his love for the monastery and its future. Would he have put so much work into his conferences for monks and for a community he despised or about which he cared little? Unlikely.

Moreover, Merton's conference notes demonstrate how deeply immersed he was in the tradition, and how seriously he took the task of imparting the tradition to his novices. Merton gave the novices thorough and comprehensive instruction in Scripture, the liturgy and liturgical feasts, the history of Christian mysticism, the history of Christian monasticism in the East and in the West, the *Rule*, the vows and observances that are part of Trappist monastic life, and the history and theology of Cistercian monasticism. And in all of these conferences, Merton included extensive quotations from and references to the primary sources of the tradition, from Clement of Alexandria to Bernard of Clairvaux to Thomas Aquinas. In so doing, he led his novices into the current of Catholic thinking, at that point on the ascendent, which focused on returning to the sources as a means of understanding and living the faith. Perhaps no other set of writings illustrates so clearly the degree to which Merton was not only acquainted with, but thoroughly immersed in, the sources of the faith as do these novitiate conference notes.

45. John Eudes Bamberger, "The Monk," in *Thomas Merton, Monk: A Monastic Tribute*, ed. Patrick Hart (New York: Sheed & Ward, 1974), 44.

Chapter 4

MERTON THE DEVOTED SON OF MARY

*Mary ever Virgin, Mother of God our Savior, I entrust myself
entirely to your loving intercession and care because you are my
Mother and I am your dear child, full of trouble, conflict, error,
confusion and prone to sin. Because my whole life must change
and because I can do nothing to change it by my own power, I
entrust it with all my needs and cares to you. Present me with
pure hands to your Divine Son, pray that I may gladly accept all
that is needed to strip me of myself and become His true disciple,
forgetting myself and loving His Kingdom, His truth and all He
came to save by His Holy Cross, Amen.*

—Journal Entry, February 12, 1966

Introduction: Merton's Marian Piety

When recounting various memories he had of Merton, Fr. John
Eudes Bamberger drew attention to Merton's devotion to Mary: "He
had a very simple faith in her, and apparently he had a very deep love
for her. It wasn't sentimental at all, very theological and so on, but it
was very real."[1] Although the Abbey of Gethsemani was consecrated

---

1. Victor A. Kramer, "Merton's Vocation as Monastic and Writer: An Interview
with John Eudes Bamberger, O.C.S.O," *The Merton Annual* 4 (1991): 32.

to Mary (its full name is Our Lady of the Abbey of Gethsemani), and although Merton himself, like all monks, was also given the name of Mary along with his monastic name (the "M" in Fr. M. Louis Merton was for Mary), Merton's own Marian piety has not received much attention. When it has received attention, the focus has been on his early writings, particularly his poetry, where his devotion is most fully on display. But Merton's love for Mary was cultivated and fostered right up to the end of his life, and in this chapter I'm going to shed some light on his devotion to Mary as he expressed it throughout his writings. I'll focus first on early manifestations of his Marian piety in his writings from 1938 to 1959, including his private journal, his letters, and his poetry. I will then delve into Merton's novitiate conferences, before exploring Merton's chapter on Mary in *New Seeds of Contemplation.* After examining a homily he preached in 1962 about Mary on the feast of the Immaculate Conception, I'll conclude the chapter by looking at his private journal and letters from the last decade of his life to get a sense of his ongoing devotion to the Blessed Mother during his last years.

Merton's Devotion to Mary from 1938 to 1959

Autobiographical Writings and Letters

We saw in the first chapter that Merton's trip to Cuba was marked by a growing sacramental awareness as his love for the Eucharist developed. It was also in Cuba that Merton's devotion to Mary blossomed. In *The Seven Storey Mountain,* when recounting his spiritual state shortly after his conversion, Merton lamented that he did not immediately cultivate an adequate devotion to Mary: "One of the big defects of my spiritual life in that first year was a lack of devotion to the Mother of God." Although he believed what the church taught about Mary, she played almost no role in his devotional practice: "I gave her no more than the kind of attention one gives to a symbol or a thing of poetry." He acknowledged that this was a grave mistake. "People do not realize the tremendous power of the Blessed Virgin," he wrote. "They do not know who she is: that it is through her hands all graces come because God has willed that she thus participate in His work for the salvation of men" (SSM, 229). He evidently developed some devotion to Mary before his trip to Cuba, as suggested by the fact that one of his main reasons for visiting Cuba was to make a pilgrimage to the shrine of Our Lady of Cobre, the patroness of Cuba, located in a small village called El Cobre. But it was in Cuba that this nascent Marian devotion grew.

In Cuba, while riding the bus from Camagüey to El Cobre, Merton caught sight of the basilica and immediately prayed to Our Lady of Cobre, asking her to intercede for him that he would become a priest and promising her that he would dedicate his first mass to her were he to become a priest: "It is you that I have come to see; you will ask Christ to make me His priest, and I will give you my heart, Lady: and if you will obtain for me this priesthood, I will remember you at my first Mass." When he arrived at the basilica, Merton knelt before the shrine where there was a statue of La Caridad del Cobre (Our Lady of Charity of Cobre), "the little, cheerful, black Virgin, crowned with a crown and dressed in royal robes" (SSM, 282). In the aftermath of this trip, Merton wrote a poem for La Caridad del Cobre, which he said came to him from La Caridad herself and was "the first real poem I had ever written" (SSM, 283). When Merton became a priest in 1948, he kept his promise to Our Lady of Cobre, offering his first Mass for her.

When Merton went on retreat at the Abbey of Gethsemani in 1941, he was not only attracted to the eucharistic life of the place, as I recounted earlier. He was also compelled by the simple Marian piety displayed by the monks. After writing in his journal that Gethsemani was the reason why the country and the universe were held together, he credited Mary with preserving the world because of the monks: "Abraham prayed to the Lord to spare Sodom if there should be found in it one just man. The Blessed Mother of God, Mary Queen of Heaven and of Angels, shows Him daily His children here, and because of their prayers, the world is spared from minute to minute, from the terrible doom" (Ji, 333: April 7, 1941). In *The Seven Storey Mountain*, Merton lamented having to leave Gethsemani, a house dedicated to Mary, to go back into the world: "How did I ever get back out of there, into the world, after tasting the sweetness and the kindness of the love with which you welcome those that come to stay in your house, even only for a few days, O Holy Queen of Heaven, and Mother of my Christ?" (SSM, 321).

Entries from Merton's private journal during his early years at the monastery reveal his continuing devotion to Mary. In a July 1947 entry, almost six years after joining the monastery, he wrote about his growing love for her: "I have been giving myself more fully to the love of Our Lady, abandoning myself more and more completely to the graces she has obtained for me from God and to her direction of my life by that grace in all things that are happening" (Jii, 92: July 30, 1947). Similar expressions of devotion are peppered throughout the journal entries from this period, a period during which he questioned whether he should leave Gethsemani for the Carthusians. He found this vocational struggle spiritually difficult, and his journals make it clear that he tried to cope with his struggle by abandoning himself more fully to the Blessed Virgin. "It is Our Lady who is working in me in these days," he wrote in November 1947, "trying to awaken things in me, bring out new worlds to light, draw me into her Christ Who is the center of all" (Jii, 131: November 6, 1947). One month later, Merton prayed to Mary, telling her that he wanted to abandon himself to her in the midst of his turmoil: "I give you my will, my judgment, my desires. I renounce all things into your hands" (Jii, 141: December 6, 1947).

His 1948 letters to the English novelist Evelyn Waugh illustrate the seriousness of Merton's Marian piety. In answer to questions from Waugh regarding prayer, Merton told him that he should pray the rosary and cultivate a devotion to Mary:

> Really I think it might do you a lot of good & give you a certain happiness to say the Rosary every day. If you don't like it, so much the better, because then you would deliver yourself from the servitude of doing things for your own satisfaction: and that slavery to our own desires is a terrific burden. I mean

if you could do it as a more or less blind act of love and homage to Our Lady, not bothering to try to find out where the attraction of the thing could possibly be hidden, and other people seem to like it. The real motive for this devotion at the moment is that the Church is very explicit: a tremendous amount depends on the Rosary & everything depends on Our Lady. (Liv, 9; TM to Evelyn Waugh: September 22, 1948)

While Merton rarely wrote about his own prayer practice, and particularly about whether and how he prayed the rosary, there is evidence that his advice to Waugh was rooted in his own devotion. More than ten years later, for example, he gave the following advice about prayer to an English schoolteacher, John Harris: "I like the rosary, too. Because, though I am not very articulate about her, I am pretty much wound up in Our Lady" (Li, 392; TM to John Harris: June 22, 1959).

In March 1949, Merton was ordained to the diaconate in the lead up to his ordination to the priesthood in May. His entries during these two months contain numerous references to the ways in which he was growing closer to Mary as he prepared for the priesthood. "Since the diaconate," he wrote, "Our Lady has taken possession of my heart. Maybe after all *She* is the big grace of the diaconate" (Jii, 296: March 27, 1949). As his priestly ordination approached, Merton wrote that he was learning how to abandon himself more fully to Mary: "Our Lady is coming gradually to be the *whole* of my interior life. The more I leave everything to her, the simpler everything becomes, and the easier I travel" (Jii, 307: May 1, 1949). A few days later, after writing that he was focused on Mary while serving as subdeacon at Mass, he wrote that he needed to "throw myself upon her mercy, leaving myself to be moved and guided by her" (Jii, 308: May 5, 1949). After Merton was ordained to the priesthood on May 26, he said the Mass he had promised in Cuba to Our Lady of Cobre. And as 1949 came to a close, the year in which he became a priest, Merton reflected on the implications of abandoning himself to the Virgin:

The fact, to give yourself to Our Lady—but really to give
yourself—seems to me to be the most obvious and simplest
way to become a saint, because if my mind and my will and
my heart and all my thoughts and all my desires become her
mind and will and heart and thoughts and desire, obviously
they will all be holy. She is *the* saint and *the* contemplative.
(Jii, 378: December 13, 1949)

Throughout the 1950s, Merton continued to appeal to Mary,
particularly during moments of distress. Merton experienced another
vocational crisis in 1952, and his journals reveal that he found solace in turning once again to the Blessed Mother. Faced again with
temptations to leave Gethsemani for another monastery, Merton
reflected on the ways in which he had experienced Mary's presence
while at the Abbey:

The choice [God] willed was for me once again to forget about
ever leaving Gethsemani. Our Lady of Gethsemani. Mary is,
in a certain sense, the community which is my Mother. It is
her love that has brought us here and keeps the community
together. It is her love I have known out under the cedars, and
working in the fields, and singing in choir. It is her love that
has made me desire solitude, and she will fulfill that desire. She
is my solitude and she is here. (Jiii, 26: November 29, 1952)

We know that this vocational crisis lasted until 1955 when he was
appointed novice master at Gethsemani. Unfortunately, this crisis
coincides with a silence in Merton's journals that lasted from March
1953 to July 1956, shortly after he was made novice master. Interestingly, his first entry after recommencing his journal contains a
recommittal of sorts to Mary in the form of a prayer: "I need to be
led by you. I need my heart to be moved by you. I need my soul to
be made clean by your prayer. I need my will to be made strong by
you. I need the world to be saved and changed by you . . . I need
to be your monk and your son. It is necessary. Amen" (Jiii, 46–47:
July 17, 1956). In December 1959, in the midst of another voca-

tional crisis during which he made a request for an indult (formal permission) from Rome to leave Gethsemani for another monastery, Merton turned once again to Mary: "Today at Mass I thought: If I have Her, nothing else matters" (Jiii, 352: December 5, 1959).

Early Poetry

These journal entries demonstrate the intensity of Merton's devotion to Mary during the first eighteen years of his time at the monastery, but his poetry from this time also underlines the depth of this devotion. Merton is best known for his prose writings, but he was also a voluminous poet; *The Collected Poems of Thomas Merton* runs to over one thousand pages in length. His first books were, in fact, books of poetry; before *The Seven Storey Mountain* was published in 1948, Merton had already published three books of poetry—*Thirty Poems* (1944), *A Man in the Divided Sea* (1946), and *Figures for an Apocalypse* (1947). One year after his autobiography came out, Merton published another book of poetry called *The Tears of the Blind Lions* (1949). A number of the poems published in these volumes have Mary as their focus, and it is worth touching briefly upon a few of these poems to illustrate Merton's early devotion to Mary.[2]

I noted above that Merton considered the poem he wrote after his visit to the shrine of La Caridad del Cobre to be the first real poem he ever wrote. This poem, "Song for our Lady of Cobre," was included in his first book of poetry, *Thirty Poems*, and while it was dedicated to Mary, the poem itself is not about her. Three other poems in this volume refer more explicitly to Mary. "The Evening of the Visitation" is a brief four stanza poem written when Merton was a novice at Gethsemani. The poem is about Mary's visitation to the home of Zachariah and Elizabeth after the annunciation, and in the final stanza, Merton wrote of Mary's ongoing care for the monastery in a manner that illustrates his love for her:

2. For an in-depth analysis of Marian themes in Merton's early poetry, and specifically in *Thirty Poems*, see Patrick F. O'Connell, "The Presence of Mary in Thomas Merton's *Thirty Poems*," *Cistercian Studies Quarterly* 47.2 (2012): 177–213.

You moon and rising stars, pour on our barns and houses
Your gentle benedictions.
Remind us how our Mother, with far subtler and more holy
    influence,
Blesses our rooves and eaves,
Our shutters, lattices and sills,
Our doors, and floors, and stairs, and rooms, and bedrooms,
Smiling by night upon her sleeping children:
O gentle Mary! Our lovely Mother in heaven! (CP, 44)

Another poem from 1942, "The Blessed Virgin Mary Compared to a Window," gives us a sense of Merton's understanding of Mary. The key theme of the poem is Mary's humility, her complete openness to God's will, which Merton (writing in Mary's voice) describes in the poem with reference to a clear window being totally open to the light of the sun to pass through it.

Because my will is simple as a window
And knows no pride of original earth,
It is my life to die, like grass, by light:
Slain in the strong rays of the bridegroom sun. (CP, 46)

Because Mary was so completely open to the will of God, she was transformed by God to become like God, in the way a window takes on the light of the sun so as to seemingly disappear:

For light, my lover, steals my life in secret.
I vanish into day, and leave no shadow
But the geometry of my cross,
Whose frame and structure are the strength
By which I die, but only to the earth,
And am uplifted to the sky my life.

When I become the substance of my lover,
(Being obedient, sinless glass)
I love all things that need my lover's life,
And live to give my newborn Morning to your quiet rooms. (CP, 47)

And in the final stanza, Merton underlines the importance of Mary's *fiat* for the salvation of the world:

> And you shall see the sun, my Son, my Substance,
> Come to convince the world of the day's end, and of the night,
> Smile to the lovers of the day in smiles of blood:
> For through my love, He'll be their Brother,
> My light—the Lamb of their Apocalypse. (CP, 48)

As Patrick O'Connell points out in his analysis of this poem, Merton's depiction of Mary in this poem illustrates how important she was to Merton as a model for him as a monk in a contemplative monastery: "In her total availability to God, Mary appears as the model of the true contemplative as well: by becoming one with the Light, she undergoes a mystical death that is also a mystical marriage, experiencing union with the 'bridegroom sun' in a relationship that merges the roles of mother and spouse" (O'Connell, "The Presence of Mary," 197).

"The Holy Child's Song" is the last of the three poems from *Thirty Poems* on Mary. Jesus is the speaker in this poem, and in the third stanza, Merton has Christ say the following:

> And when My Mother, pretty as a church,
> Takes Me upon her lap, I laugh with love,
> Loving to live in her flesh, which is My house—and full of light!
> (Because the sky My Spirit enters in at all the windows)
> O, then what songs and what incarnate joys
> Dance in the bright rays of My childish voice! (CP, 55–56)

Here we see Merton once again compare Mary to a window reflecting the light of Christ's own Spirit, but in this case "she is likened not just to the windows but to the whole house illuminated by the Spirit" (O'Connell, "The Presence of Mary," 207).

Mary continued to be present in the poetry Merton published in the late 1940s after *Thirty Poems*. *Figures for an Apocalypse*, published in 1947, contains one poem in particular with strong Marian themes.

"Canticle for the Blessed Virgin" is a thirteen-stanza poem focused specifically on Mary, and perhaps no other poem from Merton's early writing so vividly articulates his exalted understanding of and devotion to her. The poem is organized into two parts. The first speaks of Mary as one whom the entire creation praises and the one who provides protection to those under her care. The land around the monastery gives glory to Mary:

> The ox-eyed land,
> The muted lakes,
> The cloudy groves that praise you, Lady, with their blooms,
> Fuse and destroy their lights
> And burn them into gold for you, great Virgin,
> Coining your honor in the glorious sun. (CP, 161)

Indeed, the entire cosmos praises her:

> Because your Christ disposed Orion and Andromeda
> And ordered the clean spheres,
> And interplayed the chiming suns to be your toy,
> Charm you with antiphon and psalmody
> And canticle, and countersong. (CP, 161–62)

Merton then praises Mary for his own conversion:

> Because your Christ
> Fired the fair stars with argent for your raiment,
> And charged the sinner's tears
> With clean repentant lights—
> (As on the day you found me in the dens of libraries
> And crushed the jeweled head of heresy)—
> He gave you every one of the redeemed to be your dowry
> And angels for your crown. (CP, 162)

And in the final stanza of the first part, Merton beautifully describes Mary as protectress and mediatrix of grace:

Come from the compass quarter where the thunder sleeps
And let the pity of those eyes
Rout all the armies of our million dangers
Here where we lie in siege:
For you unlock the treasures of the bleeding Wood.
You hold the Mass-keys, and the locks of Calvary,
And All-grace springs in the founts of your demand. (CP, 162)

The second part of the poem is more personal. Here Merton appeals directly to Mary for himself, asking her to guide him in his theological understanding and to bestow the transforming grace that will make him worthy to be ordained a priest; the poem was evidently written while he was preparing for ordination:

Lady, whose smiles are full of counsel and theology,
Never have you withheld those seas of light
Whose surf confounds the keenest eye.
Grace me to be the soldier of your Scotus,
Arming my actions with the news
Of your Immaculate command.
You, who have saved me from the ones about to break me
On the iron wheels of sin,
And brought me from the torturer
With all the florins of the Parasceve:
If Christ will burn me clean
Of my red-handed perjuries,
Win me His blood again, and blazon me His priest. (CP, 162–63)

This small sample of Merton's early Marian poems underlines what we knew from his autobiography as well as his journals and letters about his devotion to Mary. His devotion was a very personal one, rooted in an exalted understanding of her role, not only in his own spiritual life, but in the well-being of the church and of the world. However, the poem that most fully expresses Merton's understanding of and devotion to Mary is one written in 1959 and published in 1962 called "Hagia Sophia."

"Hagia Sophia"

"Hagia Sophia" (which means Holy Wisdom in Greek) is a prose poem that Merton wrote in 1959 after seeing a painting by the artist Victor Hammer, a friend of his who lived in Lexington, Kentucky. The painting is of the boy Christ being crowned by a woman. Hammer commented to Merton that the painting was intended to be of Mary with the Christ-child, but that he was no longer sure who the woman in the painting was. According to Hammer, Merton told him that the woman was "Hagia Sophia and also the mother of Christ."[3] Hammer wrote Merton to ask him to explain what he meant, and Merton replied in a letter on May 14, 1959. Hammer's painting also led Merton to expand more thoroughly on Hagia Sophia poetically. Merton's understanding of Hagia Sophia is admittedly somewhat complicated, so I will only touch upon the non-Marian aspects of his thought, as he articulated it in both his letter to Hammer and his poem, "Hagia Sophia."[4]

At the beginning of his letter to Hammer, Merton acknowledged that "it is most difficult to write anything that makes sense about this most mysterious reality in the mystery of God." Nevertheless, he did his best in both his letter to Hammer and in his prose poem to explain who Hagia Sophia is. Sophia is, Merton told Hammer, God: "God is not only a Father but a Mother. He is both at the same time, and it is the 'feminine aspect' or 'feminine principle' in the divinity that is Hagia Sophia" (Lv, 4; TM to Victor Hammer: May 14, 1959). Merton elaborated on this notion in his poem: "As Mother His shining is diffused, embracing all His creatures with merciful tenderness and light. The Diffuse Shining of God is Hagia Sophia. We call her His 'glory.' In Sophia His power is experienced only as

3. Victor Hammer to TM (May 2, 1959) in *The Letters of Thomas Merton and Victor and Carolyn Hammer: Ad Majorem Dei Gloriam*, ed. Paul Evans Holbrook Jr. and F. Douglas Scutchfield (Lexington, KY: University of Kentucky Press, 2014), 64.

4. For a thorough analysis of Merton's understanding of Hagia Sophia, with a particular focus on Merton's poem by the same name, I strongly recommend Christopher Pramuk's excellent book, *Sophia: The Hidden Christ of Thomas Merton* (Collegeville, MN: Liturgical Press, 2009).

mercy and as love" (CP, 367). Sophia is, for Merton, inextricably tied to the love and mercy of God: "Sophia in ourselves is the *mercy* of God, the tenderness by which the infinitely mysterious power of pardon turns the darkness of our sins into the light of God's love." Hence, Merton continues, "Sophia is the feminine, dark, yielding, tender counterpart of the power, justice, creative dynamism of the Father" (Lv, 4; TM to Victor Hammer: May 14, 1959).

But as Merton mentioned to Hammer, the woman in the wood-cut was not just Hagia Sophia but was also Mary, and for Merton the two are interrelated. In "Hagia Sophia" Merton devoted the last stanza to Mary, and he elaborated here on the relationship between Sophia and Mary: "Now the Blessed Virgin Mary is the one created being who enacts and shows forth in her life all that is hidden in Sophia" (CP, 369). In other words, the mercy and love of God made manifest by Sophia is realized in created form in the person of Mary. As such, Mary "can be said to be a personal manifestation of Sophia" (CP, 369–70). Sophia is embodied, as it were, in Mary who manifests the love and tenderness of God.

And she does this through her *fiat*, her willingness to be the means by which God would be incarnate. The following lines from "Hagia Sophia" merit full quotation:

> It is she, it is Mary, Sophia, who in sadness and joy,
> with the full awareness of what she is doing, sets
> upon the Second Person, the Logos, a crown which is
> His Human Nature. Thus her consent opens the door
> of created nature, of time of history, to the Word of
> God.
>
> God enters into His creation. Through her wise an-
> swer, through obedient understanding, through
> the sweet yielding consent of Sophia, God enters with-
> out publicity into the city of rapacious men.
>
> She crowns Him not with what is glorious, but with
> what is greater than glory: the one thing greater than
> glory is weakness, nothingness, poverty.

> She sends the infinitely Rich and Powerful One forth
> as poor and helpless, in His mission of inexpressible
> mercy, to die for us on the Cross. (CP, 370)

It was Mary's "wise answer," what Merton describes as "the sweet yielding consent of Sophia," that revealed her to manifest Sophia, and it was by her consent that God entered into the world. As the personal manifestation of Sophia, Mary crowns Christ with his human nature, sending him forth in his poverty to die. In so doing, Mary reveals that Holy Wisdom is manifested not in acts of power, but in the "inexpressible mercy" and love of God.

Merton's references to Mary in "Hagia Sophia" reveal the depth of his devotion to Mary. She is, as the personal manifestation of Sophia, the one by whom our salvation came into the world, and her *fiat* revealed to us the hiddenness, humility, mercy, and love that God is. "Hagia Sophia" is a poem, and so not a work of systematic theology, but it illustrates how, in 1959, Mary continued to loom large in Merton's theology and spirituality.

Merton's Mariology

Mary in Seeds of Contemplation *and* New Seeds of Contemplation

His journals, letters, and poems tell us something about Merton's personal devotion to Mary. But while they give an indication of the esteem with which he held Mary, we need to look elsewhere to get more of a sense of his theology of the Blessed Mother. There are three key sources to which we can turn for understanding Merton's Mariology—a chapter on Mary found in both *Seeds of Contemplation* (1949) and the revised and republished *New Seeds of Contemplation* (1961); the conference notes he wrote on the liturgy, in which he focused particular attention on the liturgical celebration of the Marian feasts; and a homily he gave in 1962 on Mary, published in 1965.

In 1949 Merton published *Seeds of Contemplation*, the first iteration of what would eventually be rewritten and published as *New Seeds of Contemplation* in 1961. In both books he included a chapter on Mary; in the 1949 edition the chapter is titled "Electa ut Sol" ("As the Sun"), and in the 1961 edition it is called "The Woman Clothed with the Sun." There is a great deal of similarity between the two chapters, but the additions and deletions Merton made for his 1961 revision provide us with a glimpse of how his Mariology developed in the years separating the two publications. In both the 1949 and 1961 versions, Merton wrote of Mary in exalted terms, declaring that "hers was the most perfect sanctity outside the sanctity of God," that "the sanctity of all the saints is a participation in her sanctity, because in the order He has established God wills that all graces come to men through Mary" (SC, 87, 89). And the reason all graces come to us through her is because Mary, "of all creatures, most perfectly recovered the likeness to God." At the same time, Merton argued that Mary's exalted status as the one by whom all graces come to us is tied to her humility and nothingness, for in her nothingness she emulates "the infinitely selfless God" (SC, 89). We cannot talk about Mary's glory without simultaneously talking about her humility, her absolute willingness to give of herself to allow God to work through her.

While the 1949 version of this chapter focused some attention on Mary's humility, Merton placed particular emphasis on it in the 1961 iteration. Perhaps the reason for this had to do with the fact that, one year after publishing *Seeds of Contemplation*, Pope Pius XII proclaimed the dogma of the assumption of Mary, the dogma that declares that Mary was bodily assumed into heaven at the end of her life. While Merton happily affirmed belief in the assumption of Mary, his 1961 chapter indicates that he was concerned that Pope Pius XII's proclamation led some Catholics to elevate Mary to a place where she was viewed "as an almost divine being in her own right." However, according to Merton, such a view is contrary to the Catholic faith for, he wrote, "it forgets that Mary's chief glory is in her nothingness" (NSC, 170). "The glory of Mary," he continued, "is purely and simply the glory of God in her, and she, like anyone else, can say that she has nothing that she has not received from Him through Christ" (NSC, 170–71). Because Mary gave herself in humility so completely to God, God "was able to accomplish His will perfectly in her, and His liberty was in no way hindered or turned from its purpose by the presence of an egotistical self in Mary." Our devotion to Mary is not based on a glory she has inherently apart from God, but is rooted in the fact that she opened herself so fully to the transforming presence of God who became incarnate through her. And we believe "that the one who was closest to Him in this great mystery was the one who participated most perfectly in the gift" of the incarnation. In other words, our devotion to Mary is not due to something inherent in her, but "is to be seen in the light of the Incarnation itself" (NSC, 171). For in her we see what we can become through union with the Incarnate Word: "If human nature is glorified in her," Merton wrote, "it is because God desires it to be glorified in us too, and it is for this reason that His Son, taking flesh, came into the world" (NSC, 173).

This account of Mary's humility goes some way toward helping us understand why Merton so often turned to her, particularly during his crises about his vocation. He was not under the illusion that his crises were wholly because of the monastery. He knew that his own ego played a key role, so it's no accident that he frequently expressed a desire to abandon himself to Mary—the one who herself opened herself totally to God—when in the midst of temptations to leave Gethsemani. And while he would have none of the overly maximalist conceptions that some Catholics had of Mary—conceptions that the Second Vatican Council would itself condemn in *Lumen Gentium*[5]—both iterations of his chapter on Mary in *Seeds of Contemplation* and *New Seeds of Contemplation* illustrate that his devotion to her, rooted in her humility and nothingness, was profound. He clearly saw in her the supreme model of the Christian life. But more than that, he saw that her own humility and nothingness became themselves the reason why God uses her to communicate his grace to us. "For unless Our Lady is recognized as the Mother of God,"

---

5. See paragraphs 66–67 of *Lumen Gentium* (Dogmatic Constitution on the Church), Vatican website, November 21, 1961, https://www.vatican.va/archive /hist_councils/ii_vatican_council/documents/vat-ii_const_19641121_lumen-gentium _en.html.

he wrote, "and as the Queen of all the saints and angels and as the hope of the world, faith in God will remain incomplete" (NSC, 174).

Merton, Mary, and the Novices

Merton's most thorough and extensive treatment of Mary is found in his conference notes for the novices on the liturgy. In these conferences, Merton took the novices on an exploration of the significance of various liturgical celebrations. Merton generally described the significance of the Sunday or feast in question, before delving into the meaning of the collect prayer for the day, as well as of the Scripture readings accompanying the eucharistic celebration. As Br. Paul Quenon wrote in his introduction to a forthcoming book of Merton's liturgical conferences, Merton was a mystagogue, one who taught the mysteries of the faith by means of digging deep into the liturgy itself.[6] In his first set of conference notes on the liturgy, Merton focused attention on the Sunday liturgies, beginning with Advent and moving through to Easter, but in his second set, he devoted himself to the sanctoral cycle, the feast days found throughout the liturgical year. Merton did not cover every feast in this set of notes, so the ones he did cover give some indication of his priorities in terms of what he most wanted to communicate to the novices.[7] And the largest proportion of these conferences—fourteen out of forty-three—are devoted to Marian feasts. Merton's reflections on the Blessed Virgin in these pages, therefore, provide an important window by which we can understand more thoroughly his Mariology.

Significantly, Merton began his conferences on the sanctoral calendar with a lecture called "The Mystery of Mary and the Church." Here Merton addressed concerns raised by some that devotion to Mary takes "away something from our faith in Jesus, as if Jesus and Mary could possibly be rivals for our love and devotion." Such concerns are misplaced, Merton argued, particularly if one understands

---

6. Paul Quenon, OCSO, "Preface," NCiii, iv. Note that the page numbers NCiii are to an as yet unpublished edition. I am thankful to Patrick F. O'Connell for giving me access to this text.

7. Patrick O'Connell, "Introduction," NCiii, xxxii.

"how closely the mystery of Our Lady is connected with the mystery of the Church," both of which are tied to the mystery of Christ (NCiii, 109). If we understand that it is by the incarnation of the Son of God that humans are transformed to become daughters and sons of God through Christ, then we can understand the important role Mary played in human salvation. Indeed, Mary cooperates in the redemption of humankind both through her willingness to say yes to the angel when told that she would conceive as well as through her compassion and sorrow at Calvary when she suffered alongside of Christ. Thus, "through Mary, whom Christ willed to have as His collaborator in His great work, all grace is given to the mystical members of Christ, who therefore have her for their mother in a much more intimate sense than the natural man is united to his mother" (NCiii, 109–10). She becomes our mother in a profound way in that "we not only receive life from Mary, but we continue to receive it at every moment, remaining always in complete dependence on her for the life of grace."

Merton also spoke to the novices about the connection between Mary and the mystery of the church. Merton submitted that, just as Mary collaborates with Jesus in the work of human redemption, so we are called to collaborate with Jesus in the redemption of others: "We obtain grace for one another. We help and educate one another in the faith; we grow together in the knowledge of Christ; we share His gifts with one another, until we all become 'one Christ loving himself'" (Merton here quotes Augustine). This is the mystery of the church. We are called to collaborate with Christ in the work of the salvation of our fellow Christians, and we do so in imitation of Mary, who is the "model and center around which the church's life is built." The church begins her life in Mary, who is perfectly united to Christ in such a way that she suffered with him on Calvary, was united with him in the resurrection, and reigns with him in glory. Each of us in the church, through our union with Christ in the Eucharist, grows in our holiness and so becomes more "perfectly conformed to Mary the Co-redeemer" (NCiii, 110). And in becoming conformed to

Mary, we grow in our unity with one another, a unity rooted in the self-giving love that Mary manifests most perfectly.

Merton expanded on this understanding of Mary as co-redeemer in his conference on the feast of the Seven Dolors, the feast of Mary's sorrows. It appears on the liturgical calendar on September 15 but can also be celebrated the Friday before Good Friday. We obtain grace for one another insofar as we cooperate in the distribution of graces in various ways, but this, Merton emphasized, is a matter of what he called subjective redemption. In other words, we ourselves do not save others, but we cooperate with God in obtaining graces for others, graces made possible by Christ's death and resurrection. With Mary, however, the situation is different, as she "is the only human being who cooperated in the *objective redemption* of mankind" (NCiii, 131). She did this through her *fiat* at the annunciation, when she said yes to the angel, for in this act she participated objectively in the very incarnation of the Son of God. Moreover, according to Merton, she played a role in the redemption made possible by the crucifixion, and Merton here cited the famed nineteenth-century theologian, Matthias Joseph Scheeben (1835–1888). What Merton means by this is that she offered Jesus to the Father on our behalf, and in so doing also offered herself with him in order that all would attain salvation through him. And in this offering, she gave of herself so as to become the mother of us all, a point he made particularly clear in another conference for the novices on a day of recollection during May:

> Mary's part in the Passion was, then, to become mother of us all, mother of the whole Church, and thus Mother of Christ over and over again each time a new member is born to life in Christ. In a word, Mary's principal part in the Passion was to receive *us* from the hands of Jesus in exchange for Jesus dying on the Cross, and thus to *find and keep Jesus* in us. We are the supreme gift of Jesus to His mother. (NCiii, 137)

"Mary's participation in the Passion," Merton continued, was "not just *quantitative*, but *qualitative*—not just the sufferings themselves but the added pain that comes from knowing the *full inner signifi-cance* of each indignity visited upon the Son of God" (NCiii, 138).

In other words, Mary played a pivotal role in the plan of human salvation, not only because she said yes to the angel at the annuncia-tion, but because she suffered alongside of Christ, offering her son for the salvation of the world. Merton therefore did not hesitate to call Mary "co-redeemer and mediatrix of all grace" (NCiii, 136). In his conference on the feast of the Immaculate Heart of Mary (August 22), Merton drew on the Marian reflections of Bernard of Clairvaux to emphasize that Mary is the mediatrix of all grace precisely because she took an "active" part in our salvation by cooperating perfectly with divine grace. She abandoned herself completely to God, and as a result, God "poured out into her heart the fullness of His grace" (NCiii, 164). While we all receive something of divine grace, she received grace completely and fully. As such, she becomes the media-tor of grace, a "point of mediation between Christ and ourselves."

Because he understood Mary to play such a pivotal role in human salvation, Merton urged his novices to understand that their mo-nastic lives needed to be explicitly consecrated to her (NCiii, 165). Mary's life was one characterized by faith, obedience, purity, love, and humility, all virtues that are essential for the Christian life, and particularly important for those called to live contemplative lives as monks. By consecrating themselves to Mary, the novices hope to participate in her virtues and so gain her assistance in living out their vocation as contemplatives. "The whole of our monastic life," Merton wrote, "can be summed up as a trusting love for Our Lady, a love that seeks her face always, that always calls upon her merciful and motherly love" (NCiii, 169). Over and over in his conferences, Merton urged the novices to abandon themselves to Mary. Arguing that their vocation to the contemplative life is from her, Merton wrote that "our life and perfection depend, in fact, on how closely we reproduce in our own religious life her gift of herself to God" (NCiii, 199). Without her help, the monks cannot truly give themselves to God. At every moment, according to Merton, the monks must ask her to guide them, and she will do so as their mother.

One of the ways that Merton urged the novices to devote themselves to Mary was through the praying of the rosary, about which he spoke at length. He acknowledged that Cistercians have sometimes not prioritized the recitation of the rosary, but told the novices that it is a prayer that lends itself naturally to contemplation for it is a prayer that is easy to recite while working, walking, or even while reading meditatively during *lectio divina* (sacred reading). Merton described the value of praying the rosary this way: "The repetition of the prayers in the rosary is calming, peaceful; it lulls our minds; it creates an atmosphere of prayer; it attunes us to Our Lady's presence; it surrounds us with an aura of love in which our hearts spontaneously open themselves to the grace which she obtains for us by her motherly intercession" (NCiii, 170). By these prayers, we unite ourselves to Mary and her Son, the incarnate Word.

Mary and the Light: A 1962 Homily

In 1962 Merton preached a sermon for the feast of the Immaculate Conception of Mary (December 8) titled "A Homily on Light and the Virgin Mary." He evidently liked this homily; not only did he publish it in 1965 in a collection of essays on the liturgy but he sent a copy of it to his Muslim friend and correspondent Abdul Aziz as a means to foster dialogue about Mary.[8] In the homily, Merton placed Mary within the broad context of human creation and salvation. "God our Father and Creator," Merton wrote, "Who is pure being, pure light, in Whom there is no darkness, willed to kindle the light of His truth outside Himself and for this reason He made the universe" (SCel, 158). The universe became God's lampstand, and humanity became God's lamp. Having been created in the image and likeness of God, humans "shone with the very light of God within [themselves]" and

---

8. "I will also send a homily on the Virgin Mary which may not be in all respects relevant to you but you may find one or two common points of agreement here and there. I hope so. I know that Mary is treated with the greatest reverence in the Koran and have read these passages with deep emotions" (Li, 53: TM to Abdul Aziz; December 26, 1962).

so "came into existence with divine light dwelling in [their] inmost being." Humanity was created to participate in the divine nature, to be united with God. "But as soon as the lamp was set on the lampstand," Merton wrote, "by an act of its own perverse choice, the lamp put out the light and refused to be rekindled" (SCel, 159). God prepared for the rekindling of the light in humanity in various ways, but it was in Mary that we see "the perfect rekindling of the pure light which had been extinguished by the sin of Adam" (SCel, 163). Merton continued:

> In Mary, the lamp was once more perfectly clean, burning with pure light, standing on the lampstand, illuminating the whole house of God, restoring meaning to all God's creatures, and showing the rest of men the way to return to the light: not that Mary was filled with any light of her own but because she was the first fruit of redemption, perfectly sanctified by the sacrifice of our redemption even before it was consummated, to give greater glory to the power of that sacrifice, and to prepare a way for the Lamb of God, the Light of the world, who was to come into the world through her consent and her obedience. (SCel, 163–64)

What was this light? It was the light of God's very own Wisdom, which is why the church's liturgy applies the texts from the Sapiential books of the Hebrew Scriptures so frequently to Mary herself. "No one," Merton wrote, "has ever more perfectly contained the light of God than Mary who by the perfection of her purity and humility is, as it were, completely identified with the truth like the clean window pane which vanishes entirely into the light which it transmits" (SCel, 164). It is the light of the transfigured Christ, Wisdom incarnate, that fills Mary, and the light that fills her "is the same light that is to shine in the whole Church and in the entire cosmos recapitulated in Christ" (SCel, 165).

In short, "in Mary is perfectly realized God's whole creative and redemptive plan." He continued: "In her is all the beauty of the world, transfigured and elevated to a level beyond our comprehension." Her "littleness," which she shares with us by virtue of our humanity, was "glorified in the light of Christ" in such a way that she not only reveals what we are to become, but she becomes a conduit for that divine light such that we are transformed (SCel, 169). We ourselves need simply to open ourselves to the light that transformed her. As was the case in his other writings on Mary, Merton's homily on the Blessed Mother shows his continued devotion to her in the early 1960s. And this devotion was rooted in his understanding of Mary as the one who made possible the salvation of the world through her obedience to God. For Merton, Mary's glory is her humility.

Merton's Devotion to Mary from 1960 to 1968

Merton's vocational struggles began to be resolved in 1960 as possibilities for greater solitude at Gethsemani opened up. It was in that year that the Abbey built a small retreat house about a mile from the monastery that everyone, including Merton, knew was actually intended as a hermitage for their novice master. By October 1960, the hermitage was almost finished, and it is worth noting that Merton immediately dedicated it to the Blessed Mother, calling it "St. Mary of Carmel" (Jiv, 62: October 29, 1960). Merton already had a devotion to Our Lady of Carmel, the patroness of the Carmelite order that dated back to his time in Havana in 1940 when he saw the reflection of the church of Our Lady of Carmel in a mirror in his hotel room (see Ji, 219: May 21, 1940). Merton referred again to this experience in a prayer to Our Lady of Carmel in a July 1956 journal entry on her feast day: "I have never forgotten you. And you are more to me now than then" (Jiii, 46: July 17, 1956). And just as Merton dedicated his first Mass to Our Lady of Cobre in recognition of the prayer he made to her in Cuba, so Merton dedicated his hermitage to Our Lady of Carmel in recognition of the devotion for her that kindled in Cuba.

From 1960 to 1965, as he was given permission to spend more time at St. Mary of Carmel's hermitage, we find numerous expressions of Merton's devotion to her in his journal and letters. For example, in a 1960 letter to Pope John XXIII written to thank the pope for sending a signed photo along with a blessing for the novitiate, Merton noted that it was significant that the pope's photo and blessing came on the feast of Our Lady of Lourdes for it was as if "we received all these graces as though directly from the hands of Our Blessed Mother" (Li, 483; TM to Pope John XXIII: February 11, 1960). In a 1962 letter to the abbot general, Dom Gabriel Sortais, written on the anniversary of his ordination to the priesthood, Merton wrote that he owed much to Mary: "I think of Our Lady's intervention in my life, and my enormous debt towards her. I am glad to belong to her, too, and to hide in her Immaculate Heart" (Liii, 144; TM to Gabriel Sortais: May 26, 1962). On the feast of Our Lady of Carmel in 1963 (July 16), Merton again focused his attention on the Virgin: "With ardent hope and compunction I dedicate this day, and myself, to Our Lady" (Jiv, 339: July 17, 1963).

It was during this period that Merton exchanged a remarkable series of letters with Abdul Aziz, a Sufi Muslim in Pakistan, to which I've already made reference. These letters provide a remarkable example of interreligious dialogue and friendship, and I will have further opportunity to discuss this correspondence in a later chapter. The two discussed a wide range of topics, from trinitarian theology to prayer, and Mary came up in their conversation. Aziz asked Merton why the monastery was called Our Lady of Gethsemani, and this question led Merton to write about the role of Mary in his life and in the lives of his fellow monks given that all Trappist monasteries are dedicated to Mary: "I consider that each monastery dwells so to speak surrounded and protected by the maternal love of Mary, and by her prayers in heaven. If we are dedicated to the mystery of Gethsemani, it means to say that we are in particular to be mindful of the Blessed Virgin's solitude and sorrow of heart in her compassion for the suffering of Christ" (Li, 47; TM to Abdul Aziz: January 30, 1961). In 1962, Merton sent Aziz the homily on Mary I explored above, which he gave in the hope that they might "find one or two common points of agreement here and there." After all, Merton wrote, "I know that Mary is treated with the greatest reverence in the Koran and have read these passages with deep emotion" (Li, 53; TM to Abdul Aziz: December 26, 1962). From Merton's perspective, Mariology could be a means by which he and Aziz could better understand each other

As time went on, Merton was given permission to spend ever increasing periods of time at St. Mary of Carmel hermitage. Early in 1965, after spending an extended period of time there, Merton wrote about feeling Mary's presence at the hermitage: "The presence of Our Lady is important to me. Elusive but I think a reality in this hermitage . . . Her influence is a demand to love and no amount of talking will explain it. I need her and she is there. I should perhaps think of it more explicitly more often" (Jv, 197: January 30, 1965). In the summer of that year, Merton published an essay called "Day of a Stranger," in which he described, in a lighthearted fashion, what a day at the hermitage looked like for him. For our purposes, it's enough to note that Merton wrote that "I have the place full of ikons of the Holy Virgin" (TMSE, 237). Late in 1965, after moving to the hermitage permanently, Merton was able to add to his collection of icons of Mary when he received an eighteenth-century Greek icon of the Virgin from Marco Pallis, a Greek-British author and mountaineer. Merton's exuberant letter of thanks to Pallis indicates just what Mary's presence at the hermitage in this icon meant to him:

> Where shall I begin? I have never received such a precious and magnificent gift from anyone in my life. I have no words to express how deeply moved I was to come face to face with this sacred and beautiful presence granted to me in the coming of the ikon to my most unworthy person . . . [I]n a strange way the ikon of the Holy Mother came as a messenger at a precise moment when a message was needed, and her presence before me has been an incalculable aid in resolving a difficult problem. (Li, 473; TM to Marco Pallis: December 5, 1965)

A few months later, he described again his continued devotion to Mary: "Said mass privately as usual, and thought deeply about Our

Lady afterward, prayed much to her, saw her immense importance in my life, 'gave' myself as completely as I could. I have a great need to 'belong' to her. All this is not easily explained and easily becomes confusing if put into words" (Jvi, 16–17: February 3, 1966). A week later, in some personal notes, he composed the following prayer to Mary:

> Mary ever Virgin, Mother of God our Savior, I entrust myself entirely to your loving intercession and care because you are my Mother and I am your dear child, full of trouble, conflict, error, confusion and prone to sin. Because my whole life must change and because I can do nothing to change it by my own power, I entrust it with all my needs and cares to you. Present me with pure hands to your Divine Son, pray that I may gladly accept all that is needed to strip me of myself and become His true disciple, forgetting myself and loving His Kingdom, His truth and all He came to save by His Holy Cross, Amen. (Jvi, 360: February 12, 1966)

In April 1967, he wrote about his need for Mary: "I need to know Mary is still close to us and need her to be very close to me here, always" (Jvi, 220: April 16, 1967). One month later, he wrote that he clearly had a "[s]ense of the nearness and mercy of Mary" at the hermitage (Jvi, 234: May 13, 1967). And while his journal from the final year of his life contains fewer references to Mary, it is worth noting again that his final journal entry refers to the plans he made to say Mass for the feast of the Immaculate Conception on December 8 (Jvii, 329: December 8, 1968).

Conclusion

Each day at the Abbey of Gethsemani ends with the monks chanting the *Salve Regina*, a medieval hymn of praise to the Blessed Mother:

> Hail, holy Queen, mother of mercy,
> our life, our sweetness, and our hope.

To you do we cry,
poor banished children of Eve.
To you do we send up our sighs
mourning and weeping in this vale of tears.
Turn then, most gracious advocate,
your eyes of mercy toward us,
and after this exile
show us the blessed fruit of your womb, Jesus.
O clement, O loving,
O sweet Virgin Mary.

Merton chanted this hymn in Latin every evening as he, along with his fellow monks, committed themselves to the "mother of mercy" as they retired for the night. Thomas Merton came to the Abbey of Gethsemani in 1941 as someone already devoted to Mary, and during his first decade at the monastery this devotion grew and flowered. But his journal, letters, poetry, novitiate conference notes, and other writings illustrate that his devotion to Our Lady never wavered in the 1950s and 60s as he grew both theologically and spiritually. Mary remained for Merton the one to whom he would turn in times of need and distress, the embodiment of Sophia whose presence at the hermitage he experienced and valued, the merciful and loving mother who cared for him. And listed in the American embassy's description of Merton's personal effects to be shipped back to the monastery from Thailand—alongside his watch, glasses, and toiletries—is a revealing item: "1 Small Icon on Wood of Virgin and Child."[9] The American embassy recorded the value of this icon as "Nil," but its presence among Merton's personal effects, the fact that he carried this small icon around with him on his trip, reveals that his devotion to the Blessed Mother continued right to the end of his life.

---

9. American Consulate in Bangkok, "Inventory of Effects, Estate of Thomas James Merton," December 23, 1968, *Thomas Merton Center*, Bellarmine University.

CHAPTER 5

MERTON THE ADVOCATE FOR PEACE

I feel obligated to take very seriously what is going on, and to say whatever my conscience seems to dictate, provided of course that it is not contrary to the faith and to the teaching authority of the Church. . . . As for writing: I don't feel that I can in conscience, at a time like this, go on writing just about things like meditation, though that has its point. I cannot just bury my head in a lot of rather tiny and secondary monastic studies either. I think I have to face the big issues, the life-and-death issues.

—*Thomas Merton to Dorothy Day, August 23, 1963*

Introduction: Pope Francis and Thomas Merton on Nonviolence

On December 8, 2016, the feast of the Immaculate Conception of Mary, Pope Francis released his message for the celebration of the Fiftieth World Day of Peace. It was titled "Nonviolence: A Style of Politics for Peace." In addition to this message, Pope Francis used Twitter in the days following its release to focus more attention on nonviolence. On January 3, 2017, he tweeted, "May nonviolence become the hallmark of our decisions, our relationships and our actions." The next day he tweeted, "To be true followers of Jesus today also includes embracing his teaching about nonviolence," and he reiterated this message on January 5, tweeting "May charity

142 Man of Dialogue

and nonviolence govern how we treat one another."[1] His message and his tweets came after a conference on nonviolence took place at the Vatican in April, organized jointly by the Pontifical Council for Justice and Peace and Pax Christi International, at which the participants called on the pope to write an encyclical or "other teaching document" on nonviolence and to reject the just war tradition.[2] Pope Francis's World Day of Peace message was, in part, a response to this conference's appeal.

Pope Francis's message was not the first time a pope exhorted Catholics to nonviolence. Pope St. John Paul II forcefully opposed violence and praised those who opposed injustice nonviolently.[3] And at the Angelus on February 18, 2007, Pope Benedict XVI referred to Jesus' exhortation to "Love your enemies" (Luke 6:27) as "the *magna carta* of Christian non-violence" and spoke about nonviolence as "not merely tactical behaviour but a person's way of being, the attitude of one who *is so convinced of God's love and power* that he is not afraid to tackle evil with the weapons of love and truth alone."[4] That said, Pope Francis's World Day of Peace message was the first papal document focused specifically on nonviolence, and drew attention to it in a more sustained manner than previous papal documents.

One of the twentieth century's greatest Roman Catholic advocates for nonviolence and nonviolent resistance was Thomas Merton. His writings emerged out of a Cold War context when Catholic moral

1. Pope Francis, Twitter posts: January 3, 2017, 7:15 a.m., https://twitter.com/Pontifex/status/816256550184439808; January 4, 2017, 7:40 a.m., https://twitter.com/Pontifex/status/816625227887181824; January 5, 2017, 7:30 a.m., https://twitter.com/Pontifex/status/816985102433415168.

2. Joshua J. McElwee, "Cardinal Turkson: Papal Encyclical on Nonviolence, Just War Theory 'Plausible,'" *National Catholic Reporter* (April 26, 2016), https://www.ncronline.org/blogs/ncr-today/cardinal-turkson-papal-encyclical-nonviolence-just-war-theory-plausible.

3. See Heinz-Gerhard Justenhoven, "The Peace Ethics of Pope John Paul II," *University of St. Thomas Law Journal* 3:1 (2005): 118–21.

4. Pope Benedict XVI, Angelus (February 18, 2007), http://w2.vatican.va/content/benedict-xvi/en/angelus/2007/documents/hf_ben-xvi_ang_20070218.html. Emphasis in original.

theology was grappling with the dilemma of weaponry capable of destroying life on earth, and Merton's emphatic call to nonviolence was, and still is, considered a radical approach. This approach has, in my opinion, always merited examination, but it has unfortunately become even more pertinent in our current context. While in comparison to the Cold War era we pay far less attention to the danger of nuclear war, the reality is that little has changed in terms of our capability and willingness to use such weapons. Moreover, Catholics and others currently find themselves in a position where policies, particularly those revolving around racism and immigration, are having to be resisted nonviolently.

In this context, and with Pope Francis giving renewed attention to a politics of nonviolence, Merton's advocacy for the nonviolent approach deserves another look, particularly since, as already noted above, Pope Francis himself exhorted us to listen to Merton. Others have explored Merton's understanding of nonviolence,[5] and while I will delve into his conception of war and peace, my focus will be particularly on the theological underpinnings of Merton's peace writings as a means of illustrating that his response was not a consequence of him capitulating to secular peace movements, but was rooted principally in theological concerns.

I will begin by examining how and why Merton became interested in issues of peace, referring as well to reaction to his writings within his own monastic order. I will then look at Merton's arguments against nuclear war, paying particular attention to the theological sources on which he drew to make his arguments. From there, I'll examine his theology of nonviolence itself.

Merton's Writing on Peace

Those familiar with Merton know that his interest in peace issues in the 1960s didn't emerge out of thin air. In *The Seven Storey*

---

5. A recent excellent book on Merton's teachings on war and peace is Jim Forest's *The Root of War Is Fear: Thomas Merton's Advice to Peacemakers* (Maryknoll, NY: Orbis Books, 2016).

Mountain he recounted that, prior to his conversion to Catholicism, he joined a peace strike at Columbia University at which speakers argued that just war in our time was impossible. After his conversion, Merton grappled with his position on war given that the American government had instituted the draft in preparation for possible participation in World War II. He accepted Catholic teaching on just war, as he would for his entire life, but he had doubts about the morality of modern warfare and consequently applied to be considered a non-combatant objector. His entrance into the Abbey of Gethsemani on December 10, 1941, kept him out of the war and put a cloister wall between himself and a world at war

But the wall didn't keep him from being regularly reminded of war's existence. His younger brother, John Paul, was killed in the Second World War, and he described in his journals hearing the guns firing at Fort Knox and seeing Air Force planes flying over the monastery. But Merton's published writings from the 1940s into the mid-1950s contain few references to the problem of war, and focus instead on prayer and contemplation. His private journals are also largely silent on this issue during these years. Later, Merton describes this period as being a time characterized by a "highly unworldly, ascetical, intransigent, somewhat apocalyptic outlook" in which he operated out of a perspective that saw a "[r]igid, arbitrary separation between God and the world" (Liii, 384; TM to Sr. J. M.: June 17, 1968).

Merton's understanding of his relationship to the world began to change throughout the 1950s. Such rethinking is on display in a November 1957 journal entry: "Politics vital—even for monks" (Jiii, 135: November 12, 1957). It is, however, an experience he had on March 18, 1958, that illustrates the transformation that took place in the 1950s as he focused his attention back on the world.

On a trip into Louisville, he found himself downtown on the corner of Fourth and Walnut. There are two versions of what happened. The first is that found in Merton's journal, written the day after his trip to Louisville. The second is the version found in *Conjectures of a Guilty Bystander*, published in 1965. For this version, Merton edited and rewrote his original journal entry, which is more raw and unpolished. It is the original journal entry I want to cite here, specifically because of its rawness. The entire passage is worth quoting at length:

> Yesterday, in Louisville, at the corner of 4th. and Walnut, suddenly realized that I loved all the people and that none of them were, or, could be totally alien to me. As if waking from a dream—the dream of my separateness, of the "special" vocation to be different. My vocation does not really make me different from the rest of men or put me in a special category except artificially, juridically. I am still a member of the human race—and what more glorious destiny is there for man, since the Word was made flesh and became, too a member of the Human Race!
>
> Thank God! Thank God! I am only another member of the human race, like all the rest of them. I have the immense joy of being a man! As if the sorrows of our condition could really matter, once we begin to realize who and what we are—as if we could ever begin to realize it on earth. (Jiii, 181–82: March 19, 1958)

Here he was, a monk in an austere monastery, standing outside a lavish hotel at the corner of a busy intersection. And far from experiencing revulsion or a sense of superiority in the face of people who lived radically different lives from his own, Merton fell in love. Those who have read his autobiography, *The Seven Storey Mountain*, know the Merton who saw in the monastery a place of refuge from a world bent under the weight of sin and corruption. The monastery represented for him an escape from the world, a place where he could devote himself to a higher way of being away from the pernicious influences of others. The revelation Merton experienced on the corner of Fourth and Walnut, therefore, was just that, a revelation. It shattered his perception that his vocation was characterized primarily by its isolation from and superiority to the world. Instead, he *experienced* a profound unity with all those he saw on that street corner, a unity rooted in their shared humanity and, most importantly, in the dignity accorded humanity when God became human.

Too much should not be made of this epiphany. If you read his journals, you can see that, prior to March 18, 1958, Merton was thinking more and more seriously about the world outside the monastery. But it is clear that his experience on the corner of Fourth and Walnut compelled him to think more thoroughly about his relationship to the world, and specifically, to address various issues in whatever way was possible for a cloistered monk. Chief among these issues was the problem of war and the Christian response to it. Compelled by a strong sense of the dignity of all human life, Merton reacted with incredulity not only to the possibility that humanity would doom itself to annihilation through nuclear war, but that American Catholics—including bishops—supported American use of its nuclear arsenal in a first strike against the Soviet Union. Given this situation, he saw no alternative but to devote himself fully to the task of peace. As he wrote in a letter in 1961, "I feel that the supreme obligation of every Christian, taking precedence over absolutely everything else, is to devote himself by the very best means at his disposal to a struggle to preserve the human race from annihilation and to abolish war as the essential means to accomplish this end" (Li, 402: TM to John C. Heidbrink: October 30, 1961). And writing to Dorothy Day in that same year, Merton said, "I don't feel that I can in conscience, at a time like this, go on writing just about things like meditation . . . I think I have to face the big issues, the life-and-death issues" (Li, 140; TM to Dorothy Day: August 23, 1963).

A month after this letter, Merton ventured into the anti-war waters by sending a chapter from his forthcoming book, *New Seeds of Contemplation* (the aforementioned revision of *Seeds of Contemplation*), to *The Catholic Worker* for publication, a newspaper published by the pacifist organization created by Peter Maurin and Dorothy Day. The title of the chapter was "The Root of War Is Fear," and it had been reviewed and approved by the Trappists for publication; throughout Merton's monastic life, all of his published writings were subject to review by his religious superiors. Not reviewed, however, were the three paragraphs that he added to the beginning of the version he sent to *The Catholic Worker* "to situate these thoughts in the present crisis" (Li, 140; TM to Dorothy Day: September 22, 1963). In these paragraphs, Merton pulled no punches in calling for nonviolence:

> The duty of the Christian in this crisis is to strive with all his power and intelligence, with his faith, hope in Christ, and love for God and man, to do the one task which God has imposed upon us in the world today. That task is to work for the total abolition of war . . . [The Church] must lead the way on the road towards nonviolent settlement of difficulties and towards the gradual abolition of war as the way of settling international or civil disputes. ("The Root of War Is Fear," PFP, 12)

Two days after the article was published, Merton wrote in his journal that its publication marked a distinct and significant shift in his life, knowing as he did that he was heading into controversial territory, particularly for a monk: "Walking into a known and definite battle. May God protect me in it" (Jiv, 172: October 23, 1961). He was one of the few Catholic clerics in the United States to call for the abolition of war and the active practice of nonviolence, and he knew that there was likely to be backlash both from those inside and outside the church.

He was right. Merton followed "The Root of War Is Fear" with further essays in 1961 and 1962 on war and peace, and immersed himself as fully as a cloistered monk could in the peace movement, becoming a member of Fellowship of Reconciliation, a largely Protestant pacifist organization, as well as a sponsor of a Catholic peace organization called Pax Christi. In the spring of 1962, however, the axe came down. Dom Gabriel Sortais, abbot general of the Cistercians, asked Merton to stop publishing anything on war because he felt it was a subject about which monks should not write as it "falsifies the message of monasticism" (Jiv, 216: April 27, 1962). Two factors likely played into Dom Gabriel's silencing of Merton. First, the backlash against Merton's early writings on war and peace was intense within the American church, and it is probable that many were pressuring the abbot general to keep him in check. Second, and Merton hinted at this, Dom Gabriel does not appear personally to have agreed with Merton's assessment of nuclear weaponry.

No matter the cause, Merton obeyed his superior, at least to the letter of the law. Anything published publicly in a large forum required formal censorship by the order. Not so anything published privately on a small scale. Therefore, with his immediate abbot's knowledge, Merton mimeographed and privately circulated two books on war. The first, *Cold War Letters*, is a collection of more than one hundred letters to friends and activists about the problem of war. The second, provocatively titled *Peace in the Post-Christian Era*, was a book that was completed when the axe came down; it was not finally published until 2004. Merton also published a few articles under rather uninventive pseudonyms like Benedict Monk.

In 1963, Pope John XXIII released *Pacem in Terris*, his encyclical on peace. Writing to Dom Gabriel shortly after the encyclical's publication, Merton somewhat pointedly remarked that it was a good thing that the pope did not have to go through the order's censors, otherwise it would never have been published (Liii, 166; TM to Gabriel Sortais: Easter Day, 1963). Merton hoped that now that the pope had weighed in on the issue of war and peace in a manner similar to what Merton himself had been doing, he himself would be allowed to publish on it again. The abbot general would have none of it, arguing that it was the job of bishops and theologians to write about such things, *not* Trappist monks (Jiv, 317–18: May 10, 1962). It was only after Dom Gabriel died in November 1963 that restrictions on Merton's writing on war and peace began to be lifted.

Merton and Nuclear Weapons

From the very beginning of his anti-war writings, Merton wrote from a theological perspective, drawing on explicitly Catholic sources and ideas to argue against the use of nuclear weapons. A common misconception about Merton is that he was a pacifist. He was not. He accepted the church's teaching on just war, acknowledging that the just war tradition had deep roots in the church's tradition (see PFP,

66). However, he came to the conclusion that the just war tradition no longer had relevance in the modern age given the destructive capabilities of contemporary weaponry, including and especially nuclear weaponry.[6] "I am not a pure pacifist in theory," he wrote in 1961 to James Forest, a prominent peace activist, "though today in practice I don't see how one can be anything else since limited wars (however 'just') present an almost certain danger of nuclear war on an all-out scale" (Li, 259; TM to James Forest: November 29, 1961).[7] This was a position Merton shared with none other than Cardinal Alfredo Ottaviani, known as one of the most conservative prelates at the Second Vatican Council.[8] Before the Council, then Monsignor Ottaviani wrote forcefully about the problem modern weaponry posed to the church's traditional teaching on just war, arguing that "Modern wars can never fulfill the conditions which govern, theoretically, a just and lawful war."[9] Merton quoted Ottaviani at length on this point in a 1962 article he wrote for *The Catholic Worker*. When the Council debated the issue of war, Cardinal Ottaviani again spoke up, stating that "War must be completely outlawed."[10] While Merton's position on nuclear war raised the hackles of the American hierarchy as well as of those within his own order (for reasons we will explore below), he was not raising into question the church's traditional teaching on just war. He accepted the teaching, acknowledging both its provenance and its wisdom. However, like Ottaviani, he understood that the modern context had changed everything. Merton's writings against war and on nonviolence should

6. See "Target Equals City," PFP, 28–29, 35; "Christian Ethics and Nuclear War," PFP, 60–63; *Peace in the Post-Christian Era* (Maryknoll, NY: Orbis Books, 2004), 43–46.

7. See also Li, 145; TM to Dorothy Day: June 16, 1962; Li, 330–31; TM to Jean and Hildegard Goss-Mayr: December 17, 1962.

8. See John W. O'Malley, *What Happened at Vatican II* (Cambridge, MA: Harvard University Press, 2008), 108–9, for a brief overview of Cardinal Ottaviani's role at the Second Vatican Council.

9. As quoted in "Christian Ethics and Nuclear War," PFP, 60.

10. As quoted in O'Malley, *What Happened at Vatican II*, 264.

therefore be read, not as a challenge to the church's teaching, but as an exposition of that teaching in a nuclear world.

The intended audience for Merton's argument for nonviolence and against the use of nuclear weapons was his fellow American Catholics, many of whom—including bishops—supported the use of nuclear weapons, and even the use of such weapons in a first strike against the Soviet Union. Knowing his audience, Merton focused his attention in his earliest essays (1961–1962) on the problem of war in the church's tradition, pointing as far back as the New Testament and the teachings of Christ and as recently as Pope Pius XII, who was pope from 1939 to 1958.

Merton's first essay on war after "The Root of War Is Fear" was "The Shelter Ethic," published in *The Catholic Worker* in November 1961. He wrote the essay as a response to an article he read by a priest in *America*, a Jesuit magazine. In the article, called "Ethics at the Shelter Doorway," Fr. L. C. McHugh, SJ, argued that a person who had built a fallout shelter for his family was morally permitted to use violence against anyone who tried to enter the shelter for safety. Merton began the essay by criticizing what he saw as the "lowest common denominator" Catholic morality being preached by Fr. McHugh, and he used this as a launching pad for a discussion of nonviolence, focusing his attention on the gospels and the witness of Jesus Christ. Whereas Fr. McHugh seemed to think that Christians need only meet the most minimal standards to fulfil Catholic moral obligations, Merton argued that the New Testament put forward a much more rigorous and challenging conception of morality. In this day and age, Merton argued, "instead of wasting our time in problematic ways of saving our own skin, we ought to be seeking with all our strength to act as better Christians, as men of peace, dedicated wholeheartedly to the law of love which is the law of Christ." Given the very real possibility of nuclear annihilation, Christians needed to return to the roots of their faith, and Merton here pointed specifically to the Sermon on the Mount. Merton lamented that too often "the nonviolent resistance to evil which is of the very essence of the New Testament morality has come to be regarded as a specialty reserved for beatniks and eccentric cultists" instead of "the whole spirit and orientation" of Christian morality (PFP, 23). Pure selfishness and pragmatism are simply not options for Christians governed by the Law of Christ, modelled for us by Christ who accepted suffering out of love. Love, Merton wrote, is not passive. It is, as the crucifixion shows, a "dynamic spiritual force" capable of transforming. Such love is not optional for Christians. Rather, "A Christian is committed to the belief that Love and Mercy are the most powerful forces on earth. Hence every Christian is bound by his baptismal vocation to seek, as far as he can, with God's grace, to make these forces effective in his life, to the point where they dominate all his actions" (PFP, 25).

Merton did not believe he was developing a new or novel conception of nonviolence, but he was aware that he needed to demonstrate, through appeal to the Scriptures and to the church's tradition, that nonviolence was central to Christian teaching. In an essay he published in 1965 in *The Catholic Worker* called "St. Maximus the Confessor on Non-Violence," he described the situation in America as follows: "Christians are sometimes so disturbed by the enemies of Christianity that they become convinced that hatred of these enemies is a proof of love for Christ." Given this state of affairs, Merton argued that "it is necessary to go back to the sources and try to recover the true Christian meaning of the first and all-embracing commandment to love all men including our enemies" (PFP, 241). Knowing how seriously Catholics take tradition, or at least *should* take tradition, Merton realized that he needed to appeal to the sources of the faith as a means of demonstrating that his call to nonviolence had deep roots in Catholic theology.

Therefore, in a February 1962 essay, "Nuclear War and Christian Responsibility," published in *Commonweal*, Merton pointed specifically to the example of Christ who "brought to His disciples a vocation and a task, to struggle in the world of violence to establish His peace not only in their own hearts but in society itself" (PFP, 39–40). What about Christ's example demonstrated this? His crucifixion. Rather than defend himself as he could have done with twelve legions of angels, Christ "allowed Himself to be nailed *to the cross* and died praying for His executioners." The idea that Christians, who are to follow the example of Christ, could advocate for the use of nuclear weapons when their own Savior refused to respond in power in the face of adversity struck Merton as utterly absurd, and to press home his point, he turned not simply to Christ but to the witness of the martyrs who took Christ's words and example with utter seriousness: "The Christian is one whose life has sprung from a particular spiritual seed: the blood of the martyrs who, without offering forcible resistance, laid down their lives rather than submit to the unjust laws that demanded an official religious cult of the Emperor as God" (PFP, 40).

In *Peace in the Post-Christian Era*, the book completed in 1962 that he was forbidden to publish, Merton argued that Christ's teaching on violence and on war are rooted in Christ's teaching on the kingdom of God. According to Merton, Christ inaugurated the kingdom of God here on earth, and in so doing, emphasized a new way of being for his followers. Merton put it this way:

> War was neither blessed nor forbidden by Christ. He simply stated that war belonged to the world outside the kingdom, the world outside the mystery and the Spirit of Christ and that therefore for one who was seriously living in Christ, war belonged to a realm that no longer had a decisive meaning. (PPCE, 28–29)

Christ came to create a new political community, a kingdom of God in this world, where the "normal" rules don't apply. While power, force, and violence characterize the kingdoms of this world, the kingdom of God is governed by the Law of Love, exemplified for us by the selfless generosity of the Word made flesh. Those in the kingdom of God, Merton argued, "will take no direct part in the struggles of earthly kingdoms." He continued: "They depend on no power other than the power of God, and it is God they obey rather than the state, which tends to usurp the powers of God and to blaspheme him, setting itself up in his stead as an idol and drawing to itself the adoration and worship that are due to him alone" (PPCE, 30). This he takes to be the message not simply of the gospels, but also of the book of Revelation, a book that shows that early Christians understood that, whatever may be the battles fought by the worldly empire, the battle of the Christian was to be "nonviolent and spiritual."

Merton was arguing that nonviolence is not something novel, but actually has roots in the very foundation of Christianity, in Christ himself. And lest his interlocutors think that Christ's teaching and example were appropriate only for him and that, for example, the Sermon on the Mount is not intended to be taken literally, Merton pointed to the example of the early Christians who preferred to suffer rather than do that which was opposed to the Law of Love. As opposed to some arguments made by Christian pacifists, Merton argued that post-apostolic Christians were not absolute pacifists who "had a clear, systematic policy of pacifism which obliged them to refuse military service whenever it was demanded of them" (PPCE, 31). While the military life was not considered ideal for Christians in no small part because service in the military was tied to the idolatry of required sacrifices, there were Christians in the army. Nevertheless, prominent Christian writers like Justin Martyr, Origen, Clement of Alexandria, Tertullian, and Cyprian of Carthage all argued that killing in war was opposed to following Christ. Moreover, Christians like St. Maximilian of Tebessa were martyred for refusing to serve in the army, and St. Martin of Tours remained in service until he was asked to kill (PPCE, 32–33).

Although things changed substantially in the fourth century with the rise of Constantine, Merton didn't think that Christian nonviolence was isolated simply to Christ and his early followers before the fourth century. In a 1965 essay, Merton argued that nonviolence was an important theme in the thought of one of the most important post-Constantinian patristic writers, St. Maximus the Confessor (died 662). Born in Constantinople in the late sixth century, Maximus was a highly educated monk and theologian whose influence on theology in both the East and the West was considerable.[11] He wrote extensively, both on theological issues and on the life of prayer. In his essay, Merton provided excerpts from a treatise Maximus wrote on the ascetic life, excerpts that focus on what it means to love our enemies. It isn't necessary to go through this essay in detail, filled as it is with quotations from Maximus himself. We need only point to the conclusion Merton drew from Maximus's treatise:

> The significant thing for us, in this remarkable passage from the Greek saint, is that he portrays non-violent resistance under suffering and persecution as the normal way of the Christian, and shows that the Christian who has recourse to force and hatred in order to protect himself is, in fact, by that very action, denying Christ and showing that he has no real understanding of the Gospel. (PFP, 241)

Maximus did not understand nonviolence to be an aberration or an extraordinary and unrealistic demand on Christians. Rather, he recognized it to be the "normal way of the Christian," an essential and central component of what it actually meant to be a Christian.

At the same time, Merton had to come to grips with the fact that Christian attitudes toward war changed significantly in the fourth century. In a chapter of *Peace in the Post-Christian Era*, he explored this change by contrasting the writings of Origen, a third century theologian, and Augustine of Hippo. Origen's *Contra Celsum* (*Against Celsus*) was a response to the criticisms of Celsus, a second century philosopher and opponent of Christianity. Celsus understood Christianity to be a blight on Roman society, a parasite that

---

11. In his introduction to the selected writings of Maximus the Confessor for Paulist Press's Classics of Western Spirituality series, Jaroslav Pelikan writes: "The importance of Maximus Confessor in the seventh century is universally acknowledged by scholars representing many different traditions of scholarship and articulating several different theological perspectives—Eastern Orthodox, Roman Catholic, and Protestant." See *Maximus Confessor: Selected Writings*, trans. George C. Berthold (New York: Paulist Press, 1985), 3.

compromised the stability of the empire, and Merton noted that one of Celsus's harshest critiques was that many Christians refused to serve in the army. And because they refused to serve in the army, they demonstrated that they have no concern for peace and order. Origen responded theologically, arguing that Christians have a very different understanding of society and of their role in it than does Celsus. Origen understood "that human society has been radically transformed by the incarnation of the Logos" (PPCE, 36). Whereas Celsus saw a world that requires and necessitates war, given human incapacity to live in peace, Origen argued that the incarnation revealed the possibility for humanity to live in unity in the divine Logos. As he put it, "the presence in the world of the risen Savior, in and through his Church, has destroyed the seeming validity of all that was in reality arbitrary, tyrannical or absurd in the fictions of social life" (as quoted in PPCE, 36–37). In other words, Christians saw the world through the lens of the incarnation, recognizing that they were called to a new way of living in the world by the incarnate Word, that they must obey the law of love rather than the law of Rome should the two come into conflict. It is in obedience to Christ that Christians were united against war, and Merton quoted Origen as follows: "No longer do we take the sword against any nations nor do we learn war any more since we have become the sons of peace through Jesus who is our author" (PPCE, 37). Origen insisted that Christians would not take up arms on behalf of any one nation. Rather, they fight against war itself by praying against the forces that divide humankind and by living a way of life centered around love.

As we have seen, Origen was not alone among the early church fathers in his condemnation of war and military service, but Merton focused his attention on Origen particularly because he was so thorough in his recounting of Christian attitudes toward war. But Merton had to acknowledge that Christian attitudes toward war changed in the fourth century, as exemplified by the writings of Augustine of Hippo. While Merton had a deep admiration for Augustine and was influenced by him in many ways—not least by his *Confessions*—he was critical of Augustine on the issue of war.

Whereas Origen took it for granted that the Christian would have great qualms about serving in the military, Augustine pleaded with a soldier not to become a monk but to remain in the army and do his duty (PPCE, 39). What had changed in the intervening years? In a word, Constantine. The marriage of Christianity with political power meant that a way had to be found to develop theological justifications for the use of force by Christians for the sake of order and peace in the empire. "The question was," Merton wrote, "to find out some way to fight that did not violate the law of love" (PPCE, 41). It was out of this framework that Augustine developed the just war tradition, insisting that any cause for which Christians will fight must meet particular standards so as to be considered morally licit. I've already noted above that Merton affirmed the just war tradition and understood its value, particularly "in ages less destructive than our own" (PPCE., 43). So Merton did not attack Augustine for his role in the development of the just war tradition. Rather, what bothered him most about Augustine was the way in which he argued that war does not compromise Christ's command to love our enemies. Indeed, Augustine was clear that war may be the means by which we demonstrate our love. "Love," Merton quoted Augustine as saying, "does not exclude wars of mercy waged by the good." The key for Augustine had to do with distinguishing the interior motive from the external act. It is the former that justifies or condemns the latter. Provided our interior motive remains one of love, physical force can be used against enemies without violating Christ's law of love. Merton held this distinction between interior motive and exterior act to have disastrous consequences in the history of Christianity. "The history of the Middle Ages, of the Crusades, of the religious wars," he wrote, "has taught us what evil could have been expected from this noble principle" (PPCE, 42).

Merton did give credit to Augustine for the limits he imposed on Christian soldiers and on what constitutes a just war. But Merton noted that, by the time we get to the medieval period, constant efforts were made "to evade and rationalize the demands of the just war theory" (PPCE, 45). Without going through the entire history of the just war tradition, Merton argued that the just war tradition was distorted in the sixteenth century in ways similar to how it was being distorted in the twentieth century by those who advocate for the use of nuclear weapons against the Soviet Union:

> Let us remember, however, that in the sixteenth century, Christian Conquistadors felt themselves to be obliged by a kind of divine mission to destroy civilizations "which carried out practices contrary to the natural law" (viz., the Aztecs and human sacrifices—or any other form of idolatry. This concept of a Christian civilization with a mandate and obligation to punish and reform the lesser breeds without the law is still unfortunately prevalent in the west, even though the west is no longer Christian. It underlies the whole concept of the nuclear crusade against Communism. (PPCE, 45–46)

The just war tradition was used to justify the unjustifiable in the sixteenth century, and was being used to do the same in the twentieth.

In a later chapter in *Peace in the Post-Christian Era*, Merton focused more attention on the modern applicability of just war theory, demonstrating that it could no longer apply in a world that has nuclear weapons. The just war theory presupposes a defensive war in which the use of force is limited and non-combatants are protected, and while these principles were frequently disregarded in the medieval period, they made sense given the limited scale of warfare. But nuclear weapons are, according to Merton, "purely offensive" weapons, particularly given that so many people, including Catholics, were calling for an offensive first strike against the Soviet Union. Moreover, these are weapons that, given their destructive capabilities, cannot but kill non-combatants, and the scale of the force used is on a level that limitations are themselves meaningless. "Hence," Merton concluded, "the theologian is faced with a problem of fabulous complexity if he wants to justify nuclear war by traditional Christian standards" (PPCE, 69).

That complexity had not prevented theologians from attempting to justify just that. Moreover, as Merton noted in another essay, the sad fact is that Catholics are no different in their attitudes toward nuclear war than anyone else (PFP, 57). Not only did Merton therefore argue against this attitude through theological argument, which we looked at above, but he also argued on the basis of magisterial authority by pointing to statements made by Pope Pius XII and Pope John XXIII on the issue of nuclear war. While he acknowledged that the popes have never made an *ex cathedra* condemnation of nuclear war, Merton questioned why such a condemnation would even be necessary given what the teaching authority of the church has already said about war. He pointed out in an essay called "Religion and the Bomb" that there exist many statements by both Pius XII and John XXIII that unambiguously condemn recourse to war in international disputes. Even before the advent of the nuclear weapon, Pope Pius XII warned that war, even war that used conventional weapons, could be criminal. And in 1939, in response to the blitzkrieg in Poland, Pius XII said that the use of conventional weapons against civilians "cried out to heaven for vengeance" (PFP, 75). In his 1944 Christmas message, before the bombing of Hiroshima, Pius XII stated that "the theory of war was as an apt and proportionate means of solving international conflicts is now out of date." He went on to say that the duty of banning wars was a duty that was "binding on all," and "brooks no delay, no procrastination, no hesitation, no subterfuge." And in 1954, in an address to the World Medical Association, he unequivocally denounced nuclear annihilation as immoral. While Pius XII affirmed the right of the state to self-defense, this did not mean that he approved of nuclear weapons as a legitimate response to an aggressor, as he made clear in an address to army doctors in 1953: "If the damage caused by the war is disproportionate to the injustice suffered, it may well be a matter of obligation to suffer the injustice" (PFP, 76).

Given both the theological argument against nuclear war, as well as the statements by recent popes about the immorality of nuclear weaponry, Merton questioned how Catholics could in any way justify the use of nuclear weapons either offensively or defensively. The high stakes of nuclear war, stakes that amount essentially to global suicide, mean that Catholics should not only refuse to advocate for or participate in nuclear war. They should also work tirelessly against war. As he wrote in "The Root of War Is Fear," "There can be no question that unless war is abolished the world will remain constantly in a state of madness and desperation in which, because of the immense destructive power of modern weapons, the danger of catastrophe will be imminent and probably at every moment everywhere" (PFP, 12; italics removed). It is for this reason that Merton argued that the only option open to Christians is nonviolence, and it is to his theology of nonviolence that I now turn.

Merton's Theology of Nonviolence

As already mentioned, Merton's monastic superiors ordered him to stop writing about the problem of war in 1962. However, when the abbot general died in 1963 the restrictions on Merton's writing were slowly lifted. In 1966, Merton published his most important and insightful essay on war and nonviolence, "Blessed Are the Meek: The Christian Roots of Nonviolence." Merton wrote this essay in response to a request from Jean and Hildegard Goss-Mayr, prominent Catholic peace activists who worked with Cardinal Ottaviani to craft documents against war during the Second Vatican Council. Hildegard Goss-Mayr wanted an article on humility for the journal *Der Christ in der Welt*. Two weeks after this request, Merton wrote to Goss-Mayr to let her know that the article was completed, and that it had actually turned into an article on meekness as applied to Christian nonviolence. It was translated into German and published in the April–June 1966 issue of *Der Christ in der Welt*. In 1967 it was published in *Fellowship*, the journal of the Fellowship of Reconciliation, an important Protestant organization that advocated for nonviolence, and later that year, the Catholic Peace Fellowship published it as a pamphlet complete with a cover by Sr. Mary Corita.

Although "Blessed Are the Meek" is Merton's fullest treatment of nonviolence, it is not the first place he discussed it. In his first writing on war and peace, the aforementioned three uncensored paragraphs in "The Root of War Is Fear," Merton wrote that, to address the problem of war, "nonviolence is to be explained as a practical method, and not left to be mocked as an outlet for crackpots who want to make a show of themselves" (PFP, 12–13). Merton did not develop his thoughts on nonviolence in this early writing, but did so in "Blessed Are the Meek" a few years later, in which he provided, in essence, a theology of Christian nonviolence. In what follows, I am going to delve into his theology of Christian nonviolence, and to do so I'll focus most of my attention on his essay, "Blessed Are the Meek," while occasionally referring to other writings by Merton when necessary. I will first go into what, according to Merton, Christian nonviolence is *not*. Second, I will look at how and why humanity resorts to violence; that is, I will briefly look at Merton's account of the human dilemma. Third, I will examine the theological bases Merton established for nonviolence, focusing especially on how the incarnation of the Son of God should shape our relations to others, as well as on how the teachings of the Incarnate Son should mold our actions. The focus of the examination as a whole will be on how Merton framed his argument *theologically*. As we shall see, Merton's understanding of nonviolence is rooted in a fundamentally theological, and specifically Catholic, understanding of God, humanity, and the purpose of human life.

What Nonviolence Is Not

Merton began "Blessed Are the Meek" by describing, not what Christian nonviolence *is*, but what it is *not*. It is not, Merton writes, "a novel tactic which is at once efficacious and even edifying, and which enables the sensitive [person] to participate in the struggles of the world without being dirtied with blood." It is not "a way of proving one's point and getting what one wants without being involved in behavior that one considers ugly and evil" (PFP, 248). Nonviolence is not about prevailing over an adversary, nor is it about proving the adversary wrong and ourselves right. Christian nonviolence cannot become a form of moral aggression or "subtle provocation designed . . . to bring out the evil we hope to find in the adversary" (PFP, 249). In short, any form of nonviolence that caters to selfish and prideful inclinations to attain anything at the expense of our adversary is not *Christian* nonviolence, for reasons he outlined later in the essay. As Merton wrote, "to practice nonviolence for a purely selfish or arbitrary end would in fact discredit and distort the truth of nonviolent resistance" (PFP, 248).

The Human Dilemma: Fragmentation and Violence

Merton's comments about what nonviolence is not are rooted in his understanding of human sin and its implications for how we interact with one another. Later in "Blessed Are the Meek," Merton referred to the incessant temptation we have to demonize our adversaries, to view them as totally unreasonable, wicked, and evil, particularly when we are appealing to what we understand to be higher ideals. Such temptation emerges out of the divisiveness that characterizes human society, a divisiveness that is the root of violence. Humanity's propensity toward fragmentation, and thus toward violence, is a consistent theme in Merton's writings.

In "The Root of War Is Fear," Merton explored this propensity to divide, analyzing "the psychological forces at work in ourselves and in society" (PFP, 13). Merton here argued that one of the ways we deal with our faults and weaknesses is by exaggerating the faults and weaknesses of others. While we are willing to view the malice within us as being somehow distanced from who we really are, we do not extend this privilege to others. We instead compensate for minimizing our own sins by exaggerating the faults of others. Thus, to deal with our own sense of guilt, we create enemies who, by our assessment, are evil and who therefore need to be eliminated for the cause of "peace." We divide as a means of elevating ourselves over others who thus become our adversaries.

It is because of our divisiveness that Merton outlined precisely what nonviolence is not at the beginning of "Blessed Are the Meek." He was convinced that nonviolence has the potential to play into our inclination to divide insofar as it can be used to differentiate and further division rather than to heal the divisiveness that characterizes human relations. To make our nonviolence the means by which we conquer and subdue our enemies, to make it a way to manifest our adversary's "evil" and our "righteousness," is to turn nonviolence into a form of violence that simply caters to that which is least human in us.[12]

The Theology of Nonviolence

If divisiveness is both the consequence of sin and the cause of violence, Christian nonviolence—rooted in the person, teaching, and example of Jesus Christ—is focused squarely on fostering unity. What is required is an understanding of humanity that takes seriously the incarnation, which, according to Merton, changes everything in terms of how we understand ourselves and how we interact with one another. In essence, Merton argued that Christians need to see all people, including adversaries, in the light of the incarnation of the Son of God. The incarnation, God-becoming-flesh reveals to us the possibilities of human transformation through the radical love of a God who became one of us. In his Fourth-and-Walnut experience, to which I have already made reference, Merton expressed this point beautifully. Reflecting on this experience seven years after his epiphany, Merton wrote:

> I have the immense joy of being *man*, a member of a race in which God Himself became incarnate. As if the sorrows and stupidities of the human condition could overwhelm me, now I realize what we all are. And if only everybody could realize this! But there is no way of telling people that they are all walking around shining like the sun. (CGB, 141)

---

12. See Li, 263. TM to Jim Forest (February 6, 1962): "One of the most problematical questions about non-violence is the inevitable involvement of hidden aggressions and provocations." Similarly, in *Faith and Violence*, Merton argued that, unfortunately, "nonviolent resistance as practiced by those who do not understand it and have been trained in it is often only a weak and veiled form of psychological aggression." See *Faith and Violence: Christian Teaching and Christian Practice* (Notre Dame, IN: University of Notre Dame Press, 1968), 12.

The incarnation reveals to us the immense dignity and surpassing value of each person, such that, if we take it seriously, we come to see each person in the light of what they can be and of what they already are in God's eyes. And if we could see that, *really* see that, what would be the implications? According to Merton, "There would be no more war, no more hatred, no more cruelty, no more greed. . . . I suppose the big problem would be that we would fall down and worship each other" (CGB, 142).

The incarnation means that we cannot view anyone, including our adversary, as inherently evil or beyond hope. Rather, as Merton wrote in *New Seeds of Contemplation*, "if we believe in the Incarnation of the Son of God, there should be no one on earth in whom we are not prepared to see, in mystery, the presence of Christ" (NSC, 296). It is this new way of seeing other people that Merton insists is at the heart of Christian nonviolence. We must view all people, including our enemies, as brothers and sisters, rather than as adversaries. We must see them from the standpoint of our fundamental unity with them. For, as Merton wrote in a letter to Dorothy Day, "we justify the evil we do to our brother because he is no longer a brother, he is merely an adversary, an accused" (Li; TM to Dorothy Day: December 20, 1961).

Therefore, as Merton wrote in "Blessed Are the Meek," Christian nonviolence "is not built on a presupposed division, but on the basic unity of mankind" (PFP, 249). We must approach others not from the starting point of negation but from an orientation of affirmation, rooted in an acknowledgement of our unity with them. This does not mean for Merton the adoption of a kind of supernatural naivete that ignores the reality of conflict and division, but it does mean viewing other people eschatologically through the lens of the kingdom Jesus established, a kingdom characterized by a fundamentally new way of existing and interacting with one another. Christ assumed human nature and died out of love for *all* people, to be united in and with *all*. The kingdom of God he established is therefore a kingdom "to which *all* are summoned" (PFP, 250). The Gospel message of salvation is for every person, and this message of salvation is one focused on the reattainment of human unity in and through Christ. It is for this unity that Christian nonviolent resisters fight. They are not fighting for their own truth or their own side, as if they have a truth to which the other has no access. Rather, they are "fighting for *the* truth, common to [them] and to the adversary, *the* right which is objective and universal" (PFP, 249). They are fighting for a truth that transcends all supposed divisions between ourselves and our adversaries, that truth being that we are all—adversaries included—called to the kingdom of God. This means for Christians that they must act in a particular way toward their adversaries, recognizing that salvation extends as fully to the adversary as it does to them.

Therefore, because salvation and the potentiality for transformation is possible for all people, Merton argued that we must approach others from the orientation that they, as creatures of God for whom God became human, have a great capacity for good. As Merton wrote, "there is in [humanity] a potentiality for peace and order which can be realized provided the right conditions are there." Merton emphasizes that this attitude does not reflect a naive optimism in humankind. Evil does exist and people can indeed do evil things. Rather, this attitude based on the idea that inherent within all persons is the possibility of transformation. "The Christian knows," Merton declared, "that there are radically sound possibilities in every [person], and he believes that love and grace have the power to bring out those possibilities at the most unexpected moments" (PFP, 256).

Given this understanding of the divisiveness of sin and the possibility of human transformation, Merton argued that only nonviolence rooted in meekness can lead to the actual transformation of individuals, societies, and indeed the world. One of the most "insidious" temptations nonviolent resisters face is a "fetishism of immediate results" (PFP, 254). The question inevitably posed whenever nonviolence is raised as a possibility is, "But will it *work*?" The premise of such a question is that there is an adversary who is wrong and who therefore needs to be conquered or eliminated as quickly as possible. This is a perversion of the purpose of Christian nonviolence. The goal of nonviolence is not immediate victory over the adversary, but the transformation of human relationships—of society—through the healing and restoration of human nature.[13] This means, however, having the meekness—the humility—to recognize that you are as much in need of healing and restoration as your supposed adversary.[14]

And this is where we see that Merton's understanding of nonviolence comes with extraordinary demands. "Christ brought to His disciples a vocation and a task," Merton wrote, "to struggle in the world of violence to establish His peace not only in their own hearts but in society itself" (PFP, 39–40). Merton insisted that, not only must nonviolent resisters be unwilling to use power in any way to vanquish the adversary given his dignity and worth, and given our call to unity with him, but the nonviolent resister must enter into dialogue with the adversary in such a way as to be open to learning from and being transformed by him. If our nonviolence is characterized by an unwillingness truly to listen to the adversary, if we demonstrate our conviction that he has nothing worthwhile to say, our adversary will recognize that our concern is not love but domination. Moreover, we prove by our unwillingness to listen "that we are interested not in the truth so much as in 'being right'" (PFP, 255). Such unwillingness to enter into genuine dialogue is, according to Merton, inherently unchristian, for it presumes both an overly pessimistic assessment of the other and an overly prideful assessment of our own grasp on truth. Moreover, it violates the reality of the kingdom of God established by Christ.

Conclusion: Nonviolence as a "Style of Politics"

The title of Pope Francis's World Day of Peace message was "Nonviolence: A Style of Politics for Peace." *A style of politics.* For Thomas Merton, nonviolence was just that. It is an alternative form of politics that is governed by the ethics of the kingdom of God, inaugurated

13. See Thomas Merton, *Gandhi on Non-Violence: A Selection from the Writings of Mahatma Gandhi* (New York: New Directions: 1965), 23.

14. Merton, *Gandhi on Non-Violence*, 12.

by a Savior who chose the way of love rather than the way of power and exhorted his followers to do the same. Merton exhorted us to take seriously the message and example of Jesus as a whole, and not simply to pick and choose which aspects of Christ's kingdom ethic we wish to adopt. In his book, *Conjectures of a Guilty Bystander*, Merton held nothing back in his criticism of the dominant political climate of the 1960s and of the willingness of his fellow Roman Catholics to buy into a politics dominated by individualism and power. This Merton calls the "practical atheism" of many Christians who not only buy the dominant political culture, but who actually view power and coercion as the most appropriate and realistic approach to deal with adversaries (CGB, 222; see also CGB, 34–36). As we have seen, Merton would have none of this. Throughout his writings, he emphasized over and over again that the genuine transformation of human society can never occur through violence. At best, violence begets hatred and more violence. At worst, in a nuclear age, violence results in the destruction of all life. Thomas Merton argued that Christ came to inaugurate a new way of being, a new kingdom in which the predominant mode of doing politics in the world is rejected. Nonviolence is not, as it so often understood by Christians and non-Christians alike, "phony and sentimental" (PFP, 40). Rather, based as it is on a decidedly Christian understanding of humanity in light of the incarnation, it is the only means of being political that can actually lead to genuine transformation, a transformation rooted in love. For, as Merton declared, "Love, love only, love of our deluded fellow man as he actually is . . . this alone can open the door to truth" (CGB, 57). Not only, therefore, is it—in the words of Pope Francis—"a style of politics for peace."[15] It is for Merton the only style of politics open to us as Christians.

And to make this point, Merton drew on and engaged with the tradition as a whole, from the teachings and example of Christ to the early Christian writers through to the teachings of the twentieth-century popes, Pius XII and John XXIII. Because he was disturbed

---

15. Pope Francis, Nonviolence: A Style of Politics for Peace 1, December 8, 2016.

both by the "awful silence and apathy on the part of Catholics, clergy, hierarchy, [and] lay people" on nuclear war, and by the sometimes explicit calls for the use of nuclear weapons by Catholics against the Soviet Union, Merton wrote his essays and books on war and nonviolence specifically for a Catholic audience (Li, 139; TM to Dorothy Day: August 23, 1961). And, as such, his arguments for nonviolence and against nuclear war were intentionally and thoughtfully theological. His engagement with Christian sources demonstrates both the scope of his knowledge of these sources as well as the seriousness with which he took them.

CHAPTER 6

MERTON THE OPPONENT OF RACISM

The big thing for Christians is to live the truth that in Christ there is absolutely no distinction between Black and White, but the Adversary has made sure that a very real distinction exists (due to the sins of history). Neither can be ignored. We have to learn the reality of the difference, and emphasize Black and White identities and qualities and rights: and see beyond to the inner unity: that unity is in Christ, not in the affluent society.

—Thomas Merton to Fr. August Thompson,
April 26, 1968

Introduction

After Pope Francis gave his 2015 address to the US Congress, Representative John Lewis (1940–2020), the civil rights leader who became known nationally as one of the leaders of the 1965 Selma to Montgomery marches, published a press release, commenting on the four great Americans named by the pontiff. In the press release, a surprising detail emerged about the role Thomas Merton had in forming Rep. Lewis as a young civil rights leader:

Thomas Merton was a monk whose words I studied during non-violence training in the Civil Rights Movement. It was amazing that the Pope mentioned the Selma-to-Montgomery march because during the first attempt to march to Montgomery, now known as Bloody Sunday, I carried one of Thomas Merton's books in my backpack.[1]

On the day John Lewis led a group of protestors across the Edmund Pettus Bridge where he was brutally beaten by armed police officers, he was carrying a book by Merton. Lewis didn't mention which book he was carrying, but it is significant that he mentioned that Merton had an influence on him in his civil rights work.

Paul Pearson, the director of the Thomas Merton Center at Bellarmine University, lamented that "Merton's writings on racism are all too frequently skirted over if not completely ignored."[2] It is unfortunate that Merton's essays on racism, written during the height of the civil rights movement, are not better known. They contain penetrating critiques of his fellow white Americans and white Catholics, as well as analysis of the racial situation that contains insights that remain relevant today. In an essay about Merton, Christopher Pramuk wrote about an elderly African American woman at his parish who mentioned to him that, when she felt alienated by her church and religious community for her civil rights work in the 1960s, Merton was the white exception: "'Merton got it,' she said, 'when few others did.'"[3] I had the opportunity to speak once with Bishop Edward Braxton, who was then bishop of the diocese of Belleville, Illinois, and one of the few black Catholic bishops in the United States. I asked him what he made of Merton's writings on

1. John Lewis, "Rep. John Lewis on Pope Francis' Address to Congress," *Congressman John Lewis Official Website*, September 25, 2015.

2. Paul M. Pearson, "A Voice for Racial Justice," *The Merton Seasonal* 40.1 (2015): 46.

3. Christopher Pramuk, "Thomas Merton and the Future of Faith," *Marginalia*, April 23, 2016, https://marginalia.lareviewofbooks.org/thomas-merton-future -faith-christopher-pramuk/.

race, and he responded with one word—"Prophetic."[4] This assessment is shared by others.[5]

In this chapter, I'm going to take a look at Merton's essays on race, paying particular attention to the theological ideas undergirding his arguments against racism. I will then take readers through the powerful correspondence Merton exchanged with Fr. August Thompson (1926–2019), a black Catholic priest from Louisiana who sought Merton's advice in the face of racial prejudice within the Catholic Church. We shall see that Merton addressed the topic of race on a decidedly theological basis, one focused particularly on the implications of the incarnation on race relations. Merton's contribution to the conversation regarding racism in society and in the church was important, and remains significant enough that he can be understood to be one of American Catholicism's most important voices on the issue of race in the twentieth century.

Merton's Early Forays into the Problem of Racism

In *The Seven Storey Mountain*, Merton recounted the time he spent at Friendship House in Harlem while he was teaching at St. Bonaventure College. In 1938, Catherine de Hueck started Friendship House, a Catholic center focused on racial and socio-economic justice, and in 1941 she visited St. Bonaventure College to tell faculty and students about the kind of work she and others at the house did. Merton was struck by her message, and after the talk he asked if he could spend some time at Friendship House.

Merton's description of his time in Harlem, and particularly his description of the poverty and degradation he saw there, illustrate

4. Personal communication with Bishop Edward Braxton in Belleville, Illinois, on September 8, 2017.

5. See also Christopher Pramuk, "'The Street Is for Celebration': Racial Consciousness and the Eclipse of Childhood in America's Cities," *The Merton Annual* 25 (2012): 95–96, and Alex Mikulich, "Merton's Letters a Call for White Atonement," *National Catholic Reporter*, January 21, 2013, https://www.ncronline.org/news/theology/mertons-letters-call-white-atonement.

that the young monk who wrote *The Seven Storey Mountain* was acutely aware of racial inequality, and it merits full quotation (note that Merton used language acceptable for the time in which he was writing):

> Here in this huge, dark, steaming slum, hundreds of thousands of Negroes are herded together like cattle, most of them with nothing to eat and nothing to do. All the senses and imagination and sensibilities and emotions and sorrows and desires and hopes and ideas of a race with vivid feelings and deep emotional reactions are forced in upon themselves, bound inward by an iron ring of frustration: the prejudice that hems them in with its four insurmountable walls. In this huge cauldron, inestimable natural gifts, wisdom, love, music, science, poetry are stamped down and left to boil with the dregs of an elementally corrupted nature, and thousands upon thousands of souls are destroyed by vice and misery and degradation, obliterated, wiped out, washed from the register of the living, dehumanized. (SSM, 345)

In his 1968 bestselling collection of essays, *Soul on Ice*, Eldridge Cleaver—the civil rights advocate and prominent member of the Black Panther Party—wrote about encountering Merton's description of Harlem while serving time at Folsom Prison. In one of the "Letters from Prison" published in this book, Cleaver recounted coming under the tutelage of a teacher during his time at San Quentin, Chris Lovdjieff, who introduced him to history, philosophy, comparative religion, and economics. He also introduced Cleaver to Merton. At first, Cleaver was unimpressed. He could not figure out why anyone would voluntarily put themselves in a monastery, which to Cleaver sounded too much like prison. Although Lovdjieff tried to instill in Cleaver a love for Merton, Cleaver would have none of it. The most Lovdjieff could convince him to do was to read Merton someday. Soon afterward, Cleaver was transferred from San Quentin to Folsom where he was put in solitary confinement. He asked for something to read, and was given a list of books from which he could choose. On the list was *The Seven Storey Mountain*; here was his opportunity to fulfill his promise to Lovdjieff.

Cleaver found the book deeply compelling, and despite the fact that he wasn't all that interested in what Merton had to say about God, he came to see Merton as a companion: "I could not keep him out of the room. He shouldered his way through the door. Welcome, Brother Merton. I give him a big bear hug."[6] But what particularly impressed him was the description of Harlem quoted above, which Cleaver quoted in its entirety in his own book. Cleaver felt that it captured the oppression of black people. "I liked it so much," he writes, "I copied out the heart of it in longhand." After he left solitary confinement, he kept this passage in mind when he gave lectures to his fellow prisoners. Indeed, Cleaver says that this passage gave him inspiration in his fight for racial justice: "Whenever I felt myself softening, relaxing, I had only to read that passage to become once more a rigid flame of indignation . . . It had precisely the same effect on me that Elijah Muhammed's writings used to have, or the words of Malcolm X, or the words of any spokesman of the oppressed in any land" (*Soul on Ice*, 44).

"Letters to a White Liberal"

Cleaver noticed right away that the young Merton had an acute understanding of racial oppression. However, his passage in *The Seven Storey Mountain* stands almost alone in Merton's early writings in terms of its reference to the problem of racism. Between 1948 and 1961, Merton's references to racism were limited.[7] This started to change in

6. Eldridge Cleaver, *Soul on Ice* (New York: Dell Publishing, 1968), 44.

7. There is one brief reference to racial problems in a 1959 letter to Dorothy Day, but apart from this his journals and correspondence are largely silent on the topic. See Li, TM to Dorothy Day (July 9, 1959), 136: "I came upon a copy of *CW* [*Catholic Worker*]. The one with the piece about the Hopis in it. Again, same reaction. You people are the only ones left awake, or among the few that still have an eye open. I am more and more convinced that the real people in this country are the Indians—and Negroes, etc."

1961 and 1962,[8] but it was his exposure in 1963 to the writings of
noted author and civil rights activist James Baldwin, that propelled
him to engage the issue of racism more directly.[9] Shortly after reading
Baldwin, Merton sent a letter of appreciation to him and wrote an
essay on Baldwin for the June 1963 issue of *Liberation*, a magazine
associated with the New Left.[10] This would be his first foray into the
issue of racism, but it would only be the starting point.

Many more references to racism occurred in his private journals
and letters in 1963. Moreover, his contacts with those involved in
the civil rights movement increased. One of these contacts was John
Howard Griffin (1920-1980), a white journalist who wrote *Black
Like Me*, a book about Griffin's experiences in the Deep South when
he chemically altered his appearance so as to look like a black man.
Merton read *Black Like Me* in 1962, noting this briefly in a jour-
nal entry on March 24 of that year. Soon after Merton read James
Baldwin in 1963, Griffin came to visit Merton at Gethsemani where
Griffin shared with Merton stories of racial oppression and violence.
So began a regular correspondence between the two that continued
for the next five years until the end of Merton's life. While their

8. For example, see his entry for March 11, 1961: "The Negroes and their struggle
for integration into American society: not only do they have to face the enormity of
the whites who are completely unsettled by their irrational fears, but they have to
face fear, guilt and passivity in themselves: one of the most difficult things is for them
to admit completely in their hearts what they know intellectually: that they are in
the right. It is fine that they have a leader who can direct them in the way of nonviolence [Martin Luther King Jr.]. But the situation is so ambivalent that there remains danger of violence—as the less rational whites seem to sense intuitively. Great
admiration and compassion for the Negroes" (Jiv, 99: March 11, 1961).

9. In his journal he writes that Baldwin helped him understand the civil rights
movement was not simply about the attainment of necessary rights for African
Americans, but about the conversion and transformation of whites: "The liberation
of the Negroes," Merton wrote in summary of Baldwin's thesis, "is necessary for
the liberation of the whites and for their recovery of a minimum of self-respect,
and reality." See Jiv, 298: February 23, 1963.

10. Thomas Merton, "Neither Caliban Nor Uncle Tom," *Liberation* (June 1963):
21.

exchanges involved discussion on a variety of topics, their earliest letters focused on racial inequality.[11]

Merton became increasingly disturbed the more he learned about the problem of racism. In the spring of 1963, Edward Keating, the publisher of *Ramparts* magazine, a new Catholic literary and political magazine, approached Merton to ask him to write something on racial inequality. At first he suggested that Merton do an exchange of letters with Baldwin that would be published. Merton was initially enthusiastic about the idea, and Baldwin expressed interest through his agent, but Merton soon had second thoughts about such an exchange, particularly questioning the value of it from Baldwin's perspective. He instead suggested writing something on the race question from his own vantage point as a white monk in a cloistered monastery. The publisher said yes, and Merton spent the next two months writing. "Letters to a White Liberal" was published in the Christmas 1963 issue of *Ramparts*, and later published with a new introduction in his 1964 book of essays, *Seeds of Destruction*.[12] It is his most extensive essay on racial injustice and his most important, though I shall also refer to his later essays on racism below.

As the title of the essay indicates, Merton wrote as a white person to fellow whites, directing his argument particularly toward those who identify as "liberals." Overarching the entire essay is Merton's

---

11. For example, John Howard Griffin sent Merton a photo he took of a black woman fearful for her son that Merton found deeply moving (unpublished letter of John Howard Griffin to TM, May 9, 1963, *Thomas Merton Center*, Bellarmine University), and Merton sent to Griffin a poem about Birmingham after reading Martin Luther King Jr.'s "Letter from Birmingham Jail" (unpublished letter of TM to John Howard Griffin, May 28, 1963, *Thomas Merton Center*, Bellarmine University).

12. After receiving the essay, the editor of *Ramparts*, Ed Keating, raved about the piece to John Howard Griffin, saying that he doubted that "anyone has ever written more brilliantly, more passionately, more perceptively on the subject than has Merton in this instance" (unpublished letter of Edward Keating to John Howard Griffin, August 1, 1963, box 11, fol. 386, *John Howard Griffin Papers*, Columbia University). See also unpublished letter of John Howard Griffin to TM, August 7, 1963, *Thomas Merton Center*, Bellarmine University.

conviction that the oppression of African Americans is systemic and that white liberals (a) do not do enough to fight against the racism baked into American society and (b) that they are, in fact, guilty of propping up this racist system for their own well-being.

"Letters to a White Liberal" contains four separate "letters," each of which contains separate but interrelated arguments. The first letter contains his most explicitly theological argument, and therefore is the most important for the purposes of examining the theological foundation of Merton's argument against racism. He began the letter by referring to Pope Paul VI's speech at the opening of the second session of the Second Vatican Council. In this speech, Paul VI called the church to purity and renewal, telling the council fathers that the church needs to recognize its duty to manifest Christ in the world. It would be only after sanctification and renewal in the church that the church could show herself to the world and say "Who sees me sees Christ." But the pope insisted that, in order to become like Christ, the church must "look upon Christ to discern her true likeness" (SD, 11–12). Merton pointed out that the pope's exhortation to an examination of conscience took place two weeks after the Birmingham bombing killed four black children. While it was not a Catholic who committed the bombing, Merton argued that Catholics in the South "have explicitly and formally identified themselves with racial segregation," and he listed a number of examples of white Catholic racism, noting that in Louisiana Catholics set fire to a parochial school rather than allow it to be integrated and, in another instance, a white Catholic priest was beaten by his white parishioners for allowing both black and white children to receive first communion together (SD, 12). Merton brought up the problem of Christian racism here because, as he noted, the emphasis in the United States on "freedom" is rooted in a recognition of the dignity and rights of the person, and although the United States is not officially Christian, "this democratic respect for the person can be traced to the Christian concept that every man is to be regarded as Christ, and treated as Christ" (SD, 13). In other words, the United States justifies its international and national policies on the supposed idea "that we are supremely concerned with the human person and his rights," and we "do this because our ancestors regarded every man as Christ, wished to treat him as Christ, or at least believed this to be the right way to act, even though they did not always follow this belief" (SD, 13–14).

It is worth pointing out that Merton's most important essay on civil rights began on a theological note. His concern was not simply to articulate an argument against racism from the standpoint of human rights, as important as such an argument is. Rather, Merton began his essay christologically, a fact that should come as no surprise given what we've explored thus far regarding his understanding of the impact the incarnation of the Son of God has for how we are to view our fellow human beings. If, as Merton thought should be the case, Christians are called to view fellow humans through the lens of the incarnation, and even to conceive of them *as Christ*, then Christians have something to say about the problem of racism. To believe in the incarnation is not simply to affirm a dogmatic truth claim. Rather, to believe in the incarnation is to be transformed by our comprehension of what God-becoming-flesh means for our comprehension of God, of ourselves, and of others. And it is the reality of the incarnation that led Merton to begin his essay on the problem of racism by asking, "How, then, do we treat this other Christ, this person, who happens to be black?"

Merton's answer was blunt. In the South, where most whites consider themselves Christian, "we discover that belief in the Negro as a person is accepted only with serious qualifications, while the notion that he is to be treated as Christ has been overlooked" (SD, 17). Southerners have expressed unwillingness even to ride in the same buses as or eat alongside of African Americans. Worse still are those professed Christians who refuse to worship with their black sisters and brothers, and some Catholics have even gone so far as to refuse to receive the Eucharist with them. And when they have found themselves officially excommunicated for refusing to integrate their schools, white Catholics have been astonished even though, as Merton pointed out, "they had already by their own action manifestly excommunicated themselves, acting implicitly as schismatics, rending the unity of the Body of Christ" (SD, 18). The Eucharist, the sacrament of love that binds us together, had been weaponized by racists to become a perverse instrument of disunity and hate, the ultimate blasphemy.

It is only after setting the stage theologically that Merton proceeded to talk in broader terms about the problems posed by racism, and by the unwillingness of whites, including white liberals, to adequately address concerns raised by African Americans. Merton argued that, in both the North and the South, whites are either openly racist or they manifest an implicit racism through the tolerance they have for the injustices suffered by their fellow black citizens. They will claim that laws have been passed and supreme court decisions have been made that uphold the rights of black citizens, at least on paper. However, Merton commented that these laws and decisions are entirely reliant on the good will of white society, meaning that the execution of those laws requires whites to follow through on what the laws demand. Such has not been the case. At every step, Merton argued, whites have blocked, obstructed, or simply ignored the laws and decisions upholding black rights. The result is that black Americans have effectively not been given the rights they have been supposedly given on paper. Rather, the only right given to them has been the right to sue when they are not accorded the rights to which they are due by law, but the possibility of succeeding in such a lawsuit, given that judges and juries are made up primarily of whites, is minimal.

It was therefore a real question for Merton as to whether civil rights legislation had actually done anything to improve the situation for African Americans, or whether it was written primarily to placate the consciences of whites who felt they needed to do something, but who did not want to do anything that actually changed social structures. "I think," he wrote, "that there is possibly some truth in the accusation that we are making laws simply because they look nice on the books" (SD, 20). When challenged about their commitment to civil rights, white Americans comfort themselves by pointing to these laws to reassure their consciences, all the while turning a blind eye to violations of civil rights as if such violations had nothing to do with themselves. And when African Americans demonstrate to let others know that their rights continue to be violated, the white response has been to make more laws, all the while "knowing well enough how much chance those bills have of retaining any real significant after they have finally made it (if they make it at all)." What, therefore, are white Americans, including white Christians, doing for the cause of racial justice? Merton was damning in his assessment:

> I do not claim to be a prophet or even a historian. I do not profess to understand all the mysteries of political philosophy, but I question whether our claims to be the only sincere defenders of the human person, of his rights, of his dignity, of his nobility as a creature made in God's image, as a member of the Mystical Body of Christ, can be substantiated by our actions. It seems to me that we have retained little more than a few slogans and concepts that have been emptied of reality. (SD, 22)

Given this state of affairs, Merton began his second letter in the essay by bringing up the possibility of revolution. We are getting to a point, he wrote, where the African American struggle for full civil rights is going to amount to a revolution. Recognizing that the various pieces of civil rights legislation that passed resulted only in cosmetic changes, African Americans are coming to recognize that attaining full equality is going to mean radical change in society itself. "Much as it might distress southerners," Merton wrote, "the fact that a Negro may now sit down next to a white woman at a snack bar and order a sandwich is still somewhat short of revolution" (SD, 22). African Americans find themselves "in the presence of a social structure which [they have] reason to consider inherently unjust" (SD, 31). They have to fight against vocal racists bent on preserving white power, but they also have to fight against a group Merton referred to as the "white liberals." These are whites, including white Christians, who support civil rights, advocate for civil rights legislation, and join African Americans in protests. But in Merton's opinion, although they have a "generous, but vague, love of mankind in the abstract," white liberals have little interest in the actual equality of African Americans (SD, 33). Black civil rights leaders know that white liberals privilege "material comforts" and security over their idealism, so when push comes to shove, and white liberals are forced to choose an equality for all that will entail sacrifices for whites as opposed to the status quo, they will go with the latter every time. White liberals were at the March on Washington because they felt good about being there; it was a balm to the liberal conscience. But while white liberals perhaps thought that black people needed them to participate in the march, African Americans had mixed feelings. It was pleasant to see and experience the good will of white liberals, but black civil rights leaders know that such good will comes with a caveat. White liberals want equality, but they want it on their terms. They have nice, comfortable lives, and while they feel like they are for their black sisters and brothers, they are really only for them insofar as equality doesn't compromise their standard of living. They need to support the civil rights movement for the sake of their liberal consciences, but they need the movement to proceed slowly, patiently, and without upheaval.

Merton was convinced that the greatest threat to the civil rights movement, the greatest threat to racial equality, did not come from vocal southern racists. We know at least where the racists stand. No, the greatest threat comes from white liberals who say all the right things, but who cannot be relied upon to remain proponents of racial equality when they see precisely what this might entail for them. When they see that racial equality will mean that society will cease being dominated and governed by whites, when they see that "whiteness" will no longer be the standard by which society is measured, white liberals will slam on the breaks. Merton put it this way, directing his comments to his white liberal interlocutor:

> Are you going to say that though changes may be desirable in theory, they cannot possibly be paid for by a social upheaval amounting to revolution? Are you going to decide that the Negro movement is already out of hand, and therefore it must be stopped at any cost, even at the cost of ruthless force? In that case, you are retreating from the unknown future and falling back on a known and familiar alternative: namely the alternative in which you, who are after all on top, *remain on top by the use of force*, rather than admit a change in which you

will not necessarily be on the bottom, but in which your position as top dog will no longer be guaranteed. You will prefer your own security to everything else, and you will be willing to sacrifice the Negro to preserve yourself. (SD, 37)

Merton argued that white liberals are unprepared—and subconsciously unwilling—to give up the privilege they have in a society dominated by whites. So when they see that their power, influence, and wealth need to erode for the sake of racial equality, white liberals will turn on the civil rights movement and on African Americans in general. They will come to see the civil rights movement as a revolutionary threat that needs to be put down.

Many continue to identify racism primarily in terms of interpersonal, individual actions or behaviors against someone from another race. As the Catholic theologian and priest, Bryan Massingale, wrote in his book on racial inequality in the Catholic Church, "The commonsense understanding discusses racism as personal acts of rudeness, hostility, or discrimination."[13] By these standards, the white liberal is not a racist. However, in a way that shows how far he was ahead of his time, Merton described a society that was systemically racist. Legislation and good will simply are not going to cut it to bring about racial equality, for African Americans find themselves "in the presence of a social structure which [they have] reason to consider inherently unjust" (SD, 31). White liberals are wholly unprepared to give up the privilege they have as white people in a society dominated by whites.

Merton predicted that white liberals will ultimately "decide that it is better for the establishment to be maintained by the exercise of power which is entirely in white hands, and which ought to remain in white hands because they are white" (SD, 41). And in that vein, whites will conclude that the civil rights movement is proposing an approach to racial injustice that is far too revolutionary, and that it will need to be squelched. Merton's words about where the white

13. Bryan Massingale, *Racial Justice and the Catholic Church* (Maryknoll, NY: Orbis Books, 2010), 14.

liberal will end up were harsh and bleak. The quote begins by looking at the logic that will end up governing white liberal oppression
of the civil rights movement:

> Conclusion: revolution must be prevented at all costs; but
> demonstrations are already revolutionary; *ergo*, fire on the
> demonstrators; *ergo*. . . . At the end of this chain of thought
> I visualize you, my liberal friend, goose-stepping down Mas-
> sachusetts Avenue in the uniform of an American Totalitarian
> Party in a mass rally where nothing but the most uproarious
> approval is manifest, except, by implication, on the part of
> silent and strangely scented clouds of smoke drifting over from
> the new "camps" where the "Negroes are living in retirement."
> (SD, 41–42)

Whatever white liberals may say to signal allegiance to the civil
rights movement, white obsession with power is so pervasive that,
faced with the loss of it, even the white liberals will subscribe to a
white supremacy akin to Nazism for the cause of supposed "peace."

It is at this point that Merton drew on his reading of James Baldwin. Black civil rights leaders are well aware of the white liberal's
subconscious hold on power, and as such, the civil rights movement's
focus is not just to achieve black liberation from racial inequality,
but to achieve the redemption of the white person.[14] African Ameri-

---

14. To see how this point is influenced by Merton's reading of James Baldwin,
see Thomas Merton, "Neither Caliban Nor Uncle Tom," *Liberation* (June 1963),
21. Here Merton wrote that, while some condemned Baldwin's *The Fire Next Time*
for fomenting violence, the "book is one of the most beautiful acts of charity to the
white race." For in the book, Baldwin didn't simply focus on the justifiable anger
that African Americans should have in the face of systemic oppression, but explained
that white oppression of blacks is rooted in the white person's "incapacity to love."
Baldwin didn't say this to condemn whites outright, but to explain to his black and
white readers that white America is caught in a state of unreality from which it is
difficult to escape. Whites have lost the ability to understand their black fellow
citizens, and have instead turned to hate and fear that which they don't understand.
But Baldwin also insisted that white ignorance means that whites become less real,

cans are "seeking by Christian love and sacrifice to redeem him, to enlighten him." For white Americans are "blinded" by the "endemic sin of racial injustice," and they require conversion (SD, 45). This conversion can only take place through the kind of nonviolent protest that leads whites toward self-examination:

> The purpose of non-violent protest, in its deepest and most spiritual dimensions, is then to awaken the conscience of the white man to the awful reality of his injustice and of his sin, so that he will be able to see that the Negro problem is really a *White* problem: that the cancer of injustice and hate which is eating white society and is only partly manifested in racial segregation with all its consequences, *is rooted in the heart of the white man himself.* (SD, 45–46)

Merton's critique of white liberals and white society was unrelenting, and it provoked offense. Martin Marty, prominent Lutheran theologian from the University of Chicago, took particular exception. In his review of *Seeds of Destruction*, the book that contains Merton's "Letters to a White Liberal," Marty characterized Merton's approach to the white liberal as filled with little more than "judgmental earnestness" not rooted in the reality of things on the ground.[15] Marty criticized Merton for falling into well-worn patterns of critique that bear little resemblance to the situation as it actually existed. Instead, Merton provided what Marty argued was nothing more than a bellicose critique that lacked precision and nuance. It

---

less than who they are supposed to be. Whites need to see the African American "as a human and personal reality," and when they can do this, they will not only cease fearing and hating their black neighbors, but they will become more fully human, more complete. Baldwin did condemn whites in his book. According to Merton, he did them a service. As Merton put it: "If a man thinks another man is crazy and, instead of locking him up, he patiently and lovingly does things which he thinks can help to cure him, I think we ought to find a better way of thanking him than by comparing him with a stupid and bloodthirsty monster."

15. Martin E. Marty, "Sowing Thorns in the Flesh," *Book Week* 2 (January 17, 1965): 4.

amounted not to prophecy but to what Marty called "propheticism, a cultic kind of judgment pronounced on relative innocents."[16]

Interestingly, three years after writing this critical review of Merton's essay, Martin Marty wrote an open letter to Thomas Merton for the *National Catholic Reporter*, in which he expressed regret for so quickly dismissing Merton's argument. Having recently reread Merton's "Letters to a White Liberal," Marty acknowledged that what bothered him now was the accuracy of Merton's predictions. What changed Marty's mind was witnessing the racial tension on display during the summer of 1967 as well as watching Congress in action. With regard to the latter, Marty noted that he had now seen that the majority of politicians do "not want to get at the causes of unrest but only at false and arbitrary cures" ("TO: Thomas Merton. RE: Your prophecy," 6). They are interested in alleviating their own consciences, not in making systematic changes, changes that Marty agreed must occur for racial equality to become a reality. Moreover, Marty noted that a refusal to make systematic societal changes was not the only failure of white society, for his observations since writing his critique of Merton's original essay confirmed that built into American society is the possibility of the kind of state-sanctioned violence that Merton warned about: "Not only is [the white person] failing to come through with an alternate social system," Marty wrote, "the system *we* have is undergoing a transition toward brutalization of the type which makes the American Auschwitz at least remotely conceivable" ("TO: Thomas Merton. RE: Your prophecy," 7).

Fr. August Thompson and Thomas Merton

"Letters to a White Liberal" appeared in the Christmas 1963 issue of *Ramparts* magazine. The entire issue was devoted to the problem of racism, and Merton was not the only Catholic featured prominently in it. Included in the issue was an extended interview by John Howard Griffin with Fr. August Thompson, a black priest in the diocese

16. Martin E. Marty, "TO: Thomas Merton. RE: Your prophecy," *National Catholic Reporter* 3.43 (July 30, 1967): 6.

of Alexandria, Louisiana, and one of American Catholicism's most important civil-rights leaders. Merton and Thompson developed a relationship in the aftermath of the publication of this issue, and their correspondence not only tells us a great deal about the bigotry faced by Thompson but it also illustrates the role Merton played in trying to shape American Catholic responses to racism.

Thompson was born in 1926 into a poor Catholic family in Baldwin, Louisiana, a small town two hundred miles west of New Orleans. His parents were devout Catholics who said grace before and after meals, and led the children in a family rosary each day. Thompson discerned a calling to the priesthood, and while his white priest was supportive, his own diocese of Lafayette was not. He graduated from seminary in 1957, but his bishop would not accept him as a priest. Bishop Charles Greco of the neighboring diocese of Alexandria did accept him, and he became the first black priest to be ordained there.

While Thompson was grateful to Bishop Greco for being the only southern bishop willing to ordain him, the two frequently quarreled, particularly about the treatment of black Catholics in the diocese. Thompson became so frustrated that he agreed to an interview with Griffin for *Ramparts*, an interview that did not sit well with the bishop.

Fr. Thompson held nothing back in the interview.[17] His description of what life was like for black Catholics in the South at the time, including black priests, makes for painful, sometimes shocking reading. Unlike their white Catholic counterparts, black Catholics could not attend retreats or days of recollection, both important aspects of Catholic devotional life. Moreover, black Catholics could only attend a white parish if the distance to the closest black parish was considered inordinate. In one town where there was only one black Catholic and no black parishes, the white parish went so far as to pay someone to drive the black Catholic to a black parish in another town. And even if a white parish allowed black Catholics to

17. John Howard Griffin, "Dialogue: Father August Thompson," *Ramparts* (December 1963): 24–33. Hereafter referred to as Dialogue parenthetically in the text.

join them because the distance to "their" parish was too far, they sat in a section segregated from the white parishioners and were allowed to receive the Eucharist only after the white Catholics had done so.

Thompson told Griffin that he was frequently treated as a second-class citizen within his own church, despite being a priest. Some white Catholics refused to call him "Father," and he was often prohibited from attending certain churches even for first communions or confirmations. He was not even allowed to say Mass at many white parishes. And as the only black priest in the diocese, he was rarely invited to events with his fellow priests. He summed up how white Catholics in the Deep South viewed him as a black Catholic priest: "a Negro first, a Negro second and finally a priest."

When asked by Griffin about whether he had spoken to other priests or those in the hierarchy about the treatment of black lay Catholics and black Catholic priests, Thompson simply replied that he had "done [his] share of speaking frankly. Unfortunately, the hierarchy met his concerns with indifference. "It is suggested," Thompson said, "that I do not appreciate the complexities of the problem" ("Dialogue," 30). And while some bishops spoke out, Thompson explained to Griffin that the response of the church to racism both inside and outside of it was largely silence: "I fear that the silence in some areas is quite loud. Many people think that this silence is a sign that those in authority agree with the situation as it exists" ("Dialogue," 31).

Thompson refused to acquiesce, to remain silent in the face of such hatred. Moreover, black Catholics were unwilling to put up with prejudice in the church any longer. Thompson's concluding comments on this point are stark:

> There are many Catholics who do not go to Church because the pain of this kind of humiliation is simply unbearable. Think of going to Church, going to Communion, and in order to receive Christ you must wait until every white Catholic has gone to the Communion Table and returned to his seat— knowing that you might well be skipped if you approach the

altar while some white person was still there. Think of that encouraging people to receive Communion. Many do, of course, but with a deep sense of sickness, and then resentment that even this great Sacrament should be clouded in indignity for them. ("Dialogue," 33)

Unless the church took a radically different approach, both speaking out and taking action against racism, Thompson envisioned the small black Catholic population becoming even smaller—a dire possibility that would have consequences for the entire church. "Each day we see more Negroes disillusioned with what they call 'the white man's Christianity,'" he said. "And each day we see more whites disillusioned by the same scandal; let's not forget that" ("Dialogue," 33).

Bishop Charles Pasquale Greco was bishop of the Diocese of Alexandria from 1946 to 1973. He continues to be a much beloved figure among Catholics in the diocese, though his record on civil rights was somewhat mixed. While he personally favored integration of schools and parishes, he was reluctant to push for it, instead arguing that the church in Alexandria needed to move slowly toward integration so as not to scandalize white parishioners.[18] So it did not go over well with the bishop to have one of his own priests speak so openly about racism within his diocese and within the broader church. Before the interview was published, Greco tried to stop the publication of the interview by legal means, and when that proved impossible, he turned to canon law.[19] By the fall, he believed that he had succeeded in convincing the publisher not to run the interview, and was livid to learn that this was not the case.[20]

18. See Mark Newman, "The Catholic Diocese of Alexandria and Desegregation," *Louisiana History: The Journal of the Louisiana Historical Association* 52.3 (2011): 282–83, and Adam Fairclough, *Race and Democracy: The Civil Rights Struggle in Louisiana, 1915–1972* (Athens, GA: University of Georgia Press, 1995), 176.

19. Unpublished letter of August Thompson to John Howard Griffin, August 17, 1963 (box 11, fol. 380, *John Howard Griffin Papers*, Columbia University).

20. Unpublished letter of August Thompson to John Howard Griffin, October 7, 1963 (box 11, fol. 380, *John Howard Griffin Papers*, Columbia University).

On November 21, shortly after the interview was published, Bishop Greco wrote a scathing letter to Fr. Thompson from Rome. His anger is palpable from beginning to end. It begins as follows:

> It is with keenest disappointment and displeasure that the current issue of "Ramparts" comes to my attention. I am sincerely and totally convinced that your appraisal of the Church—her Bishops, Priests, Religious and Laity—in her relation to the racial problem in the South is exaggerated, distorted and misleading, and constitutes a defamation of the Church.[21]

Bishop Greco went on to express his anger not only about the content of the interview itself, but also about what he considered to be the duplicitous way in which it was published. He argued that he granted permission to Thompson for the interview with Griffin only under the condition that it would not be published without Greco's approval. But while the supposed deception bothered him, he was clear that it was the content of the interview itself that he found most offensive, particularly since "unjustified slander" against the church was expressed by a priest "consecrated to protect her interest." He ended the letter as follows:

> The Church had done much for you as a Catholic and as a priest, and you owe her all that you are today. But the image of Your Mother the Church which you, her son, have projected to the world is unfair, is a disservice to her and has inflicted a deep wound upon her. We pary [sic] God we may be able to heal it.

The letter came as a shock to Thompson, and he immediately turned to Thomas Merton for guidance about how to respond. This is why we have a copy of Greco's letter; Thompson sent it to Merton to get direction. It is interesting that he turned to Merton, a white

---

21. Unpublished letter of Bishop Charles Greco to August Thompson, November 21, 1963, *Thomas Merton Center*, Bellarmine University.

monk in a contemplative monastery. The two had met a month previously when Thompson was at the Abbey of Gethsemani for a visit, and Thompson expressed gratitude for Merton's guidance in a letter to Merton shortly after that visit. It is unclear whether Thompson read Merton's "Letters to a White Liberal" before their meeting, or indeed if he read it before writing to Merton for advice. Nevertheless, whether he read the essay or not, Thompson evidently understood Merton to be someone who could provide guidance to an oppressed black priest, this despite the fact that Merton was white. He understood that Merton "got it" in a way many other white Catholics did not. So began a correspondence between Thompson and Merton that continued until the year of Merton's death in 1968, and it is worth looking at this correspondence as a way to understand more thoroughly the perspective Merton brought as a white Catholic priest and a contemplative regarding the problem of racism in and outside the church.

In his letter to Merton about Greco's response to his interview, Thompson told Merton that he was not quite sure how to respond.[22] It was the bishop's accusation of defamation that most bothered Thompson. He did not intend to defame the church but simply spoke honestly about the experience of black Catholics and of his experience as the only black Catholic priest in a diocese in the Deep South. How can one be guilty of defamation when one is simply speaking the truth, particularly when he had previously spoken directly to the bishop himself about these matters? Thompson believed that he needed to answer Bishop Greco's letter, but he wanted to do so in a way that would not inflame the already elevated tension between himself and his bishop. He therefore asked Merton for advice about whether and how he should respond.

Merton responded immediately to Thompson's letter and he did so in detail. Merton began by affirming Thompson for speaking out the way he did. He found the interview "to be very frank and fair,"

22. Unpublished letter of August Thompson to TM, November 26, 1963, *Thomas Merton Center*, Bellarmine University.

not at all "extreme."[23] It was, in fact, "historic," "something really first rate and it was very badly needed." He continued: "Far from dishonoring the Church, I think you have borne witness to the fact that Catholics can think and speak out for the truth in these matters." I can imagine that these words from Merton were great comfort to Thompson. While he was being attacked by his bishop and by other white southern Catholics—including his fellow priests—for "stepping out of line,"[24] here was a prominent American Catholic priest, arguably *the* most prominent American Catholic figure at the time, telling him that his voice was an important one, that he needed to speak the truth, and that he was justified in doing so.

In addition to offering his assurances, Merton took seriously the concerns Thompson raised and provided as much guidance as he could from his vantage point. He focused attention on how to navigate the complicated waters of conflict with a superior in such a way that Thompson could acknowledge love for and fidelity to the bishop without betraying his convictions. That is, he instructed Thompson on how to do what he had been doing throughout his monastic life—remain obedient to his superiors without relinquishing the calling he feels he has to speak forthrightly and prophetically.

Moreover, and even more importantly, Merton's advice centered on how Thompson could respond to his bishop in such a way as to lead Greco to the kind of conversion about which Merton wrote in "Letters to a White Liberal." In that vein, he cautioned Thompson against responding angrily to the bishop by appealing to the bishop's limitations as a white southerner:

> You have to take into account the absolute blindness and absolute self-righteousness of people who have been scooled [*sic*]

23. Unpublished letter of TM to August Thompson, November 30, 1963, *Thomas Merton Center*, Bellarmine University.

24. August Thompson as quoted in John Howard Griffin, *The Church and the Black Man* (Dayton, OH: Pflaum Press, 1969), 11: "As Father August Thompson, a black priest, remarked recently when he was chided by white religious colleagues for 'stepping out of line' by telling it too bluntly and by black men for telling it too mildly, 'Blessed are the peacemakers, for they will catch it from all sides.'"

by centuries of prejudice and injustice to see things their way
and no other. I would say that now your job is to have, if you
can, some compassion for the Bishop, and if you refrain from
goading him, refrain for his sake even more than for your own.
He can't handle it rightly. In so far as obedience can at the
moment help him to calm down, it can be of some help to
you and to the cause of the Negro. At least I hope so.

On the one hand, if read in a certain way, Merton could be seen to
be making excuses for Greco's intransigence. Even worse, this advice
could be interpreted as Merton advising Thompson to go easy on
his bishop, to do what so many white authorities, including white
bishops and priests, had been telling black people to do—be patient.
However, given the vehemence of Merton's "Letters to a White Liberal" and his criticism there of precisely this white exhortation to
patience, we can be certain that this was not what Merton was trying
to do here, nor was he trying to make excuses for Greco. Rather,
he called Thompson to work for his bishop's conversion. As we saw
in the previous chapter, Merton was a great proponent of dialogue,
which he understood to be central to the task of nonviolence. He
saw dialogue, whereby we endeavor to understand the perspective of
another, even of those who are our enemies, as the primary way to
express love for one another. Indeed, as already noted in a previous
chapter, he understood such dialogue to be a specifically *Christian*
approach to conflict, an approach deeply rooted in the Catholic
tradition. In his advice to Thompson to recognize Greco's limitations
and so have compassion for him, Merton was not telling his friend
to be silent and acquiescent in the face of oppression. Rather, he
exhorted Thompson to understand his engagement with his bishop
in terms of the purposes of nonviolence. The possibility of conversion, of transformation, remained open only if Thompson engaged
his bishop in love without antagonizing him.

Thompson's reply to Merton indicates that he appreciated the
advice. Along with his own letter, he included the letter he wrote
to Bishop Greco in which he declared his unwavering love for him
and the church. He apologized for offending the bishop, while still

maintaining that he did little but speak the truth: "I said what I said because I was honestly convinced I was giving an honest answer to the questions asked not only for the good of the Negro but for the good of the whole Church."[25] He ended the letter by again professing his love for the bishop.

A little over two months after he sent this letter to Bishop Greco, Fr. Thompson wrote Merton to update him on how things were going with his bishop as well as to let him know how things were going more generally. According to Thompson, the bishop never responded directly to his letter. They conversed in person, and Thompson wrote that the bishop "has been most gracious never once mentioning Ramparts."[26] Greco had instead directed his attention to a center for catechesis and recreation he wanted Thompson to open, presumably for black Catholics in the diocese. And while he was glad to have support for this, Thompson admitted to Merton that he was still disappointed with the bishop's reaction, especially given that other members of the hierarchy had expressed support: "As the Bishop of the Houston Galveston Diocese told me [Greco] might have been glad that someone said something. Well, you would not have been able to tell he was glad from his letter to the press and to me."

At the same time, Thompson wrote that reaction from other Catholics had been very positive, both locally and nationally. Locally, not only had he not experienced any ill will from anyone, but "it seems most of the people are becoming more friendly towards me." And nationally, Thompson received an invite from another priest in the Catholic Interracial Council to participate in a workshop with Jewish and Protestant clergy on protesting for civil rights. The workshop was secret, and Thompson wrote that he did not plan on telling Bishop Greco about participating in it. He told Merton that he knew he needed to tread lightly right now given the bishop's displeasure,

25. Unpublished letter of August Thompson to Bishop Charles Greco, December 7, 1963, *Thomas Merton Center*, Bellarmine University.

26. Unpublished letter of August Thompson to TM, February 20, 1964, *Thomas Merton Center*, Bellarmine University.

but also that he felt the need to follow his own conscience. He asked once more for any guidance Merton could give him.

Merton again responded immediately to Thompson's letter. While he did not have any specific guidance to give Thompson regarding his participation in the workshop, about which Merton was enthusiastic, he took the opportunity to lament the state of the church in the United States regarding the race issue and to advise Thompson again regarding his relationship with Bishop Greco. His words are worth quoting at length:

> Looking at the broad perspective of the whole problem, from the point of view of the priest, I think we have to face the very serious fact that in the Church today "obedience" is invoked constantly to frustrate the real work that ought to be done for genuine issues (war, race, etc). The principles remain perfectly true: a subject does lack information, perhaps cannot judge sufficiently well, etc but when the decision is constantly pushed back higher up and when no decision comes from higher up except to play safe and do nothing, there is a real problem.[27]

One of Merton's major frustrations as a monk and as a writer was the problem of obedience to his superiors when they made what he understood to be unreasonable demands. As noted in a previous chapter, Merton was prohibited from writing about war by the abbot general who considered the issue of nuclear war to be an inappropriate topic for a contemplative monk to tackle. But the problem, as Merton saw it, was that no one else in the church was writing about nuclear war, so it appeared to him that religious superiors were simply kicking the can further down the street without actually addressing the issues and using "obedience" as a handy excuse to stay silent. Merton saw the same thing happening with Thompson and civil rights. Thompson had been asked, under obedience, to refrain from speaking out on civil rights, yet there were few in the church who

27. Unpublished letter of TM to August Thompson, February 27, 1964, *Thomas Merton Center*, Bellarmine University.

were actually confronting the problem of racial injustice. Indeed, as Thompson's interview showed, the church, particularly in the South, was implicated in the continuance of racial prejudice, and as a black priest in the South, Thompson was in a unique position to speak to racial injustice within his own church. Unfortunately, he was also in a unique position as a priest under obedience to his bishop. If he went too far, he would be silenced. Merton knew from his own experience that Thompson would get nowhere if his superior simply viewed him as a troublemaker; this would lead to the bishop being unwilling to listen to anything Thompson had to say. The key for Thompson, Merton wrote, will be to refrain from all violence—physical or verbal—in the face of the violence being committed against African Americans:

> All I can say is that I certainly hope God will protect you and your people, and that something can be done to change things. You will need an awful lot of courage and trust, and that is why you must see to it as far as you can that there is as little as possible of the same violence in your own heart. The courage that is without violence is the greatest of all, because it relies completely on God and not on man's strength. The Psalms are surely the real expression of the sufferings and conflicts that you face there. Fill your heart with them and Christ will live and fight in you.

Over three years went by before Merton and Thompson corresponded again. In September 1967, Fr. Thompson contacted Merton to get his feedback on recent correspondence between himself and Archbishop John Dearden, the archbishop of Detroit. Thompson had taken offense at something Archbishop Dearden had said in the August 30 issue of the *National Catholic Reporter*, which Thompson felt showed a lack of understanding of the church's complicity in racial injustice. In this issue, Dearden was quoted as responding to the problem of recent race riots as follows: "racial riots made it clear that the Catholic Church will have to allocate large amounts of money and personnel to the service of non-Catholics." He added, "If the Church does not do so . . . then it will fail to meet her responsibilities."²⁸ Thompson took offense at these statements, and his response to the archbishop runs for almost six single-spaced pages. We do not need to go through the entire letter paragraph by paragraph. It is sufficient to note that Thompson took issue with Dearden's words predominantly because it appeared to show a lack of understanding of what was going on within his own church in terms of racial injustice. It sounded to Thompson like Dearden wanted to focus the church's resources on racial injustice for non-Catholics, and while this at least demonstrated some cognizance of racism, it showed no understanding of the problem of racism within the Catholic Church itself. What business does the Catholic Church have to speak against racism to non-Catholics when racism remains a plague within the church?

> It is the old problem of racism and until we can straighten that out, first [in] our own house, we cannot speak about our helping non-Catholics, financially or personally because our problem is not with the non-Catholic, but first with the full acceptance of the black man, even in the Church, or may I go further and say especially in the Church. Consequently, until we have allocated a large amount of sincere, honest, unequivocal love first in the Catholic Church to Negro Catholics, white Catholics, nor Negro Catholics nor anyone else will understand what we are saying or doing.

To illustrate just how problematic racism was within the church, Thompson listed all of the ways he, as a black Catholic priest, as well as his fellow black Catholics were treated as second-class Catholics throughout the United States. Many of them were included in the *Ramparts* interview. But he emphasized that black Catholics in his diocese continued to experience prejudice, and he told Dearden that this was not isolated to the South, illustrating this point with an experience he had in the North. Earlier that year, when he went to Minneapolis to give a series of sermons for a parish mission, the

28. Unpublished letter of August Thompson to Archbishop John Dearden, September 1, 1967, *Thomas Merton Center*, Bellarmine University.

priest at this parish called another priest in the diocese to ask if Thompson could come speak to his CCD (Confraternity of Christian Doctrine) class. The shocking response he received was, "I don't want any nigger priest talking to my kids." Given the pervasiveness of racism within the church, Thompson asked Dearden what right the Catholic Church had to say anything to non-Catholics about civil rights. "Can we show the non-Catholic that the Negro is integrated in every phase of Catholic life? I fear if we went out now and tried to show the non-Catholic Negro we are interested in him as a person he might refer us back to what is happening in our own Church and say something like this: 'Baby get your own home straight first.'"

I have not located a response directly from Archbishop Dearden. However, Thompson did receive a letter one month later from a priest in the Archdiocese of Detroit asking him, on behalf of Archbishop Dearden, if he would be willing to volunteering some of his time to come up to the archdiocese to help with the inner-city parishes in the city, many of which had substantial black populations. In this letter we discover the astonishing detail that there was at the time only one black priest in the entire archdiocese.[29]

Thompson again wrote to Merton for advice, attaching both his letter to Dearden and the one from the archdiocese. In two different letters, Merton suggested that perhaps Thompson should go to Detroit, but acknowledging that his understanding of the situation was limited.[30] Either way, he told Thompson that he would support him no matter what he decided to do, and he praised Thompson for his "extremely powerful" letter to Archbishop Dearden, which clearly made an impression on the bishop.[31] Indeed, echoing some of what he said in a previous letter, Merton wrote that Dearden and other

29. Unpublished letter of Fr. Norman P. Thomas to Fr. August Thompson, October 23, 1967, *Thomas Merton Center*, Bellarmine University.

30. Unpublished letter of TM to Fr. August Thompson, October 30, 1967, *Thomas Merton Center*, Bellarmine University.

31. Unpublished letter of TM to Fr. August Thompson, November 9, 1967, *Thomas Merton Center*, Bellarmine University.

bishops actually want to understand what is going on, but there were so many barriers preventing them, as white men, from truly understanding that they rarely got "more than a quarter of the picture." Thompson's letter evidently filled in more of that picture for Dearden.

Four months after this exchange of correspondence about Detroit, Thompson wrote what would be his last letter to Merton. In it he described a conversation he had recently with Bishop Greco that demonstrated to him that Greco still does not understand the situation of black Catholics.[32] Merton responded to Thompson's letter a month later in what would be his final letter to the priest. He did not respond directly to Thompson's conversation with Bishop Greco, but instead focused on the tragedy that occurred shortly after Merton received Thompson's letter, the assassination of Martin Luther King Jr. While Merton and King never met, the two knew of one another, and in the run-up to Memphis, John and June Yungblut, friends and co-workers of King, encouraged him to make a retreat at the Abbey of Gethsemani.[33] This retreat would, of course, never occur. In his letter to Thompson, Merton expressed some measure of despair about the future of race relations in a post-King America. "There is a great sickness," he writes, "the sickness of decaying western civilization."[34] In this vein, Merton wondered what Christians were to do now in the face of racial injustice. His answer merits full quotation:

> The big thing for Christians is to live the truth that *in Christ* there is absolutely no distinction between Black and White, but the Adversary has made sure that a very real distinction exists (due to the sins of history). Neither can be ignored. We

32. Unpublished letter of August Thompson to TM, March 20, 1968, *Thomas Merton Center*, Bellarmine University. Thompson included a transcription he made of the conversation he had with Bishop Greco ("One hour conference with Bishop Charles P. Greco by Father Thompson," February 27, 1968, *Thomas Merton Center*, Bellarmine University).

33. See Jvii, 79: 6 April 1968.

34. Unpublished letter of TM to August Thompson, April 26, 1968, *Thomas Merton Center*, Bellarmine University.

> have to learn the reality of the difference, and emphasize Black
> and White identities and qualities and rights: and see beyond
> to the inner unity: that unity is in Christ, not in the affluent
> society.

We have already seen how, in "Letters to a White Liberal," Merton
highlighted the scandal of Catholic bigotry by pointing to the incarnation and what God-becoming-flesh tells us about the value
and dignity of all people, regardless of race. In this, his last letter to
Thompson, Merton again focused on the theological, arguing that
Christians need to take seriously the implications of the incarnation for race relations. It was not enough for Christians merely to
affirm the reality of God-becoming-flesh; Christians must actually live this truth out. And for Merton this meant recognizing the
fundamental unity of humankind that the incarnation reveals. In
becoming human, God demonstrated that all humanity has a value
and dignity that transcends and encompasses all races. In his letter
to Thompson, Merton argued that Christians needed to live out this
truth, that they needed to understand that Christ gave us an identity
that transcends and encompasses all the ways in which we divide
ourselves from one another, including along race. In Christ, therefore, "there is absolutely no distinction between Black and White."
Merton did not mean that there are no differences between white
and black Americans. Differences exist, and they matter. They are
what make each individual and each culture distinct. But beyond
the differences is, Merton argued, an "inner unity" rooted in Christ
himself, and it is up to Christians to live this unity out.

Conclusion

Thompson and Merton never corresponded again after this letter.
Twenty-four years later, in an interview with the local Alexandria
paper, *The Alexandria Town Talk*, Fr. Thompson reflected on his
relationship with Thomas Merton. Noting that Merton "was very
much concerned about race," Thompson said that Merton's letters

"gave me courage to keep going."[35] He also told his interviewer that, after Merton's death, Thompson visited Merton's hermitage and said Mass, using Merton's chalice.

In the years following Merton's death, Fr. Thompson continued to fight for racial justice in the Catholic Church. In a 1972 interview, he lamented the state of things in the church. He mentioned that he continued to be criticized by white Catholics for being too outspoken and criticized by black Catholics for not doing more. And while he acknowledged that progress had been made, he lamented that the progress was slow and always forced. "White people ask, 'What do we need to do for you?'" he said, "The question should be, 'What can we do to make the Church more Christian?'"[36] In a 1982 interview about the Silver Jubilee of his ordination to the priesthood, Thompson again acknowledged progress, but noted that black Catholics were still not fully included in the life of the Catholic Church. "All we want," he said, "is a chance to be truly Catholic."[37] And in a 1997 interview with the distinguished Vatican reporter John Allen about his interview with John Howard Griffin in *Ramparts* thirty-five years earlier, Thompson continued to criticize the church, both for its history of racial prejudice and its continued reluctance to be countercultural when it comes to race relations. "I really feel for the most part that the church has been a follower instead of a leader," he lamented.[38]

In examining the correspondence between Merton and Thompson, I have only scratched the surface in telling about the kind of oppression Fr. Thompson experienced throughout his life. In an unpublished journal John Howard Griffin kept from 1964 to 1966

35. Sidney Williams, "Local Priest Will Be Watching Merton Special with Interest," *The Alexandria Town Talk* (September 20, 1992): 32.

36. Helen Derr, "Father August Thompson: One Man With Courage," *The Alexandria Town Talk* (January 8, 1972): 7.

37. Tom Haywood, "25 Years in 'Integrated-Segregated' Church," *The Alexandria Town Talk* (June 5, 1982): 14.

38. John L. Allen Jr., "Black Priest Lives with Hope, Resignation," *National Catholic Reporter* (November 21, 1997): 16.

about Fr. Thompson, Griffin described in detail the threats Thompson faced on a daily basis. Thompson's friends and neighbors had businesses and homes bombed, and Thompson received regular threats against his life. "[Thompson] told me that he had been told the Klan promised to get three Negroes in Ferriday," Griffin wrote, "one of whom was 'that nigger priest.' "[39] But throughout it all, Thompson's primary concern was for those under his care. He feared for the lives and well-being of his black parishioners, but also expressed concern for the white racists. In the aforementioned interview with John Allen, Thompson talked about his unwillingness to go uninvited to the homes of dying white Catholics for "fear that person would commit an act of hatred on his or her deathbed" and so put their soul in peril because of their racist reaction to his presence.[40] As for his own safety, Thompson told Griffin that he was willing to die if God willed it. "Don't worry so much," he said. "Think how nice it will be if they get me—I can go to Heaven young."[41]

It was out of this context that Fr. August Thompson turned to Thomas Merton. Faced with a bishop who seemed unwilling to listen to him and a church in which he experienced life as a second-class Catholic even as a priest simply because he was black, Thompson found in Thomas Merton a fellow priest who understood. They were both priests of the Catholic Church, yet priests in vastly different cultural and racial contexts. While Thompson experienced daily oppression, Merton existed as a contemplative in the woods of Kentucky. And yet, from his vantage point and despite his own identity as a white American, Merton wrote about and responded to the problem of systemic racism in a prophetic way that led civil rights activists like Fr. August Thompson to recognize that Merton understood the plight of African Americans. Merton's argument

39. "Journal Notes Re: His Interview with Father Thompson and Its Aftermath, December 1964–January 1966," box 8, fol. 266, *John Howard Griffin Papers*, Columbia University.

40. Allen Jr., "Black Priest Lives with Hope, Resignation," 16.

41. "Journal Notes."

against racism was not revolutionary. He simply drew upon the very basics of Catholic teaching on the incarnation both to illustrate the sinfulness of racism and to remind the church that it could in no way be complicit in the sin of racism. Lamentably, Merton's arguments remain relevant, and Catholics would do well to delve more deeply into Merton's writings on race to understand more thoroughly what is going on in society today.

CHAPTER 7

MERTON THE LOVESTRUCK

I have no intention of keeping the Margie business entirely out of sight. I have always wanted to be completely open, both about my mistakes and about my effort to make sense out of my life. The affair with Margie is an important part of it—and shows my limitations as well as a side of me that is—well, it needs to be known too, for it is part of me. My need for love, my loneliness, my inner division, the struggle in which solitude is at once a problem and a "solution." And perhaps not a perfect solution either.

—Journal Entry, May 11, 1967

Introduction: A Controversy Renewed

In the April 2019 issue of *Harper's Magazine*, Garry Wills—a prolific Catholic writer of *Papal Sin: Structures of Deceit*, *What Jesus Meant*, *Why I Am a Catholic*, and many other books—reviewed a recent book on Thomas Merton by the famed author of both fiction and nonfiction, Mary Gordon.[1] Wills used his review of Gordon's book to attack Merton as a shallow monk and thinker.[2] According

---

1. Mary Gordon, *On Thomas Merton* (Boulder, CO: Shambala Press, 2018).
2. Garry Wills, "Shallow Calls to Shallow: On Thomas Merton, Fifty Years after His Death," *Harper's Magazine*, April 2019, https://harpers.org/archive/2019/04/on-thomas-merton-mary-gordon-review/.

to Wills, Merton was little more than a disgruntled pseudo-ascetic who enjoyed cultivating an adoring fan club that included celebrities, Catholic and non-Catholic alike. He was not so much a monk as he was a writer in a monastery that gave him special treatment only because his books provided the Abbey with income. Such special treatment included a hermitage—which Wills describes as "a state of virtual secession within the monastery"—where Merton was able to get away from an abbot and a monastery he detested.

Wills wrote that the isolation of the hermitage came in handy when he entered into an illicit relationship with a nurse named Margie Smith during the summer of 1966. This relationship is for Wills the ultimate example of Merton's shallowness as a monk who felt he deserved special treatment. He recounted that Merton used trips into Louisville to meet influential friends as an excuse to see her and that, after he was ordered to end the relationship by his abbot, he continued to meet with her clandestinely because he didn't feel that the rules applied to him. This struck Wills as horribly smug and is further evidence of the "webs of lies" that "is at one with a pattern built into his 'apostolate' as the with-it monk."

The reaction by conservative Catholics to Wills's piece was perhaps predictable. A piece in *The Catholic Herald* by Chad Pecknold, a professor of theology at The Catholic University of America, epito- mized the reaction.[3] Despite admitting that he hasn't actually read Merton, Pecknold argued that such an affair is precisely what one would expect from someone like Merton, a "Catholic icon of six- ties optimism—an icon which was morally and spiritually deleted enough to seek solace in the 'round hull of hips'" of his lover. And to hammer home his point that Merton should in no way be vener- ated, Pecknold ended the piece by asking his readers to pray for all the souls in purgatory like Merton.

---

3. Chad Pecknold, "Thomas Merton's Illicit Affair and the Weakness of 60s Zen Catholicism," *The Catholic Herald*, April 10, 2019, https://catholicherald.co.uk /thomas-mertons-illicit-affair-and-the-weakness-of-60s-zen-catholicism/.

There's a flippancy to the way that Gordon, Wills, and Pecknold all treat Merton's relationship with Smith. Gordon's treatment was sympathetic, but so brief as to gloss over the entire relationship as being of little consequence, while both Wills and Pecknold used the relationship as a bludgeon for condemnation. None of them actually delved into what happened, at least from Merton's perspective. None of them examined Merton's agonized thoughts about his love for Smith, her love for him, and the threat this relationship posed to his vocation. And none of them looked at what Merton had to say about the relationship in the years after it ended.

I'm not interested in defending Merton's relationship with Smith, nor do I think it merits a sympathetic treatment. It is important to note that we only possess Merton's narrative of the affair. Smith has remained silent about this relationship to this day. Moreover, while he chose to preserve an account of this relationship in his journals for posterity, he still—even unconsciously—was under pressure to put forward an account that put himself in a light that was consistent not only with who he understood himself to be, but who the world understood him to be. But if we should, as I've been arguing in this book, take seriously Merton's status and contributions as a Catholic thinker and writer, then Merton's description of his relationship with Margie Smith needs to be taken into account. And from Merton's account we not only get a sense of his own shortcomings—his journal entries from this time show him at his most selfish and self-absorbed—but we see him grappling with these shortcomings with a measure of honesty and humility.

The Beginning of the Relationship

On March 25, 1966—the feast of the Annunciation—Thomas Merton had an operation on his back at St. Joseph's hospital in Louisville. A little less than a year earlier, Merton was given permission to live permanently as a hermit with the blessing of his abbot and his community, not because he merited some sort of special treatment, but because the Cistercian order had come to acknowledge its own tradition of solitaries and understood Merton to be someone who had a calling to the hermit life. A number of other monks at Gethsemani also became hermits soon thereafter, including Merton's own abbot in 1968 after his retirement.

Merton loved the hermit life, but it took a physical toll and his back began to give him trouble. Necessary tasks like chopping wood soon became difficult for him and an operation proved inevitable. Merton was nervous about the procedure, yet in a journal entry written two days before the operation, he talked about his faith in Christ: "I know I have to die sometime and may this not all be the beginning of it? I don't know, but if it is I accept it in full freedom and gladness. My life stands offered with that of Christ my brother." He concluded the entry by reflecting on his monastic brethren: "Certainly the spirit of the community is excellent and the place is blessed" (Jvi, 32, 33: March 23, 1966).

The operation was successful, though recovery was slow. His first journal entry after the operation was written at the hermitage a little over two weeks after his operation. He recounted in the entry his slow and ongoing recovery, and his description contains the first reference to Smith. It's clear that the two hit it off from the start:

> I got a very friendly and devoted student nurse working on my compresses etc. and this livened things up considerably. In fact we were getting perhaps too friendly by the time she went off on her Easter vacation, but her affection—undisguised and frank—was an *enormous* help in bringing me back to life fast. (Jvi, 38: April 10, 1966)

The care he received from Smith and the other nurses was life-giving, and indeed, Merton wrote that their friendship led him to realize he had a need for "feminine companionship and love" that he didn't know he had.

A week and a half went by. Perhaps Merton was thinking about Smith, but his journal contains no references to her during these days. However, on April 19, a letter from Smith appeared. We don't know exactly what was in the letter, but Merton was clearly flattered and had to admit that the affection she expressed for him in her letter was mutual. Upon receiving this letter, he knew he had to grapple deeply with the love he had for her, knowing that he was called to a life dedicated to God.

> The question of love: I have to face the fact that I have simply side-stepped it. Now it must be faced squarely. I cannot live without giving love back to a world that has given me so much. And of course it has to be the love of a man dedicated to God—and selfless, detached, free, completely open love. (Jvi, 42: April 19, 1966)

Merton seemed to think that the love he felt for her could be incorporated in some way into his life as a hermit, that this love could be channeled into a general love for the world. It's hard to say what Merton meant; perhaps he was simply trying to justify this love to himself. What is clear is that he had very little clue about what to do with Smith's feelings for him nor what to do with his feelings for her.

Two days later, things became more serious when Smith wrote to tell him that she would like to see him. Merton admitted to himself that he wanted to see her too. "I tell myself it is because I want to help her," he wrote, adding that he couldn't become emotionally attached (Jvi, 43; April 21, 1966). Two days after her letter, they had a long illicit phone conversation; Merton used one of the monastery phones to chat with her. They spoke again about wanting to see one another, and Merton realized that with this phone call, and his unwillingness to stop communicating with her, he had crossed a line he knew he should not have crossed: "In my heart I know it would really have been better if I had followed my original intuition and been content with a couple of letters and nothing more" (Jvi, 33: April 24, 1966). Both knew that a relationship between them could have no future, and Merton wrote that he should end it before things became more complicated.

He didn't.

"I Am Not as Smart or as Stable as I Imagined"

His journal entry for April 27, 1966, begins with a harsh realization: "There is no question that I am in deep" (Jvi, 45: April 27, 1966). Smith met him in the doctor's office when he was in Louisville for an appointment, and afterward the two of them sat alone for a half hour in Cunningham's, a popular downtown eatery. It was during this lunch that, according to Merton, they both realized they were in love. The realization both thrilled and terrified him:

> More than ever I saw how much and how instantly and how delicately we respond to each other on every level. Also I can see why she is scared. I am too. There is a sense of awful, awesome rather, sexual affinity—and of course there can be no hesitation about my position here. I have vows and I must be faithful to them. And I told myself that I can and will be, but I have moments of being scared too. Apart from that, though, we had a very good talk and once again it was clearer than ever that we are terribly in love, and it is the kind of love that can virtually tear you apart. (Jvi, 45–46: April 27, 1966)

Merton was clearly very attracted to her. He brought up his vows immediately, acknowledging that their relationship had the potential to threaten his faithfulness to them. But at this point, he naively thought he could maintain a relationship with her without violating his vows. He went on to write in the entry that he wanted simply to be friends, but he knew that things had gone too far and he had no idea how to respond. She "is so tragically full of passion and so wide open," he wrote. "My response has been too total and too forthright, we have admitted too much, communicated all the fire to each other and now we are caught." He sums up the situation with a succinct realization of himself: "I am not as smart or as stable as I imagined" (Jvi, 46: April 27, 1966).

Their relationship lasted two months. Merton entered the relationship thinking the two could simply be friends, but from the beginning he knew he was in love with her, the first time he had ever truly loved or been loved by a woman. Without playing too much of the amateur psychologist, I would suggest that any assessment of the affair needs to take into account the fact that Merton's relationships with women prior to entering the monastery appeared to be uniformly poor. Merton remembered his mother as a harsh, demanding, and distant presence. His relationships with women as a teenager and as a college student appeared not to be on a deep level. Somewhat famously, Merton had a reputation as a womanizer during his one and only year at Cambridge University, and the rumor persists that he fathered a child that year. Merton's description of his life while studying at Columbia University contain few references to relationships with women; his close friends were all men. Thomas Merton entered the Abbey of Gethsemani apparently never having experienced genuine love for or from a woman, and when this love appeared unexpectedly in 1966, he had no clue how to react.

His journal entries early in the relationship are almost embarrassingly euphoric. "I respond so much to her now," he wrote after speaking to her on the phone, "to the inflections of her voice, her laughter, everything, that I was flooded with peace and happiness and wanted just to talk to her forever." He continued, "All I know is that I love her so much I can hardly think of anything but her" (Jvi, 47: April 28, 1966). He somehow felt that his relationship with Smith could "become a harmonious part of [his] vocation" as a hermit, though he didn't offer any explanations as to how the two could possibly work together (Jvi, 49: May 2, 1966). In another entry he acknowledged that, by all standards, his relationship with Smith "is all wrong, absurd, insane." And yet, "I can't help coming back again and again to the realization that somehow it is not crazy—it makes sense" (Jvi, 50: May 4, 1966). A week later he wrote, "Clearly this love is not a contradiction of my solitude but a mysterious part of it. It fits strangely and without conflict into my inner life of meditation and prayer" (Jvi, 59: May 12, 1966).

Merton seemed to think that his relationship squared with his vocation as a hermit in part because he believed the relationship benefited Smith. She loved him, and returning that love brought "her joy and support and help" (Jvi, 45: April 27, 1966). He sometimes talked about the relationship as if it was solely an opportunity to bring her happiness: "Of course I would be more peaceful, secure and safe just minding my own business in the hermitage and trying to forget her—but thank God for this blessed disturbance, for this love that sometimes upsets me, which, at a certain cost to me, makes another person happier" (Jvi, 51: May 4, 1966). However, Merton also understood that he was being transformed both by her love for him and by the love he didn't know he could express: "I realize that the deepest capacities for human love in me have never even been tapped, that I too can love with an awful completeness. Responding to her has opened up the depths of my life in ways I can't begin to understand or analyze now" (Jvi, 54: May 9, 1966). The relationship was proving to be revelatory in ways he did not feel he could ignore or set aside.

Even as the relationship began to take on more physical expressions, Merton wrote about the way in which their love was helping him to come to terms with his own sexuality. While his sexual encounters before his conversion to Catholicism were marked by an unhappiness that was the result of his own desire for sexual conquest, such was not the case with Smith. After describing an afternoon of physical intimacy (Merton is clear that their intimacy, at least that afternoon, did not involve the consummation of their physical relationship),[4] Merton wrote that his "sexuality has been made real and decent again" (Jvi, 67: May 20, 1966).

Nevertheless, the tension between his monastic solitude and his love for Smith soon became obvious to him. In an entry on May

---

4. Merton's description of the afternoon is somewhat cringe-inducing. While it is clear that their relationship took a decidedly physical turn, he's also clear that there were limits to the physical expression of their love, at least to this point: "We ate herring and ham (not very much eating!) and drank our wine and read poems and talked of ourselves and mostly made love and love and love for five hours. And though we had over and over reassured ourselves and agreed that our love would have to continue always chaste and this sacrifice was essential, yet in the end we were getting rather sexy. We now love with our whole bodies anyway and I have the complete feel of her being (except her sex) as completely me." See Jvi, 66 (May 20, 1966).

24, he admitted the limitations of their relationship. Each of them was holding back something of themselves from each other, perhaps recognizing that the relationship compromised something essential about their identity. In Merton's case, he knew that his deepest calling was to the solitude of the hermitage.

> The thing is that we do *not* meet completely in our love: it is partial, not whole. There are aspects of ourselves, sides of ourselves that come together, are in harmony, respond deeply. But there are other sides which do not. And where we *do* meet we try to pull ourselves wholly together and fail—each tries to envelop the whole self of the other—and this is where my own ambiguities come into play. My deepest self evades this and is jealous of absolute freedom and solitude. Hers too has its reservations—the freedom to love others and perhaps this is why we both protest so much about our love, the wholeness of it, the totality of it. Have any two people ever sworn to each other such total and unending love? I guess all lovers do. But do we really mean it? Are we in a position to mean it? I think we are desperately trying to persuade ourselves and failing. Why do we think it necessary to persuade ourselves in the first place? (Jvi, 69–70: May 24, 1966)

A few days later, Merton wrote about his "confusion, anguish, indecision, and nerves" in the wake of their afternoon of passion. He couldn't bring himself to end the relationship; he loved her, and he knew that she loved him. He mused that perhaps the most merciful thing for both of them would be to have his superiors end the relationship. He acknowledged the sexual temptation to be overwhelming, and while they had both agreed to keep their relationship chaste, he had to admit that "we are not safe with each other" (Jvi, 70: May 27, 1966). The next day, in an anguished entry that both celebrated and lamented the love he felt for Smith, Merton wrote, "I should never have got in love in the first place" (Jvi, 72: May 28, 1966).

The conflict between his vocation and his relationship heated up as May gave way to June. A long passage from his June 2 entry merits full quotation, if only because it so clearly demonstrates the depth of the internal conflict Merton experienced:

> This love *cannot* be a matter of playing around. I wrote in a way that it could. It's altogether serious. It scares me at times. She has given up saying we should live together and fully accepts my vows, etc. but love demands contact and much communication and this remains a constant problem here. My phone calls are illegal and so too are some of our meetings. This does not make for peace, but it meets the demands of love and I think in conscience—and in love—I must meet them. The sincerity and depths of all this will probably be tested, and God knows I will need help!! There's something in me that wants freedom at any price and can claim all sorts of religious justification. More or less clear sightedly [*sic*], at least now, I am going in the opposite direction. I am taking a course that can be harmful to me as a monk, a contemplative and a writer. And I am doing it for love. Not out of passion and enthusiasm, but out of simple love for Margie. However, I think it is understood that when a show down with the vows comes, I have to stick by the vows. (Jvi, 76: June 2, 1966)

The next day he wrote, "There is a real danger of my cracking up under the pressures and contradictions of love in my absurd situation" (Jvi, 77: June 3, 1966). On the feast of Corpus Christi six days later, Merton wrote shamefully about concelebrating the Mass with his fellow monk-priests: "I stood there among all the others, soberly aware of myself as a priest who has a woman." In the entry, Merton expressed a realization that, sooner or later, the relationship would have to come to an end. "Today especially I was thinking we must be realistic in our expectations for the future," he wrote. "There just is no real future for our love as a real *love* affair" (Jvi, 79: June 9, 1966). At the same time, he couldn't bring himself to end it himself because he was convinced that the love the two had for each other was genuine and true. Just how complicated the situation was for Merton is made clear from his June 10 entry. He acknowledged that he loved her more than he had ever loved another woman, another human being. And, as he wrote, "she tells me over and over that she loves me totally with a love she has never known before for anyone and a love that she could not possibly give to anyone else." But he did not want to give up who he was called to be, a hermit at the Abbey of Gethsemani, and he wrote about the ways in which the relationship was pushing him in uncomfortable directions: "Scruples about my vocation and worries about preserving my old identity are the two things that get in the way," he wrote, "for this love will eventually change me completely and is changing me already, and unconsciously with great anguish sometimes, I resent it." And that evening, as he meditated before the Blessed Sacrament, he faced fully the challenge the relationship posed to his identity and vocation: "Her love is not just 'another question' and 'another problem'—it is right at the center of all my questions and problems and right at the center of my hermit life" (Jvi, 81: June 10, 1966).

Merton travelled to Louisville the next day to get a bursitis shot in his elbow. While in town he arranged with his psychologist and friend, Jim Wygal, to meet Smith alone in his office. In order to protect the privacy of those still living, as Smith is, the entry describing this meeting has been censored,[5] and the Merton Legacy Trust—the trust established by Merton to oversee the publication of his work—continues to withhold access to it. The reason appears to be that Merton and Smith experienced a level of physical intimacy they had not had together before,[6] and the Trust sees no need to violate Smith's privacy by allowing Merton's description of their physical

5. The general editor for Merton's private journals, Br. Patrick Hart, wrote the following note at the end of Christine Bochen's introduction to the volume containing entries about Merton's relationship with Margie: "For the sole purpose of protecting the privacy of persons still living, the members of the Merton Legacy Trust and the Abbot of Gethsemani have asked Christine Bochen, the editor of this volume of the journals, to delete a very few passages involving the invasion of other persons' privacy, and to indicate the deletion ellipses within editorial brackets" (Jvi, xxiv).

6. See Jvi, 94 (July 12, 1966). A brief sentence in this entry is suggestive: "I keep remembering her body, her nakedness, the day at Wygal's, and it haunts me."

intimacy to be made public. Whatever took place in Wygal's office, Merton realized that the relationship could not continue: "We can't go on like this. I can't leave her. I have to try to live the life I have chosen. Yet I love her" (Jvi, 81: June 12, 1966).

The End of the Affair

Two days later, the beginning of the end came. On June 13, Merton's abbot returned home from a trip. When Merton went to the cellarer's office to phone Smith illicitly, he was told that another monk had listened in on one of his calls to Smith and reported the relationship to the abbot. Far from experiencing anger about this outcome, Merton expressed relief: "I have to face the fact that I have been wrong and foolish in all this. Much as I loved Margie, I should never have let myself be carried away to become so utterly imprudent . . . Well, it is clearly over now" (Jvi, 82: June 14, 1966). Truth be told, the relationship didn't end immediately upon the abbot's discovery. Merton wrote that Dom James Fox was kind and understanding about the relationship, but he ordered a complete and immediate break. Merton felt in conscience that he couldn't do so immediately without doing irreparable harm to Smith. The relationship needed to taper off. She was, by his telling, heartbroken at the end of their relationship, and he felt that he had an obligation to her to console her. There were a few more clandestine phone calls, as well as some meetings in Louisville. But Merton realized that the relationship was effectively over. "I am alone and I love her," he wrote on July 8, "but the choice between her and solitude presented itself and I chose solitude" (Jvi, 93: July 8, 1966). Four days later, he reflected on their relationship as follows: "I realized that no matter how much I may love Margie and be attached to her, there has never for a moment really been any choice. If it is a question of leaving Gethsemani and trying to live with her, and staying here in solitude and doing whatever it is I am supposed to do, then the answer is easy. There is not even a credible question" (Jvi, 94: July 12, 1966). On July 16, he met with her in Louisville at Cherokee Park for one last meeting. The two spoke of the love they shared for one another, and according to Merton she proposed that he leave the monastery so that they could spend the rest of their lives together. Merton, however, knew the impossibility of this, and felt that perhaps her impressions of him were based less on reality than on the ideals she had of him. This was to be their final meeting, and while it was difficult for Merton not to see her, he realized that this was the choice he had to make.

Merton's Later Reflections

In his review of Mary Gordon's book, Garry Wills argued that Merton felt no compunction about this relationship, that it was simply part of a life of deception. In reality, careful reading of Merton's private journals reveals a more complex, indeed human, situation. Merton was not a man searching for love, but, by his own telling, was someone who experienced the love from and for a woman for the first time. Caught in the throes of this love, Merton acted recklessly, and his journal entries from this time read more like the reflections of a heart-struck teenager than a fifty-one-year-old respected monk and writer. But in the months and years after the relationship ended, Merton's assessments of the relationship were sober. Wills didn't refer to any of these assessments. Rather, to prove that Merton was simply playing around with his vows, he pointed to the fact that Merton called Smith from a payphone in the days following the vow Merton made before Dom James Fox on September 8 "to live in solitude for the rest of my life in so far as health may permit" (Jvi, 129: September 10, 1966) as proof that Merton wasn't taking seriously his need to enter into the monastic life more fully. Wills pointed also to a moment in December 1966 when Joan Baez came to visit Merton at his hermitage and Merton told her about his love for Smith and how Baez was willing to drive Merton to go see her in Cincinnati and how Merton was almost willing to go (see Jvi, 168: December 10, 1966).

These events demonstrate that Merton still didn't quite know what to do with the love he had for Smith in the months following the end of their relationship. But as time went on, Merton's reflections on this relationship indicate that he felt no small measure of shame about it. In an entry written ten months after his relationship was discovered by the abbot, Merton wrote about what might have occurred had the relationship gone too far. While wandering through the woods, Merton reflected on their moment of intimacy in Wygal's office and how this affected him at the time. We can see that Merton was far more conflicted internally than he perhaps let on in his journal entries from that summer:

> That Sunday I was literally shaken and disturbed—knowing clearly that I was all wrong, that I was going against everything that made sense in my life, going against all that was true and authentic in my vocation, going against the grace and love of God. Struggling desperately in my heart and knowing I was helpless, that things were moving in a certain direction and I had gone too far to turn back. (Jvi, 217: April 10, 1967)

And as he looked back on the end of their relationship, Merton expressed relief: "After that, only the grace of God saved us from a really terrible mess. It was fortunate that we were simply not able to see each other when we wanted to. And finally it *was* a good thing that we stopped altogether, though it ought to have been done differently" (Jvi, 217: April 10, 1967). A few weeks later, Merton expressed further regret about the relationship:

> I experience in myself a deep need of conversion and penance—a deep repentance, a real sense of having erred, gone wrong, got lost—and needing to get back on the right path. Needing to pray for forgiveness. Sense of revolt at my own foolishness and triviality. Shame and amazement at the way I have trifled with life and grace—how could I be so utterly stupid! (Jvi, 234: May 13, 1967)

More than a year later, just before he left for his ill-fated trip to Asia, Merton's thoughts on the relationship were even more stark:

"Today, among other things, I burned Margie's letters. Incredible stupidity in 1966! I did not even glance at any one of them" (Jvii, 157: August 20, 1968).

Conclusion: The Humility of Vulnerability

Thomas Merton established the Merton Legacy Trust in 1967 to oversee his literary estate and to take responsibility for the publication of his works after his death. The trust stipulated that his private journals could be published only after the publication of an authorized biography and twenty-five years after his death. Merton put no other restrictions on the publication of the journals. He was uninterested in having them purged of anything unsavory, not least because he was disturbed by what he saw took place after the publication of *The Seven Storey Mountain*. While he never disowned the autobiography that propelled him to fame, he found the book to be overly pious and lent itself to an image of himself that lacked reality. "Unfortunately, the book was a best-seller," he said in an interview with the journalist Thomas McDonnell, "and has become a kind of edifying legend or something. This is a dreadful fate. I am trying my best to live it down . . . I rebel against it and maintain my basic human right *not* to be turned into a Catholic myth for children in parochial schools."[7] Merton did not want the same thing to happen with his journals. If he was going to be known, he was going to be *known*.

It is the forthrightness of his journals that continue to attract readers like myself. To read Merton's private journals is to be given unique access to the kind of inner thoughts, compulsions, and emotions that all of us experience, but often don't understand or communicate to others. Merton allowed himself to become an open book, warts and all. His self-assessments were brutally honest and frequently unflattering, and his unflattering gaze could occasionally fall on others,

7. Thomas P. McDonnell, "An Interview with Thomas Merton," *Motive* 28 (October 1967): 33.

including his abbot and his fellow monks. Like a few other writers, Garry Wills chose to focus attention on Merton's negative comments about the community at Gethsemani, even going so far as to suggest that Merton intentionally distanced himself from his fellow monks, that he wanted special treatment not extended to them. Not included in Wills's assessment of Merton are the hundreds of hours of audio tapes we have of him teaching the incoming monks as their novice master, to which I've already referred in a previous chapter. One need only listen to a small sample from these tapes to hear evidence of the clear love his novices had for him, and the abundant love and care he had for them as their teacher and their spiritual director. Nor did Wills take into account the numerous places in Merton's journals in which he wrote movingly about the community at Gethsemani. For example, after walking near the monastery in the fall of 1966, Merton wrote: "I realized how much good there really is in this community—not only in so many individuals . . . but in the community as it is organized. I know this is a 'good community' and a fortunate place in which to be today" (Jvi, 145: October 4, 1966). And less than a month before his death, while travelling in Asia, Merton wrote in his journal about how much he missed and loved Gethsemani (see Jvii, 281–82: November 17, 1968). None of this negates the negative things he said about the community and his fellow monks in other pages in the journal, but it does fill out a complicated picture that is too often presented in an uncomplicated manner. Merton doesn't allow for that kind of simplistic assessment.

In a 1967 journal entry, Merton wrote honestly about why he was choosing to leave all references to the relationship in his journal:

> I have no intention of keeping the Margie business entirely out of sight. I have always wanted to be completely open, both about my mistakes and about my effort to make sense out of my life. The affair with Margie is an important part of it—and shows my limitations as well as a side of me that is—well, it needs to be known too, for it is part of me. My need for love, my loneliness, my inner division, the struggle in which solitude

is at once a problem and a "solution." And perhaps not a
perfect solution either. (Jvi, 234: May 11, 1967)

There is no doubt that Merton acted irresponsibly, not simply in
terms of compromising his vow of chastity but also in terms of
entering into a relationship in which there was a substantial power
differential between himself and Smith. While Merton clearly understood his moral misstep in entering into the relationship, it's not
clear that he fully appreciated the implications of this affair given
their substantial difference in age and stature. Nevertheless, there
is a humility on display in his words above that shows Merton's
unwillingness to be known apart from his foibles, apart from the
complexity of who he was as a human being striving to do God's
will. Merton had had enough of the pious legends that often mark
the ways we talk about our saints. As he wrote in a 1963 book, *Life
and Holiness*, too often our saints are depicted in ways that mask
their humanity. The stereotypical plaster saint looks like this: "The
saint, if he ever sinned at all, eventually became impeccable after a
perfect conversion, Impeccability not being quite enough, he is raised
beyond the faintest possibility of feeling temptation. Of course he is
tempted, but temptation provides no difficulties. He always has the
absolute and heroic answer" (LH, 22–23). There's a lack of reality to
these saints that make them unapproachable. Moreover, and Merton
pulls no punches here, "such caricaturing of sanctity is indeed a sin
against faith in the Incarnation. It shows contempt for the humanity
for which Christ did not hesitate to die on the cross" (LH, 24–25).
Merton would have none of this for himself. If people were going
to know him, they were also going to have to know his failings, his
failings as a Christian, as a monk, and as a priest.

Perhaps this is why many people find in Merton the kind of figure
to whom they can relate. Each time I go to the Abbey of Gethsemani,
I make a visit to Merton's grave. And each time I'm struck by ways
in which pilgrims venerate his burial place. Surrounding the simple
Trappist cross marking his resting place are rosaries, prayers, guitar
picks, sobriety tokens, art, and wood carvings. I have a sense that

this kind of veneration would make very little sense to some who immediately dismiss Merton for his moral failings. But there are many, and I include myself among them, who understand Merton to be the kind of saint who speaks profoundly to them precisely *because* he was human, but a human who strove throughout his life to be transformed by the love and grace of the God he had come to know so well.

CHAPTER 8

MERTON THE DIALOGIST

*For, you see, when "I" enter into a dialogue with "you" and each
of us knows who is speaking, it turns out that we are both Christ.
This, being seen in a very simple and "natural" light, is the beginning and almost the fullness of everything. Everything is in it
somewhere. But it makes most sense in the light of Mass and the
Eucharist.*

—Thomas Merton to John Harris, January 31, 1959

Introduction: The Pope, Merton, and Dialogue

In his 2013 interview with Fr. Antonio Spadaro shortly after his
election, Pope Francis named Peter Faber, SJ (1506–1546), when
asked about which Jesuit figures have most influenced him. When
asked what it was about Faber that he admired, the pope replied that
it was his "dialogue with all, even the most remote and even with his
opponents" that most impressed him.[1] In other speeches and writings
from early in his papacy, the pope continued to emphasize dialogue,
and so set the tone for his papacy. "When leaders in various fields
ask me for advice," he said in a July 2013 speech, "my response is

---

1. "A Big Heart Open to God: An Interview with Pope Francis," *America Magazine* website, September 30, 2013, https://www.americamagazine.org/faith/2013
/09/30/big-heart-open-god-interview-pope-francis.

always the same: dialogue, dialogue, dialogue."[2] And in his 2013 apostolic exhortation on evangelization, *Evangelii Gaudium*, the pope referred to dialogue more than fifty times, and exhorted us to walk along "the path of dialogue," enumerating various ways in which the church and individual Christians could embark on this path.[3] His focus on dialogue has continued throughout his pontificate. In his 2015 encyclical on the environment, *Laudato Si'*, his 2016 apostolic exhortation on the family, *Amoris Laetitia*, and his 2020 apostolic exhortation on the Amazon, *Querida Amazonia*, Francis referred to dialogue repeatedly. And appeals to dialogue appear over and over again in his speeches, morning homilies, and audiences.

Francis's emphasis on dialogue has not been appreciated by all Catholics. In October 2015, as the second session of the Extraordinary Synod on the Family was about to begin, a new parody Twitter account emerged—Dr. Dialogue, SJ. The Doctor immediately began tweeting about "dialogue" in ways that demonstrated the anonymous creator's deep suspicion of it. "Remember, you can't spell 'dialogue' without 'U' and 'I' but the 'I' always has to come first!" he tweeted on October 2. On October 8, after the Synod began, he tweeted, "Join us Saturday at the St. Robert Bellarmine Center for Dialogue and Ecumenism. We're having a fun-filled celebration of Calvin's Geneva!" And on October 15, referring to Pope Francis's repeated condemnation of "doctors of the law," Dr. Dialogue tweeted, "Don't be a doctor of the law! Be a doctor of dialogue!"[4]

In an essay for the *National Catholic Register* titled "Dubious About Dialogue," Msgr. Charles Pope raised questions about Francis's exhortation to dialogue, arguing that most people who

2. Meeting with Brazil's Leaders of Society: Address of Pope Francis, Vatican website, July 27, 2013, http://w2.vatican.va/content/francesco/en/speeches/2013/july/documents/papa-francesco_20130727_gmg-classe-dirigente-rio.html.

3. *Evangelii Gaudium*, Vatican website, November 24, 2013, https://w2.vatican.va/content/francesco/en/apost_exhortations/documents/papa-francesco_esortazione-ap_20131124_evangelii-gaudium.html.

4. You can find Dr. Dialogue, SJ's Twitter account here: https://twitter.com/DrDialogueSJ.

advocate dialogue only seek "to avoid a conclusion by steering a conversation or line of reasoning toward uncertainty; a conversation that is not really interested in truly disclosing or sharing the truth." R. R. Reno at the magazine *First Things* included "dialogue" in a list of what he considered to be embarrassing "buzzwords used at corporate retreats and in human resource departments" that are now being used uncritically in official church documents.[5]

Criticisms of Pope Francis's calls to dialogue as un-Catholic are significant for our purposes largely because the pope made clear during his 2015 visit to the United States that he views Thomas Merton's conception of dialogue as being in line with his own. During this visit, Francis referred to the importance of dialogue repeatedly, including during his address to the US bishops at the cathedral in Washington. Telling the bishops that "I cannot ever tire of encouraging you to dialogue fearlessly," Francis exhorted the bishops—and, frankly, all of us—to be unafraid to articulate our viewpoints boldly and clearly, but to do so from a position of genuine encounter by which we approach others in love. Such encounter means that we affirm others first and foremost as persons, "to realize deep down that the brother or sister we wish to reach and redeem, with the power and the closeness of love, counts more than their positions, distant as they may be from what we hold as true and certain."[6] It was therefore significant that Pope Francis referred to Thomas Merton as a "man of dialogue" and drew attention to Merton's "capacity for dialogue" in his 2015 speech to the joint session of the US Congress. When he did so, he made it clear that he viewed Merton's example as worthy of emulation.

5. Monsignor Charles Pope, "Dubious about Dialogue," *National Catholic Register* website, November 6, 2015, https://www.ncregister.com/blog/msgr-pope/dubious-about-dialogue; R. R. Reno, "Instrumentum Laboris," *First Things* website, October 4, 2015, https://www.firstthings.com/web-exclusives/2015/10/instrumentum-laboris.

6. Meeting with the Bishops of the United States of America: Address of the Holy Father, Vatican website, http://w2.vatican.va/content/francesco/en/speeches/2015/september/documents/papa-francesco_20150923_usa-vescovi.html.

Unfortunately, Catholics suspicious of Pope Francis are generally the same Catholics suspicious of Thomas Merton, so the pope's nod to Merton did little to appease those who view Merton as a syncretist whose call to dialogue threatened Catholic tradition and led him away from the church. In this chapter, I'm going to argue that Merton's understanding of the preeminence of dialogue, far from compromising him as a Roman Catholic, was actually rooted in his eucharistic theology and was, in fact, the natural result of his understanding of the implications of the Eucharist. That is, I'm going to posit that Merton's conception of dialogue was rooted deeply in Catholic tradition, and specifically, in an intensely Catholic understanding of the Eucharist. While there is little in Merton's eucharistic theology original to him—thereby showing his rootedness in the tradition—he articulated this theology in a manner that is beautiful, profound, and compelling. And for Merton, the Eucharist demonstrated to him that to be Catholic is necessarily to be called to dialogue.

Merton's Eucharistic Theology: The Sacrament of Love

To explore Merton's eucharistic theology, it is necessary first to examine his account of humanity's creation and fall, which he addressed at length in a book published in 1961 called *The New Man*. Here Merton delved into the Genesis creation stories, reading them poetically for what they tell us about the purpose of human creation. In his interpretation, Merton drew particular attention to Genesis 2:7's reference to God breathing the "breath of life" into the first human, arguing that the "breath of life" is a reference to the Holy Spirit and that this verse points to the idea that humanity "was meant from the very first to live and breathe in unison with God." According to Merton, this means that humans were created to be contemplatives who had the ability, through the indwelling Spirit, "to see things as God saw them, to love them as He loved them" (NM, 53). Such contemplation was to be at the heart of humankind's relationships to God, to one another, and to the created order in that these relationships "were transfigured by divine insights and by an awareness of the inmost reality and value of everything" (NM, 71). In other words, humans were created to see things *as they really are*, in light of God's loving union with them.

Merton spelled out the implications of this in his interpretation of the creation of Eve out of Adam's rib (Gen 2:23-24), which he argued tells us something pivotal about the nature and purpose of human creation. He wrote:

> Adam, perfectly whole and isolated in himself, as a person, needs nevertheless to find himself perfected, without division and diminution, by the gift of himself to another. He needs to give himself in order to gain himself. The law of self-renunciation is not merely a consequence of sin, *for charity is the fundamental role of the whole moral universe.* (NM, 90; emphasis mine)

To be created in the image and likeness of God is not to be created as isolated monads. Rather, Merton argued, relationality is at the very heart of human createdness; we were created for one another, to give of ourselves to one another. For we were created to love, to see and love as God sees and loves, "to be moved in all things ecstatically by the Spirit of God" to give of ourselves in love just as God gives of God's self to us in the breath of life (NM, 53). Merton therefore insisted that, even before the introduction of sin, humans could not be fully themselves as humans created in the image and likeness of God without going out of themselves toward others. To be self-focused would be to be less than human, less than what we were created to be.

And this, according to Merton, is the problem of sin. The story of the fall is a story of humanity's descent into prideful self-centeredness. "By an act of pure pride," Merton wrote, "Adam put an abyss between himself and God and other men. He became a little universe enclosed within itself" (NM, 105). He withdrew from God into himself and so became less than what he was created to be. As Merton writes, he "fell *beneath himself* into the multiplicity and confusion of external things" (NM, 114; emphasis mine). As such he reoriented himself away from the common good and toward his own private good, "which had to be first restricted to itself, entrenched within itself, and then defended against every rival" (NM, 115).

What emerged was what Merton referred to as a "false self," a self that, contrary to the purposes for which humanity was created, attempts to exist as entirely self-sufficient and private. Merton often used the language of the "true" and "false" self in his writings when talking about spiritual transformation, and he devoted significant attention to these selves in *New Seeds of Contemplation*. Here Merton posited that each of us "is shadowed by an illusory person: a false self." "My false and private self," he writes, "is the one who wants to exist outside the reach of God's will and God's love" (NSC, 34). This is a self that is self-focused, self-obsessed, and oriented entirely toward maintaining the illusion of its separateness from God. As such, it's a "self that exists only in my own egocentric desires" (NSC, 35), but it's a self that has no actual reality, based as it is on premises that are opposed to human createdness (NSC, 47). A humanity focused on self-gratification cannot but be confronted with what Merton called its own "nonentity," its lack of reality (LB, xiv).

This focus on the self—this living into the non-reality of the false self—not only alienates us from God, but also from one another, thus resulting in the deep fragmentation of a humanity created to exist in unity. All attempts to find my identity in this false self leads inevitably to conflict with others as I seek to find myself by asserting myself—my "desires and ambitions and appetites"—against others and appropriating for myself a private share of the common good (NSC, 47). I thus find my identity by accentuating the differences between myself and others. As Merton wrote, people whose lives are centered on themselves "can only conceive one way of becoming real: cutting themselves off from other people and building a barrier of contrast and distinction between themselves" and others (LB, xiv). The satisfaction of our material needs and desires over and against the other cannot bring happiness or peace, for the pursuit of such things against the other is based on a lie that is opposed to the purposes of human createdness. However, instead of this compelling us to live differently, we become burdened by what Merton called "an agony of ambivalence," and we project onto our neighbors our dissatisfaction and self-hatred (LB, xiv). We hate them primarily because we see in them what we see in ourselves, namely "selfishness and impotence, agony, terror and despair" (NSC, 123). We fear and hate others because we recognize in them the same destructive, and ultimately dissatisfying, pursuit of identity in non-reality that we see in ourselves. But, as Merton argued in his famous essay "The Root of War Is Fear," it is far more satisfying to hate these things in another than to hate these things in ourselves. Fear, distrust, and hatred thus dominate our fragmented societies.

Yet humanity, even in its fragmentation, recognizes the futility of this existence and longs for something more. Merton wrote in his 1956 book on the Eucharist, *The Living Bread*, that "we know in the intimate depths of our being that our life must recover some unity, stability, and meaning. We sense instinctively that these can only come to us from union with God and with one another" (LB, xv). And according to Merton, "the Eucharist is the great means which God has devised for gathering together and unifying" humankind (LB, 156). The purpose of the Eucharist is to transform human beings to become what they were created to be, people who exist in unity with God and one another.

The manner in which the Eucharist transforms us is multifaceted. According to Merton, it reveals to us the very nature of God as love and so reveals to us that we are profoundly loved; it draws us into the love that is God through union with God, thereby transforming us to discover our true selves in God; and in so doing, it transforms us individually and communally to imitate and manifest in concrete ways the love that is God. I shall address each of these points.

The Eucharist Reveals the God Who Is Love

Merton, as did Augustine and others, tied 1 John 4:8's statement that "God is love" to our conception of God as triune (see LB, 47–51). To understand that God is love in light of the mystery of the

Trinity is to recognize that God exists as three persons who infinitely give of themselves to one another in an eternal embrace of total self-givenness. God is love because God exists eternally loving. We know that God is love through the incarnation of the Son, for through his life and sacrifice, the Son revealed to us the utterly self-giving love that is at the heart of who God is eternally. The intertrinitarian love that characterizes God's self-existence bursts forth and is made known in the incarnation. Christ's sacrifice on the cross is the fullest expression of this self-giving divine love, for in this sacrifice the Son revealed his total love for the Father and for all humankind. The selflessness that is at the heart of God is made manifest in the selfless sacrifice of the Son of God. Thus, in "the death of Jesus on the Cross we see the One Love which is God and we see the Three Divine Persons loving one another" (LB, 52).

The profundity of the Mass is that it makes present this sacrifice to us, manifesting, "in mystery, the *agápe* which is the secret and ineffable essence of God Himself." "What we behold at Mass," Merton wrote, "is the very reality of God's own love" (LB, 53). In the Eucharist, God reveals to us, over and over again, that "God is love," that God's nature is self-giving love, for in the Eucharist God gives of himself fully to us. And to recognize in the Eucharist that God is love is simultaneously to be confronted with the reality that we are ourselves divinely loved. The Eucharist is "the ineffably perfect embodiment" of Christ's love for each one of us (LB, 4), and in the Mass Christ comes to us individually with "a most ardent and personal love for each one of us" (LB, 46). This love is not simply the love that God has for all without exception, but a specific love that reveals Christ to love us as individuals with a love that "reaches out to each one in the inscrutable hiddenness of his own unique individuality" (LB, 70).

Transformation through Union with Christ

This love transforms us, and it does so both by compelling and empowering us to love in return. Merton was clear that we never lose our "natural instincts" to love (LB, xviii). But because we are "pene-

trated through and through by the mystical fire of Christ's charity"
(LB, 10) in the Eucharist, our natural instincts to love are awakened
by Christ's love (LB, 9). However, Christ's presence in the Eucharist
does more than simply awaken these instincts to love. By uniting
himself to us fully, Christ "penetrates our whole being, transforming
and divinizing us by His power" (LB, 70). Our natural instincts to
love are therefore not only awakened, they are elevated and made
like God's own love. Merton emphasized that the Eucharist brings
about an actual and intimate union with the Word made flesh, "as if
He were the soul of our own soul and the being of our own being"
(LB, 110). The divine life of Christ himself is thus poured into us,
and this divine life is nothing else than the intertrinitarian love that
God is. Our love becomes intermingled with the divine love and
so transfigured:

> The charity that is communicated to us in the Eucharist by
> the Heart of the Divine Savior is at once the formal and effi-
> cient cause of the love which it arouses in our own hearts. And
> our response of charity is like a flame communicated to us by
> the Divine Victim burning in the fire of the Holy Spirit.
> United to him, we are consumed in the glory of one and the
> same flame. (LB, 111)

Plunged into the very life of God who is love, we enter into the reality of that love. We thus love God in return, and we do so by loving
with the love that Christ bestows on us in the Eucharist, the love that
God is in God's essence. For in the Eucharist, we are transformed
into Christ, becoming that which we consume, and in loving the
Father with the same love that Christ has for the Father, we come
to know him intimately.

Merton connected the transforming power of the Eucharist to
the language of the true and false self that we encountered above. In
being transformed to become like Christ, to whom we are united in
the Eucharist, we discover our true selves. While the fall is a descent
into fragmentary false selves that exist in opposition to God and to
others, the "problem of sanctity and salvation is in fact the problem

of finding out who I am and of discovering my true self" (NSC, 31). To discover our true selves is to discover our identities once again in union with God, the God who loves us and transforms us to love him in return. The union is so complete that we discover that "Christ is our own deepest and most intimate 'self,' our highest self, our new self as sons of God" (LB, 68), for through his intimate presence in us the false self "is burned away by the fervor of charity" (LB, 119). We discover our true selves by loving God, by returning to the intimacy with our creator that we were intended to have from the beginning. In short, we discover our true selves by being transformed into Christ's image through union with Christ.

However, the transformation does not occur magically. The sacrament may be objective in its operation, but its grace is not communicated to those not properly disposed (see LH, 79–80). To be drawn into and transformed by the divine love of God embodied in the Eucharist requires our active participation. Merton wrote: "In order for the sacraments and the Mass to achieve their full effects in the hearts of the faithful, each one must make personal and interior efforts to dispose his own heart and bring it into union with the Heart of Christ" (LB, 79). We must strive as far as possible to yield ourselves to the divine action in the Eucharist, to unite ourselves to God's will made manifest in the Eucharist. And this will is not simply that we love God, but that we live out the love we experience in the Eucharist by loving others.

Individual and Communal Transformation through the Eucharist

Merton insisted that there is more at stake in the Eucharist than the transformation of the individual. As the sacrament of love that awakens and empowers us to love, the Eucharist is also the sacrament of unity that reforges a humanity that had splintered into pieces. There is, therefore, a deep connection between the Eucharist and the church, the Mystical Body of Christ. Merton warned against "the narrow limitations of an individualistic piety which treats Communion as a refuge from the troubles and sorrows of communal living and ends by cutting us off, spiritually, from the Mystical Christ" (LB, 85–86). To understand the Eucharist merely as a means of personal consolation apart from loving engagement with our fellow communicants is drastically to misunderstand the very purposes for which Christ instituted the sacrament as well as to misunderstand the nature of the church itself. The church is not only a social organization that provides access to necessary sacraments. It is "principally a Living Mystical Body" (LB, xvi), and through the Eucharist we are absorbed into the Mystical Body of Christ (LB, xviii). Through the sacrament we become united to our sisters and brothers in Christ through a bond of love; Merton described this beautifully as members of the mystical body being welded together "in the flame of an infinite charity" (LB, 44). The conversion to the self-giving love of God that takes place through our individual union with Christ in the Eucharist manifests itself in a self-giving love for our sisters and brothers. We thus go out of ourselves to others, and in so doing we recover the relationality that is part of human createdness. But more than this, in giving ourselves to one another in love, we as a church manifest the relationality that is at the heart of who God is as three in one: "For by selfless charity we reproduce on earth, and in time, the circumincession of the Three Divine Persons, each in the others, which is the glory and the joy of the Blessed in eternity because it is the joy of God Himself" (LB, 132). We love with God's own love, offering ourselves to one another with the same love by which the Persons of the Trinity give of themselves to one another in its eternal embrace of self-givenness.

Merton was emphatic that the love engendered by the Eucharist is "more than gentleness, kindness, and affability" (LH, 114). Rather, it is love that is concrete in its expression, a love that involves each of us individually going out of ourselves to the other such that we discover our true selves not only in loving God but in living for others in Christ (LB, 149). United in the love that is God, the Mystical Body of Christ thus offers to the world an icon, not only of the intertrinitarian unity of love that characterizes God, but also of a recreated community of love that demonstrates to a fragmented world another way of existing, one that is more *fully human*. But even more than that, Merton argued that the eucharistic life by its very nature "is oriented towards an apostolate of charity which will effect a visible union of all" humankind (LB, 156). The Eucharist calls the church to unity among her members, but also calls the church to work for the unity of a humanity suffering the consequences of continual fragmentation. There is a continual temptation to reduce the Eucharist to a matter of individualistic piety or to an object of theological speculation, or to focus principally on the liturgy to the neglect of its meaning and purpose. Merton would have none of this. "Of what use is it" Merton asked caustically, "to hold seminars on the doctrine of the Mystical Body and on sacred liturgy, if one is completely unconcerned with the suffering, destitution, sickness, and untimely death of millions of potential members of Christ?" (LH, 117–18). Pointing to Pope John XXIII's encyclical *Mater et Magistra*, Merton argued that the Eucharist is directed primarily toward the creation of a just society, focused on building the kingdom of God on earth (LH, 127–28). For Merton this meant that our growth in love is characterized also by a growth in vision whereby we are able "to see Christ now not only in our own deep souls, not only in the Psalms, not only in the Mass, but everywhere, shining to the Father in the features of men's faces" (BW, 92). The Eucharist compels us to recognize in all people the overwhelming love of Christ poured out upon all, to see them as Christ himself sees them, and indeed to see Christ *in* them. And it therefore calls us to work concretely to build a just world.

The Eucharist and Merton's Fourth-and-Walnut Experience

Merton's understanding of the implications of the Eucharist was not unique only to him. His references to the Eucharist throughout his writings are punctuated by references to patristic, medieval, and contemporary sources that illustrate the degree to which Merton was steeped in the tradition. What is perhaps unique to Merton was the existential depth of his understanding. Merton did not merely possess an intellectual comprehension of the meaning of the Mass he celebrated each day. He *experienced* the profundity of the Mass in a manner that perhaps few of us ever will. I've already made brief reference to Merton's Fourth-and-Walnut experience in a previous chapter. Here I want to talk about this experience as a flowering of his eucharistic theology. Standing at the corner of Fourth and Walnut, gazing at the people surrounding him, Merton "was suddenly overwhelmed with the realization that I loved all those people, that they were mine and I theirs, that we could not be alien to one another even though we were total strangers" (CGB, 140). Whereas he had previously supposed that he was separate from them by virtue of his living in isolation from the world in a monastic cloister, he was instead struck by the realization that he was in fact profoundly united to them. This union was based on more than simply a shared humanity. Merton's eyes were opened to see his fellow humans as God sees them, to see them as immeasurably loved, to see them as so overwhelmingly loved by God that God "gloried in becoming a member of the human race. A member of the human race!" (CGB, 141). Merton wrote that

> it was as if I suddenly saw the secret beauty of their hearts, the depths of their hearts where neither sin nor desire nor self-knowledge can reach, the core of their reality, the person that each one is in God's eyes. If only they could all see themselves as they really *are*. If only we could see each other that way all the time. There would be no more war, no more hatred, no more cruelty, no more greed. . . . I suppose the big problem would be that we would fall down and worship each other. (CGB, 142)

And in seeing them as God sees them, Merton recognized that his own existence was inextricably bound to theirs: "[T]hey are not 'they' but my own self. There are no strangers!" (CGB, 142).

Merton had been writing about the purpose and meaning of the Eucharist for years prior to this experience, but there's a sense in which we can say that Merton understood, more profoundly and deeply than ever before, the implications of the Mass he celebrated each day. That which he knew theologically he experienced deeply on a street corner in downtown Louisville where Merton realized that his attempts to find his identity and purpose apart from his fellow humans was based on an illusion that catered to his false self. Using words that hearken back to his writings on the implications of the Eucharist as the sacrament of love, Merton recounted that, on that street corner, he fell in love with his fellow humans, that he suddenly saw them as the God of love sees them, and that he could no longer live as if his life was somehow separate from theirs.

It is no accident that we see Merton near this date turn his gaze more consciously to the world, focusing on the injustices of a humanity seemingly bent on tearing itself to shreds. The cloister separated him from the world physically, but Merton realized that it could not compromise his essential unity with humanity; he could not but see Christ in his fellow humans. And it was this that would lead Merton not only to write on issues of justice, but also to engage in dialogue with a wide variety of people and to write about dialogue as being at the heart of the Christian life. This emphasis on dialogue emerged in part from his experience and understanding of his unity with his fellow humans, but a letter to a schoolteacher in England in 1959 illustrates that Merton understood this experience of unity and the importance of dialogue to be rooted in the Eucharist:

> For, you see, when "I" enter into a dialogue with "you" and each of us knows who is speaking, it turns out that we are both Christ. This, being seen in a very simple and "natural" light, is the beginning and almost the fullness of everything. Everything is in it somewhere. But it makes most sense in the light of Mass and the Eucharist. (Li, 387; TM to John Harris: January 31, 1959)

Merton clearly understood dialogue to be rooted in the logic of the Eucharist, a logic rooted in our shared identity in Christ and the necessity of finding our true selves in radical openness to both God and others.

In *Conjectures of a Guilty Bystander*, Merton argued that to refuse dialogue with others, including dialogue with our adversaries, is to fall prey to the narrative of a world that fragments rather than unites. A "rigid, defensive, and negative attitude which refuses all dialogue" with adversaries and those with differing beliefs is not open to those of us called to unite and to see others as Christ himself sees them (CGB, 198). Our starting point must be respect for persons in their beauty and worth who merit being given a hearing even when their positions are opposed to our own. To do otherwise is to be guilty of what Merton called the "heresy of individualism," which is nothing else but the very sin of which Adam was guilty and that results only in fragmentation:

> The heresy of individualism: thinking oneself a completely self-sufficient unit and asserting this imaginary "unity" against all others. The affirmation of the self as simply "not the other." But when you seek to affirm your unity by denying that you have anything to do with anyone else, by negating everyone else in the universe until you come down to *you*: what is there left to affirm? Even if there were something left to affirm, you would have no breath left with which to affirm it. (CGB 128–29)

Those guilty of this heresy refuse to find their identity in the other, refuse to go out to the other, but instead seek to find their identity in themselves over and against the other. "The true way is just the opposite," Merton wrote. "[T]he more I am able to affirm others, to say 'yes' to them in myself, by discovering them in myself and myself in them, the more real I am. I am fully real if my own heart says *yes* to *everyone*" (CGB, 129). To dialogue is to reject the insularity that characterizes a world fragmented by original sin. It means to find one's self in the other, to affirm what one really can in the others. Merton spelled out the implications of this as follows:

> I will be a better Catholic, not if I can *refute* every shade of Protestantism, but if I can affirm the truth in it and still go farther. So, too, with the Muslims, the Hindus, the Buddhists, etc. This does not mean syncretism, indifferentism, the vapid

and careless friendliness that accepts everything by thinking of nothing. There is much that one cannot "affirm" and "accept," but first one must say "yes" where one really can. If I affirm myself as a Catholic merely by denying all that is Muslim, Jewish, Protestant, Hindu, Buddhist, etc., in the end I will find that there is not much left for me to affirm as a Catholic: and certainly no breath of the Spirit with which to affirm it. (CGB, 129)

Merton argued that the Christian approach to the other is one rooted in openness and acceptance. It is to begin from a standpoint of affirmation rather than immediate condemnation. That said, he was forthright in recognizing that there were limitations to this. There is, he admitted, much that we can't affirm or accept, but the point is that we must begin by saying yes where we can, and so approach the other as a sister, a brother, an equal. For the moment we do that, the adversary—the other—ceases to be an adversary and an other, for we approach him on the solidly Christian ground of love that affirms and respects him as a person who is divinely loved and who merits a hearing. "If we fear to meet him on what is really our own ground," Merton pointedly asks, "is this not perhaps because we ourselves are not sufficiently Christian?" (CGB, 198).

Conclusion: A Eucharistic Call to Dialogue

In 2007, Pope Benedict XVI published his post-synodal apostolic exhortation, *Sacramentum Caritatis*, on the Eucharist as the source and summit of the church's life and mission. In this beautiful text, the pope drew attention to the transformation the Eucharist is to enact in our relations with others both within and outside the church:

> The union with Christ brought about by the Eucharist also brings a newness to our social relations: "this sacramental 'mysticism' is social in character." Indeed, "union with Christ is also union with all those to whom he gives himself. I cannot possess Christ just for myself; I can belong to him only in

union with all those who have become, or who will become, his own." The relationship between the Eucharistic mystery and social commitment must be made explicit. The Eucharist is the sacrament of communion between brothers and sisters who allow themselves to be reconciled in Christ, who made of Jews and pagans one people, tearing down the wall of hostility which divided them. Only this constant impulse towards reconciliation enables us to partake worthily of the Body and Blood of Christ. In the memorial of his sacrifice, the Lord strengthens our fraternal communion and, in a particular way, urges those in conflict to hasten their reconciliation by *opening themselves to dialogue and a commitment to justice.*[7]

In these lines, Pope Benedict XVI pointed to the heart of the eucharistic theology about which Merton wrote and out of which Merton lived. In the midst of a fragmented world, the Eucharist is the great sacrament of reconciliation, of unity, of love. It binds us together in love, teaches us that we are loved and that we must ourselves love concretely, and for Merton (and, as we can see, for Pope Benedict XVI), this meant going out of ourselves toward the other to dialogue.

Far from compromising him as a Roman Catholic, Merton's clarion call to dialogue was rooted in his Catholicism, and specifically in his understanding of the unifying nature of the Eucharist, the sacrament of love. He did not understand dialogue to mean capitulating to the world, but understood it to be opposed to the logic of a world bent on perpetual enmity and fragmentation. To dialogue is to engage in the decidedly otherworldly and countercultural activity of approaching the other from the standpoint of love. It is to seek to transcend the limitations of selfish individualism that characterizes a fallen world. It is, in short, to live out the implications of the Eucharist, the sacrament whose divinely instituted purpose was,

---

7. *Sacramentum Caritatis* 89, Vatican website, February 22, 2007, http://w2 .vatican.va/content/benedict-xvi/en/apost_exhortations/documents/hf_ben-xvi _exh_20070222_sacramentum-caritatis.html. Emphasis mine. In the passage above, Pope Benedict XVI quoted from his 2005 encyclical, *Deus Caritas Est.*

according to Merton, to open us up more fully to others and so to become more fully ourselves. No wonder Pope Francis lifted him up as an example to us all.

CHAPTER 9

MERTON THE PILGRIM TO THE EAST

I believe that by openness to Buddhism, to Hinduism, and to these great Asian traditions, we stand a wonderful chance of learning more about the potentiality of our own traditions, because they have gone, from the natural point of view, so much deeper into this than we have. The combination of the natural techniques and the graces and the other things that have been manifested in Asia and the Christian liberty of the gospel should bring us all at last to that full and transcendent liberty which is beyond mere cultural differences and mere externals.

—Thomas Merton, December 10, 1968
(From his final talk)

Introduction: "We Don't Know All the Details"

In 2006 the US Conference of Catholic Bishops (USCCB) published the *United States Catholic Catechism for Adults*, a book intended to provide an exploration of the faith for adults. Each of the chapters opens by telling the story of a prominent figure, often an important American Catholic. The catechism features brief accounts of the lives of figures such as Sr. Thea Bowman (1937–1990), Cesar Chavez (1927–1993), Fulton Sheen (1895–1979), Dorothy Day (1897–1980), as well as of Catherine de Hueck Doherty (1896–1985), a woman who played an important role in Merton's life. Noticeably absent from the catechism is any account of the life of Thomas Merton, one of the most important American Catholics of the twentieth century, and one of the most well-known. As noted in the introduction, this was a deliberate choice by the editorial board, chaired by then-Bishop Donald Wuerl. Merton was originally to be included among those honored in the catechism, but was deleted. When asked why, Bishop Wuerl replied that "we don't know all the details of the searching at the end of his life."[1]

In October 1968, Merton boarded a plane from San Francisco bound for Asia. He spent the next two months travelling through India, Sri Lanka, and Thailand learning about Buddhism and engaging in dialogue with significant Buddhist figures, including the Dalai Lama. Merton had been studying Buddhism for years prior to his voyage to the East, and he understood his trip to Asia as an opportunity to experience, rather than simply read about, a faith that fascinated him. Although Merton was clear in his private journal and his letters to friends that he had no intention of leaving the Abbey of Gethsemani, and therefore had no inclination to abandon Catholicism for Buddhism, his fascination with Buddhism continues to raise suspicion among some Catholics who, like Bishop Wuerl, wonder just what Merton was up to during the last few months of his life.

In this chapter, I'm going to examine Merton's engagement in interreligious dialogue during the last decade of his life, paying particular attention to his engagement with Eastern religions. Much has already been written about Merton's engagement with Buddhism,[2] and it's impossible to delve into every facet of his dialogue with Buddhism, as well as of his interreligious dialogue in general, here. What I will address are the concerns occasionally raised by critics of Merton that his interreligious dialogue led him, if not to a rejection of Catholicism,

---

1. "Catholic Bishops Approve National Adult Catechism," *Pittsburgh Post-Gazette*, November 19, 2004, http://old.post-gazette.com/pg/04324/414174.stm.

2. For a thorough bibliography of studies on Merton and Buddhism see Paul M. Pearson, "Merton and Buddhism: A Bibliography," in *Merton and Buddhism: Wisdom, Emptiness, and Everyday Mind*, ed. Bonnie Bowman Thurston (Louisville, KY: Fons Vitae, 2007), 243–55.

at least to a watering down of his Catholicism and his adherence to Catholic orthodoxy. In the previous chapter, I demonstrated that his conception of the importance of ecumenical and interreligious dialogue, as well as of the centrality of dialogue with adversaries, emerged out of a deeply Catholic eucharistic theology, and so was rooted in a Catholic understanding of God and humanity. In this chapter, I will examine what interreligious dialogue looked like for Merton in the last few years of his life, focusing particularly on what he hoped to gain through such dialogue. Moreover, given that critiques of Merton revolve in part around concerns about whether he was planning to convert to Buddhism and reject Catholicism, I will devote some space to looking at what he had to say about his own identity as a Catholic and as a monk in his letters and private journals during the last few years of his life, and particularly during his final few months in Asia.

Merton and Interreligious Dialogue

"I Am Fully Real if My Heart Says Yes to Everyone"

While Merton began seriously to engage in ecumenical and interreligious dialogue during the 1960s, his encounter with and interest in other religions began early in his life, as we have already seen. His reading of Aldous Huxley's *Ends and Means* prior to his conversion brought him into contact with Eastern religions as did his meeting with Bramachari, the Hindu monk from India. Nevertheless, it was not until the mid-1950s that Merton began to delve more deeply into the study of Eastern religions. As already noted, there's a four-year gap in Merton's private journals between 1952 and 1956. There are few references to Buddhism or other Eastern religions prior to 1952, but by 1956, when he recommenced keeping a journal, Merton displayed a growing interest in Buddhism, particularly Zen Buddhism, through his reading of D. T. Suzuki (1870–1966), a Japanese author who endeavored to bring greater understanding of Zen to the Western world.[3] It's important to note that Merton's exploration of

---

3. See Jaechan Anselmo Park, *Thomas Merton's Encounter with Buddhism and Beyond: His Interreligious Dialogue, Inter-Monastic Exchanges, and Their Legacy*

Eastern religions during this time did not come at the expense of his reading and study of Christian theology and spirituality. Not only do his novitiate conference notes illustrate how immersed he was in the study of Christian theology and history, but his journals from this period show the sheer breadth of his reading. For example, at the same time as he was reading Suzuki, Merton was reading Origen, Diadochos of Photiki (a fifth-century monk), Thomas Aquinas, Hans Urs von Balthasar, and Josef Pieper, among others.

In 1959, Merton was completing a book of sayings from the Desert Fathers, the early monks from the beginnings of Christian monasticism in the desert, and his study of these monks along with his reading of Suzuki led him to see convergences between Zen Buddhism and early Christian monasticism. He wrote to Suzuki for the first time both to tell him of his appreciation for his work and to ask whether he would be willing to write a preface for his book on the Desert Fathers' sayings. Merton included in his letter a few pages from these sayings, telling Suzuki that "I feel very strongly that you will like them for a kind of Zen quality they have about them" (Li, 562: TM to Daisetz T. Suzuki; March 12, 1959). This convergence between Zen Buddhism and Christian monasticism convinced Merton that contemplative monks had much to gain from dialogue with Zen Buddhists, and over the next nine years, Merton came to understand further that monks, and Catholics in general, had much to gain from dialogue with those in other religious traditions.

To understand what Merton hoped to gain from such dialogue, it is worth exploring an important passage from his *Conjectures of a Guilty Bystander*, published in 1965. In a passage I've already cited when looking at Merton's eucharistic theology and his understanding of dialogue, Merton wrote about how we should engage with those in other Christian traditions and other religions. After referring to the "heresy of individualism," Merton recounted what the "true way" should look like for Catholics vis-à-vis non-Catholic Christian traditions and religions. The passage is worth quoting again:

(Collegeville, MN: Liturgical Press, 2019), 63–73, for an account of Merton's exposure to and engagement with Buddhism and Buddhist thinkers during his life.

The more I am able to affirm others, to say "yes" to them in myself, by discovering them in myself and myself in them, the more real I am. I am fully real if my own heart says *yes* to *everyone*. I will be a better Catholic, not if I can *refute* every shade of Protestantism, but if I can affirm the truth in it and still go further. So, too, with the Muslims, the Hindus, the Buddhists, etc. This does not mean syncretism, indifferentism, the vapid and careless friendliness that accepts everything by thinking of nothing. There is much that one can "affirm" and "accept," but first one must say "yes" where one really can. (CGB, 129)

Merton's Fourth-and-Walnut experience illustrates that he came more fully to understand the essential unity of humankind and so to understand how thoroughly we violate human unity by refusing to see ourselves as having anything to do with one another. What this insight meant for ecumenical and interreligious dialogue, as the quote above illustrates, is that such dialogue should be undertaken with a willingness to affirm whatever we can in those from a different tradition or religion. I will say a bit more shortly about what this looked like practically for Merton, but I want first to draw attention to his comments about syncretism and indifferentism. Syncretism is the willingness to amalgamate religious ideas or practices from different religions indiscriminately, and indifferentism involves viewing all religions and traditions as essentially all the same without recognizing difference or varying levels of truth. Merton rejected both. He understood that there are real differences that have to be acknowledged and respected. We get nowhere by pretending that we can affirm and accept everything in another religion; Merton described such an attitude as a "vapid and careless friendliness that accepts everything by thinking of nothing." Dialogue necessarily involves studying and understanding the other tradition, and therefore grappling with the incompatible differences that exist. It does not mean watering down one's own tradition or truth claims for the sake of attaining an imagined agreement.

Merton provided many examples of what this could look like, but there are two in particular that are worth highlighting. The first example is found in his correspondence with Abdul Aziz, a Muslim from Pakistan, to which I've made brief reference previously. The second example is found in his 1968 book *Zen and the Birds of Appetite*, and particularly in a chapter in the book called "A Christian Looks at Zen." I turn to the former first.

Abdul Aziz was a Pakistani Muslim who had a deep interest in mysticism, and so devoted himself to the study of Sufism, a tradition within Islam focused on mystical experience of God. In the 1950s, Aziz purchased and read Merton's *The Ascent to Truth*, a book about St. John of the Cross's mysticism. It was not a book Merton liked, but Aziz was deeply impressed by it. In 1959 Aziz met Louis Massignon (1883–1962), a Catholic priest and respected scholar of Sufism, and he asked Massignon if he knew a Christian mystic with whom he could correspond. Massignon gave him Merton's address, and from 1960 to 1968, Aziz and Merton engaged in correspondence.

In his first letter, Aziz introduced himself and told Merton both of his own interests in Sufism and of his admiration for *The Ascent to Truth*. He also asked some questions about St. John of the Cross as well as more general questions about Christian mysticism. Merton responded with a long and enthusiastic letter. Given the volume of his correspondence—the Merton Center possesses over twenty thousand pieces to over twenty-one hundred correspondents—and given that Merton frequently complained in his journals and letters that he was overwhelmed with mail, it is noteworthy that he responded the way he did to Aziz. Clearly Merton saw in Aziz the opportunity to engage in serious dialogue. In addition to having some of his own books as well as some of the writings of St. John of the Cross sent to Aziz, Merton responded by expressing his own interest in Sufism and his hope that Aziz could assist him in understanding Sufism more thoroughly. Most importantly, Merton gave us an example of what he meant when he wrote about saying " 'yes' where one really can" in the final paragraph of the letter:

> As one spiritual man to another (if I may so speak in all humility), I speak to you from my heart of our obligation to study the truth in deep prayer and meditation, and bear witness to the light that comes from the All-Holy God into this world of

darkness where He is not known and not remembered. The world we live in has become an awful void, a desecrated sanctuary, reflecting outwardly the emptiness and blindness of the hearts of men who have gone crazy with their love for money and power and with pride in their technology. May your work on the Sufi mystics make His Name known and remembered, and open the eyes of men to the light of His truth. (Li, 45–46: TM to Abdul Aziz; November 16, 1960)

Note how Merton did not begin his dialogue with Aziz by emphasizing the differences between their two religions. He did not focus on the doctrinal issues that separated and differentiated them. Rather, Merton recognized himself in Aziz and affirmed their common identity as "spiritual" men who understood that prayer, meditation, and mysticism had something to say in a world increasingly turned away from the spiritual life. In other words, according to Merton, he and Aziz possessed a common understanding of the life of prayer, and it was upon this foundation that he wanted to engage in dialogue.

Later letters show Merton continuing to focus on their shared understanding of God as "Compassionate and Merciful," and their shared identities as "brothers in prayer and worship no matter what may be the doctrinal differences that separate our minds" (Li, 49: TM to Abdul Aziz; May 13, 1961). When Aziz provided a brief outline of Islamic theology, Merton affirmed what they held in common. "I can certainly join you with my whole heart in confessing the One God (Tawhid) with all my heart and all my soul," he wrote, also expressing a common faith "in the angels, in revelation, in the Prophets, the Life to Come, the Law and the Resurrection." At the same time, while acknowledging that it is important to understand each other's theologies, Merton emphasized that dialogue should be rooted in their shared experience of God rather than on points of doctrine: "Much more important is the sharing of the experience of divine light, and first of all of the light that God gives us even as the Creator and Rule of the Universe. It is here that the area of fruitful dialogue exists between Christianity and Islam" (Li, 54: TM to Abdul Aziz; June 2, 1963). Nevertheless, in answer to Aziz's questions about the intricacies of Christian theology, Merton did not shy away from trying to explain the Trinity, and to do so in a way that he felt would be coherent to his Muslim friend, emphasizing that the Trinity does not compromise the unity of God, a unity much valued in Islam:

> Here I think I can take an example that may enable you to approach the idea of the Trinity. I note that Ahmad Al'-Alawi [an Algerian Sufi who lived from 1869–1934] thought that the Trinity could be made comprehensible to Moslems, but the book did not say how. My approach would be this. Just as you (and I too) speak with reverence of Allah Rahman and Rahim [the latter two refer to attributes or names of God referring to God's mercy], so I think you can see that speaking of Father, Son and Holy Ghost does not imply three numerically separate beings. The chief thing that is to be stressed before all else is the transcendent UNITY of God. Now as this unity is beyond all number, it is a unity in which "one" and "three" are not numerically different. Just as Allah remains "one" while being compassionate and merciful, and His compassion and mercy represent Him in different *relations* to the world, so the Father and Son and Holy Spirit are perfectly One, yet represent different relations. (Li, 56: TM to Abdul Aziz; October 18, 1963)

It's clear from this quotation that Merton had no qualms about affirming his own belief in the Trinity to his Muslim correspondent, a fact that should be unsurprising given that he frequently wrote about the importance of Trinity for Christian faith and for his own understanding of God. That said, it's worth noting that Merton used Islamic terminology as a springboard for explaining the Trinity as a way to make this complicated doctrine more comprehensible to Aziz, as well as in order once again to affirm what they hold in common—the unity of God—rather than what separates them. At the same time, Merton was clear that, despite the similarities, "enormous" doctrinal differences exist, most notably revolving around the incarnation (Li, 57). As he noted, the doctrine of the Trinity goes hand-in-hand with Catholic understanding of the incarnation, and the differences on this point of theology cannot be ignored.

In 1965 Aziz sent Merton a translation of the *Qur'an* and sug-gested to him that he might want to incorporate chanting the *Qur'an* daily as part of his spiritual practice. Although he appreciated Aziz's gift, Merton's response to Aziz's suggestion illustrates his concerns about adopting such a practice: "It seems to me that here again, my task is rather to chant the sacred books of my own tradition, the Psalms, the Prophets, etc., since I know the proper way of doing this. But on the other hand I read the Koran with deep attention and reverence" (Li, 61: TM to Abdul Aziz; November 7, 1965). It's clear that Merton felt that affirming the other as much as one fully can should not translate into appropriation of religious practices foreign to one's own religion, particularly if, as was the case here, the chanting of Scriptures was already practiced by him. This reticence speaks to the point Merton made about syncretism and indifferent-ism in *Conjectures of a Guilty Bystander* where he emphasized that differences have to be acknowledged and respected, albeit in a way that does not diminish the very real unity that exists.

Nevertheless, the unity and friendship shared between Merton and Aziz is on full display in a beautiful 1966 letter in which Merton, responding to Aziz's request for a description of his daily life at the hermitage, provided intimate details about his daily schedule and spiritual practices. Near the end of the letter, he described his way of meditating, one of the few places in all of Merton's writings where we get a glimpse of his method of prayer:

> Strictly speaking I have a very simple way of prayer. It is cen-tered entirely on attention to the presence of God and to His will and His love. That is to say that it is centered on *faith* by which alone we can know the presence of God. One might say this gives my meditation the character described by the Prophet [Muhammad] as "being before God as if you saw Him." Yet it does not mean imagining anything or conceiving a precise image of God, for to my mind this would be a kind of idolatry. On the contrary, it is a matter of adoring Him as invisible and infinitely beyond our comprehension, and realizing Him as all. My prayer tends very much toward what you call *fana*. There

is in my heart this great thirst to recognize totally the nothingness of all that is not God. My prayer is then a kind of praise
rising up out of the center of Nothing and Silence. If I am still
present "myself" this I recognize as an obstacle about which I
can do nothing unless He Himself removes the obstacle. If He
wills He can then make the Nothingness into a total clarity. If
He does not will, then the Nothingness seems to itself to be an
object and remains an obstacle. Such is my ordinary way of
prayer, or meditation. It is not "thinking about" anything, but
a direct seeking of the Face of the Invisible, which cannot be
found unless we become lost in Him who is Invisible. (Li,
63–64: TM to Abdul Aziz; January 2, 1966)

Again we find Merton trying to make himself comprehensible by
appealing to Islamic examples and ideas. But more importantly, the
intimacy of his description displays how seriously Merton took his
dialogue with Aziz and illustrates that he understood vulnerability
and openness to be central to interreligious dialogue. "I do not
ordinarily write about such things," Merton wrote after his description above, "and I ask you therefore to be discreet about it. But I
write this as a testimony of confidence and friendship. It will show
you how much I appreciate the tradition of Sufism" (Li, 64: TM to
Abdul Aziz; January 2, 1966).

Merton's letters to Aziz illustrate some key principles of his understanding of interreligious dialogue. First, he began from a position of
affirmation. He was wholly unwilling to condemn Aziz's adherence
to Islam, and while this might give pause to some Catholics, this was
the approach taken by the Second Vatican Council both in terms of
Islam and in terms of other religions. The Second Vatican Council's
Dogmatic Constitution on the Church, *Lumen Gentium*, specifically
affirmed Muslims as being in some way included in God's plan of
salvation and united with the church insofar as they "along with us
adore the one and merciful God."[4] The council fathers elaborated on

---

4. *Lumen Gentium* (Dogmatic Constitution on the Church) 16, Vatican website,
November 21, 1964, https://www.vatican.va/archive/hist_councils/ii_vatican_council
/documents/vat-ii_const_19641121_lumen-gentium_en.html.

the church's relationship to Islam in its Declaration on the Relation of the Church to Non-Christian Religions, *Nostra Aetate*, in which, as Merton himself advocated, the church affirms rather than negates:

> The Church regards with esteem also the Moslems. They adore the one God, living and subsisting in Himself; merciful and all- powerful, the Creator of heaven and earth, who has spoken to men; they take pains to submit wholeheartedly to even His inscrutable decrees, just as Abraham, with whom the faith of Islam takes pleasure in linking itself, submitted to God. Though they do not acknowledge Jesus as God, they revere Him as a prophet. They also honor Mary, His virgin Mother; at times they even call on her with devotion. In addition, they await the day of judgment when God will render their deserts to all those who have been raised up from the dead. Finally, they value the moral life and worship God especially through prayer, almsgiving and fasting.[5]

This focus on affirming what is held in common rather than on focusing on differences is further on display in what *Nostra Aetate* has to say about other non-Christian religions:

> The Catholic Church rejects nothing that is true and holy in these religions. She regards with sincere reverence those ways of conduct and of life, those precepts and teachings which, though differing in many aspects from the ones she holds and sets forth, nonetheless often reflect a ray of that Truth which enlightens all men. (2)

Certainly Merton was ahead of the curve with his approach to ecumenical and interreligious dialogue, but it's worth pointing out that his approach effectively received a stamp of approval from the

---

5. Declaration on the Relation of the Church to Non-Christian Religions: *Nostra Aetate* 3, Vatican website, October 28, 1965, https://www.vatican.va/archive /hist_councils/ii_vatican_council/documents/vat-ii_decl_19651028_nostra-aetate _en.html.

fathers of the Second Vatican Council. It's also worth noting that
this was the approach modelled by Pope St. John Paul II (who was
pope from 1978 to 2005) when it came to ecumenical and interreligious dialogue.[6]

Second, Merton did not in his dialogue with Aziz water down his
own Christian faith. Rather, he articulated his beliefs clearly and in
a way that he hoped would be most comprehendible for Aziz, and
did so without glossing over the real differences that exist between
Christianity and Islam. Connected to this, just as he made himself
vulnerable in articulating his faith and practices, so he expressed a
total willingness to understand Aziz's faith and practices as fully as
possible. Third, Merton focused the dialogue less on the matters of
theology that could potentially divide them, but on their shared
experiences of the divine.

This emphasis on dialogue rooted in experience is echoed in the
chapter called "A Christian Looks at Zen" in *Zen and the Birds of
Appetite*. I'm not so much interested in what Merton had to say about
Zen Buddhism in this chapter,[7] but more in how he characterized
the ways in which Christians can and should understand Zen and
what Zen can teach Christians about their own faith. From the outset
of the chapter, Merton acknowledged that setting Christianity and
Zen side by side to compare them is an immensely difficult and
even foolhardy task. "This would almost be like trying to compare

6. For an overview of Pope St. John Paul II's approach to interreligious dialogue,
see Pontifical Council for Interreligious Dialogue, Dialogue and Proclamation:
Reflection and Orientations on Interreligious Dialogue and the Proclamation of
the Gospel of Jesus Christ, Vatican website, May 19, 1991, https://www.vatican
.va/roman_curia/pontifical_councils/interelg/documents/rc_pc_interelg_doc
_19051991_dialogue-and-proclamatio_en.html.

7. It is worth pointing out briefly that some scholars have raised questions in
recent years about the degree to which Merton really understood Zen Buddhism,
mainly because much of his knowledge of Zen came through his reading of D. T.
Suzuki, and there are questions about the accuracy of his depiction of Zen. See in
particular John P. Keenan, "The Limits of Thomas Merton's Understanding of
Buddhism," in *Merton and Buddhism*, 118–32, especially 123–27.

mathematics and tennis," he wrote (ZBA, 33). If dialogue remains on the level of doctrine and theology, it will go nowhere as Christianity and Zen have two quite different metaphysical landscapes. Moreover, as Merton pointed out, "Zen cannot be properly judged as a mere doctrine, for though there are in it implicit doctrinal elements, they are entirely secondary to the inexpressible Zen experience," an experience of reality as it really is (ZBA, 35). However, Merton argued that it is on this level of experience that Christians can engage with Zen and even come more fully to understand the essence of Christianity itself. Too often, Merton argued, Christianity focuses too much on "doctrinal formulas, juridical order and ritual exactitude" to the neglect of understanding that, like Zen, Christianity is rooted in experience, namely the experience of "entering fully into the life of hope and love consummated by union with the invisible God 'in Christ and in the Spirit,' thus fully sharing in the Divine Nature" (ZBA, 39, 40). Because Christianity begins with the revelation of God communicated to us in words and statement, and because "everything depends on the believer's accepting the truth of these statements," we've tended to reduce Christianity "to a world view, at times a religious philosophy and little more, sustained by a more or less elaborate cult, by a moral discipline and a strict code of Law" (ZBA, 39, 40). Zen's focus on experience, according to Merton, can help us recognize that, however important doctrine, liturgical rubrics, and moral theology may be, "Christianity is much more than the intellectual acceptance of a religious message by a blind and submissive faith which never understands what the message means except in terms of authoritative interpretations handed down externally by experts in the name of the Church." On the contrary, Merton continued, "faith is the door to the full inner life of the Church, a life which includes not only access to an authoritative teaching but above all to a deep personal experience which is at once unique and yet shared by the whole Body of Christ, in the Spirit of Christ" (ZBA, 56). In essence, Merton emphasized a point that Pope Benedict XVI made in his 2005 encyclical on love, *Deus Caritas Est*. "Being a Christian," Benedict wrote, "is not the result of an ethical choice or a lofty idea, but the encounter with an event, a person, which gives life a new horizon and a decisive direction."[8]

Is Merton's point that the experience of the Christian is the same as that of the Zen Buddhist? No. Acknowledging that there are some who believe that mystics "in all religions are all experiencing the same thing and are all alike in their liberation from the various doctrines and explanations and creeds," Merton insisted that experiences cannot be so easily divorced from beliefs, which themselves shape and emerge out of those experiences (ZBA, 43). Differences in experience and beliefs exist and need to be acknowledged. Nevertheless, as was the case in his exchange with Abdul Aziz, Merton suggested in this chapter that we can come to a deeper understanding of another religion or tradition, as well as a deeper understanding of our own tradition, on the level of experience rather than by focusing on matters of theology or law. While experience necessarily differs, experiences of the transcendent or of the divine have at least a commonality, even a common language, that allows for genuine engagement to occur between persons of different religious traditions. Merton wasn't willing to abandon his own Christianity or that which was distinctive about Christianity for the sake of dialogue. Rather, as was the case for the fathers of the Second Vatican Council, he saw no contradiction between his Christian identity and his willingness to recognize and affirm the truth, beauty, and goodness found in other religious traditions. Indeed, as we saw in the previous chapter, Merton understood such dialogue to be fundamentally rooted in his identity as a Catholic shaped and transformed by Christ's presence in the Eucharist.

Salvation Outside the Church

When it comes to interreligious dialogue, the question of salvation—particularly whether those in non-Christian religions are

---

8. *Deus Caritas Est* 1, Vatican website, December 25, 2005, http://www.vatican .va/content/benedict-xvi/en/encyclicals/documents/hf_ben-xvi_enc_20051225 _deus-caritas-est.html.

saved—emerges sooner or later for Catholics. This question understandably came up for Merton. It is important to point out that although the Second Vatican Council did not deal with this question explicitly, it did address the question implicitly through the statements I have already quoted above from both *Lumen Gentium* and *Nostra Aetate*. Rather than demarcating salvation in strictly juridical terms by saying that salvation is only possible for those within the juridical boundaries of the Roman Catholic Church, the fathers of the Second Vatican Council talked about the church's relationship with non-Catholic traditions and religions more in terms of levels of communion. The council was clear in its articulation that the fullness of truth, goodness, and beauty—the fullness of salvation itself—was found in the Roman Catholic Church, but this didn't prevent the fathers from acknowledging that those in non-Catholic traditions and religions have a participation in this truth, goodness, and beauty.

There is at the moment continuing debate about the church's teaching on salvation outside the church, and the question is one that has not been definitively settled. Suffice it to say, I do not have space here to delve into the intricacies of this complicated debate. My goal here, rather, is to examine Merton's understanding of this question, and specifically, to address the criticisms sometimes levelled against him that he was a religious relativist who therefore placed himself outside the boundaries of Catholic orthodoxy. The idea that Merton understood all religions to be essentially the same, that they are all individual manifestations of the same basic truths, is a misconception he himself was careful to avoid. Moreover, we'll see that Merton never questioned his own Catholicism or his belief that the fullness of salvation was found within the Catholic Church.

Perhaps the best place to start would be to revisit briefly Merton's exchange with Abdul Aziz. After two years of dialogue through correspondence, Aziz brought up the question of salvation in an August 1963 letter. In particular, Aziz brought up a quotation by Pope Pius XI (1922–1939) found in a book Merton sent to him. In 1934

Pope Pius XI was said to have made the following statement when dispatching the apostolic delegate to Libya, Cardinal Camillo Vittorino Facchinetti (1883–1950): "Do not think you are going among infidels. Muslims attain to salvation. The ways of Providence are infinite." Aziz wanted to know what Merton made of this statement.

Merton's reply merits full quotation:

> It should be perfectly clear that Christian doctrine on this point is in accord with common sense and the ordinary religious feeling of all believers: obviously the ultimate destiny of each individual person is a matter of his personal response to the truth and to the manifestation of God's will to him, and not merely a matter of belonging to this or that organization. Hence it follows that any man who follows his faith and his conscience, and responds truthfully and sincerely to what he believes to be the manifestation of the will of God, cannot help being saved by God. There is and can be no question in my mind that every sincere believer in God, no matter what may be his affiliation, if he lives according to his belief, will receive mercy and, if needed, further enlightenment. How can one be in contact with the great thinkers and men of prayer of the various religions without recognizing that these men have known God and have loved Him because they recognized themselves loved by Him? It is true that there are different ways to Him and some are more perfect and more complete than others. It is true that the revelation given to the "People of the Book," Christians, Jews and Muslims, is more detailed and more perfect than that given through natural means only to the other religions. (Li, 58: TM to Abdul Aziz; June 28, 1964)

Merton understood Pope Pius XI's remark to Cardinal Facchinetti to be fully in accord with Catholic theology. He felt no need to explain it or suggest that it could be at odds with certain perspectives found within Catholicism. Rather, he unambiguously recognized the truth in the pope's comments. That people in non-Christian religions have genuine experiences of God and come to know God was a point Merton understood to be obvious to anyone who had actually read and studied the great thinkers in these traditions. At the same time, as the last two sentences of the quotation illustrate, Merton was clear that this does not mean that all religious pathways are the same or are of equal value, and he specifically draws attention—as did the Second Vatican Council—to both Judaism and Islam as being particularly close to Christianity and so more "complete" and "perfect" in comparison to other religions.

Merton expressed similar ideas in a 1965 letter to a member of a Rama Krishna order in California named Philip Griggs. Griggs took exception to a book by a Benedictine monk for which Merton wrote the preface. In the book, Dom Denys Rutledge made assumptions about the superiority of Christianity to other religions that Griggs found offensive and he wrote Merton asking why he wrote the preface. Griggs also wondered about whether, in Merton's opinion, a devout Sadhu (Hindu holy man) would be closer to God than a superficial Christian, or whether the latter's identity as a Christian automatically means he has a closer knowledge of God. Merton was unwilling to talk about the issue in such a zero-sum manner. He did not feel the necessity to adhere either to a rigid perspective on salvation in the church *or* total relativism. Neither were satisfactory. Rather, as Merton noted in his nuanced reply to Griggs, one can affirm that non-Christians have a direct experience of God without compromising belief in the church.

> You ask about the relative nearness to God of a fervent Sadhu and a superficial Christian. The Church's teaching on nearness to God is that he who loves God better, knows Him better, and is more perfectly obedient to His will, is closer to Him than others who may love, know and obey Him less well. Since it is to me perfectly obvious that a Sadhu might well know God better and love Him better than a lukewarm Christian, I see no problem whatever about declaring that such a one is closer to Him and is even, by that fact, closer to Christ. The distinction lies in the fact that Catholics believe that the Church does possess a clearer and more perfect exoteric doctrine and sacramental system which "objectively" ought to be more secure and reliable a means for men to come to God and save their souls. Obviously this cannot be argued and scientifically proved, I

simply state it as part of our belief in the Church. But the fact remains that God is not bound to confine His gifts to the framework of these external means, and in the end we are sanctified not merely by the instrumentality of doctrines and sacraments but by the Holy Spirit. And I repeat my conviction as a Catholic that the Holy Spirit may perfectly well be more active in the heart of a Hindu monk than in my own. (Li, 337–38: TM to Philip Griggs; June 22, 1965)

Merton steered a middle path between the extremes of relativism and exclusivism in his response to Griggs, and he did so by simultaneously affirming the objective completeness of Catholic doctrines and sacraments while acknowledging that the Spirit of God is free to work outside the confines of the sacraments. From Merton's perspective, the church acknowledges that members of non-Christian religions can come to know and love God, and therefore, that mere membership in the church does not guarantee that a person automatically has a more profound and deeper relationship with God than someone outside the church. As Merton wrote in a 1965 letter to Marco Pallis, whose primary interest was in Buddhism, "there is every solid reason even within the framework of Catholic orthodoxy to say that all the genuine living religious traditions can and must be said to originate in God and to be revelations of Him, some more, some less" (Li, TM to Marco Pallis; Easter 1965). God is to be found outside the Catholic Church, but at the same time, Merton was unhesitant in affirming his belief that the Catholic Church provided the fullest and most complete means of bringing people to the saving knowledge and love of God, pointing specifically to the sacraments. But neither the doctrines nor the sacraments of the Catholic Church guarantee nearness to God, particularly in the case of someone who is merely lukewarm in their faith and practice. As Merton wrote, God is not tied down by the sacraments. It is the Holy Spirit who transforms and sanctifies, and while the Spirit does both through the sacraments, the Spirit it not bound to transform only through them. That the Holy Spirit works in the hearts of those outside the confines of the church seemed to Merton to be obvious. But this didn't lead him to question his conviction regarding the objective fullness of Catholic doctrines and sacraments.

He was not oblivious to the very real differences that existed between his Catholicism and the religions he was studying. "I may be interested in Oriental religions, etc.," he wrote, "but there can be no obscuring the essential difference—this personal communion with Christ at the center and heart of all reality, as a source of grace and life" (Jv, 259: June 26, 1965). He was aware that his study of and dialogue with those in other religions brought concern about his own orthodoxy. Critically important, he wrote in a 1966 journal entry, "is the question of the purity of my own faith—my willingness to risk compromises perhaps with other doctrines? This must be faced." However, he continued in the entry, he saw no disjunction between his Catholicism and his interreligious study and dialogue:

> But I can say here I have no hesitation in firmly desiring and intending to *be a Catholic* and to hold with all my heart to the true faith of the living God manifested in Christ and in his Church. And no monkeying! Amen. Whatever I seek in other traditions is only the truth of Christ expressed in other terms, rejecting all that is *really* contrary to His Truth. (Not what is irresponsibly and hastily *said* to *be* contrary to it). (Jvi, 358–59: February 4, 1966)

He was not interested in facile syncretism. There was always going to be much that could not be affirmed. But Merton believed strongly that there was much that could be affirmed, that Christ was manifested in these other traditions, that he could see the truth, beauty, and goodness of his own faith reflected back at him in the faiths of others.

Merton's Criticisms of the Church

Merton was also clear that the Catholic Church all too often failed to manifest Christ, and he wasn't shy in his criticisms of the church throughout the 1960s. His criticisms were due in part to what he perceived to be the failures of the church, particularly the American church, to address the crisis of possible nuclear annihilation adequately. Too often he saw American clergy and theologians defending or even advocating for what to Merton was unthinkable—the use of nuclear weaponry against the Soviet Union. However, his criticisms of the church weren't rooted only in his concerns regarding peace issues. Rather, throughout the 1960s, Merton took the church to task for what he saw as being too great a focus on juridical matters and on the church as an institution. He saw the church too often emphasize law over love, dogma over people.

Given that the focus of this chapter is to address the concerns raised by some regarding the depth of Merton's devotion to Catholicism, and particularly about whether he was tempted to leave the church during the years leading up to his death, it's important to examine briefly the criticisms Merton levelled against the Catholic Church in order to understand more thoroughly his attitude toward the church as well as his self-understanding of his place within it. The time period during which he was most vocal in his criticisms of the church coincided with the period of his greatest exploration of other religions, particularly of Buddhism, leaving some to wonder whether Merton was looking for a path out of Catholicism. The question that needs to be addressed, therefore, is whether these criticisms amounted to an implicit rejection of the church.

In a 1968 letter, Merton assessed the progression of his thought, making a distinction between two different "Mertons" in the minds of people: "one ascetic, conservative, traditional, monastic. The other radical, independent, and somewhat akin to beats and hippies and to poets in general" (Liii, 385: TM to Sr. J. M.; June 17, 1968). While he disputed this characterization, he did acknowledge a progression in his thought from what he described as a "highly unworldly, ascetical, intransigent, somewhat apocalyptic" approach in his early writings, including in *The Seven Storey Mountain* (Liii, 384: TM to Sr. J. M.; June 17, 1968). One cannot read his autobiography without confronting the triumphalist manner in which Merton described his conversion to Catholicism that manifests in a kind of unquestioning approach to the church and a critical attitude toward other Christian traditions and non-Christian religions. This is one of the reasons that more conservative Catholics continue to read and appreciate *The Seven Storey Mountain*, even if they question his later writings and theology. After his autobiography, however, and coinciding in no small part with criticisms he received from Catholics—both from clergy and laity—in the wake of his writings on peace, Merton often criticized the church in his letters and journals.

In 1961, influenced by his reading of *Resurrection* by the theologian François-Xavier Durrwell (1912–2005), Merton brought up what he understood to be the problematic focus too many Catholics, including bishops, place on the institutional juridical structure of the church. By this, he meant an understanding of the church that revolves primarily around authority, law, and dogma. From Merton's perspective, Durrwell did a good job of illustrating that the institutional aspect of the church does not express the totality of what the church is; in fact, Merton wrote, "too many evils are excused by a passionate and one-sided attachment to the Church as a juridical institution" (Jiv, 108: April 16, 1961). This critique of a "juridical" understanding of the church is one that would be repeated by Merton until the end of his life. In journal entries in which he declared that he had "not the slightest inclination to be anything other than a Catholic" (Jiv, 236: August 9, 1962), and that he had "never had any doubts about my Christian faith or about the Church as the Body of Christ" (Jiv, 265: November 16, 1962), he was at the same time critical of limited conceptions that reduced the church to power and authority as manifested institutionally. However important the institutional aspect of the church is—and he always acknowledged and, as we have seen, frequently appealed to magisterial authority, particularly in his arguments about nuclear war—Merton believed that the church's fullest identity was found in love, not power (see Jiv, 289–90: January 17, 1963). As he put it in a 1967 circular letter to friends, to emphasize love does not mean to reject the institutional church, but rather to endeavor to reform the church to look more Christ-like by "accepting *people* as well as dogmas" (Lii, 101–2: Circular Letter; Easter 1967).

Merton's criticisms of the church are perhaps best summarized in a 1962 letter that he also included in his *Cold War Letters*. In it, he criticized those Christians within the church, many of them clergy, who advocated an understanding of Christianity that was, to Merton, incompatible with what Christianity actually is. His criticism revolved primarily around the issue of nuclear war, but it's clear that he understood the problem to be more far-reaching:

> Without wanting to be in conflict with the truth and with the will of God, we are actually going against God's will and His teaching. We are actually refusing Him what He asks of us as Christians, while at the same time proclaiming to heaven and earth that we are the best of Christians. We are, however, without knowing it, adhering to a Christianity that is scarcely Christian. It is infected with worldly values, and it is corrupted by love of wealth and power. In fact, the Christianity which we have subtly substituted for the will of God and for true Christian tradition is really the Christianity of the rich, the powerful, the selfish. It is a Christianity of individualism, of greed, of cruelty, of injustice, which hides behind specious maxims and encourages a kind of spiritual quietism. It is a Christianity of formulas, which are to be accepted blindly and repeated without understanding, a Christianity of passive conformity, in which under the name of obedience we are often brought into subjection to the most worldly influences and powers. (Lv, 79: TM to Evora Arca de Sardinia; January 31, 1962)

Merton's criticism of Catholicism here boils down to this: The church looks far too much like the world and so has ceased to become a countercultural witness to another way of being, to God's way of being. The church focuses on power, authority, and obedience, as if these were the only things that were to characterize the Body of Christ. And as a consequence, as Merton put it in *Conjectures of a Guilty Bystander*, the church ends up looking exactly like the world it supposedly condemns. The worldly church condemns the world, but it does not condemn the world for its abuse of power or its individualism or its cruelty. Rather, "contempt for the world became not contempt for the objectives of the world, but competition with the world on its own ground and for the same power, with contempt for its motives" (CGB, 35).

Attempts were made to reform the church at the Second Vatican Council, and Merton was initially enthusiastic about the prospect. But he soon found himself disillusioned. Despite the council's attempts at reform, Merton felt that the church was still hamstrung and "paralyzed by institutionalism, formalism, rigidity and regression" (Liv, 192: TM to Pablo Antonio Cuadra; June 30, 1964). He felt that the backlash of conservatives against the council's reforms dampened the possibilities for genuine reform, for these conservatives clung to those aspects of the church most in need of reform:

> The extreme conservatives seem to me to be people who feel themselves so menaced that they will go to *any length* in order to defend their own fanatical conception of the Church. This concept seems to me to be not only static and inert, but in complete continuity with what is most questionable and indeed scandalous in the history of the Church: Inquisition, persecution, intolerance, Papal power, clerical influence, alliance with worldly power, love of wealth and pomp, etc. This is a picture of the Church which has become a scandal and these people are intent on preserving the scandal at the cost of greater scandal. (CGB, 286)

At the same time, while he expressed frustration over the efforts of the conservatives to derail needed reform, he also expressed profound frustration with progressives who want to push reform even at the cost of charity for their fellow Catholics:

> On the other hand, the refusal of the extreme progressives to pay any attention to *any* traditional teaching which would give them a common basis for rational discussion with conservatives is surely scandalous also—especially when it is allied with an arrogant triumphalism of its own, and when it simply ridicules

all opposition. This is not only foolish, but seems to show a serious lack of that love to which they frequently appeal in justification of their procedures. (CGB, 286–87)

The church needed to be reformed away from triumphalism and rigidity, but, Merton argued, reform can't occur when one triumphalism is replaced by another, and when the very principle of genuine reform—love—is disregarded. It was his distaste for both conservatives and progressives that led Merton to emphasize that he could not and would not identify with either. Rather, he wrote, "I would like to think I am what Pope John was—a progressive with a deep respect and love for tradition" (CGB, 285).

As can be seen, Merton was critical in his appraisals of the church, and he knew that these criticisms upset people (see Lv, 144: TM to Naomi Burton Stone; March 13, 1964). But was his voice of criticism one that came from someone ready to jump ship? Not if we take his own words seriously. In his 1963 preface to the Japanese translation of *The Seven Storey Mountain*, Merton clarified for readers the ways in which he had changed since writing his autobiography. While acknowledging that his compassion for and understanding of the world had grown since he wrote the book, Merton insisted that his own identity as a Catholic, a monk, and a priest remained central, and he bore no regrets for his decision to convert and to become a monk. Moreover, he made it clear that he never experienced the temptation to reverse course: "Certainly I have never for a moment thought of changing the definitive decisions taken in the course of my life: to be a Christian, to be a monk, to be a priest" (HR, 63). He continued:

> My conversion to the Christian faith, or to be more precise my conversion to Christ, is something I have always regarded as a radical liberation from the delusions and obsessions of modern man and his society . . . I am still in the monastery, and intend to stay here. I have never had any doubt whatever of my monastic vocation. If I have ever had any desire for change, it has been for a more solitary, a more "monastic" way. (HR, 64, 65)

This public profession of continued fidelity to his Catholicism and his monastic identity was echoed in his private journals. In a 1962 journal entry in which he wrote about issues he had with the church, Merton still made it clear that, despite his issues, he remained a Catholic: "I find in myself not the slightest inclination to be anything other than a Catholic, simply because any further question of organizations and categories is ludicrous and *I believe in the Body of Christ*" (Jiv, 236: August 9, 1962; emphasis mine). It was not that he was stuck in the church but wouldn't leave because it was at least an organization with which he was familiar. Rather, he remained Catholic because he believed what the church said about itself as being the Body of Christ on earth, an identity rooted in the Eucharist. He was a Catholic because he believed in the church.

In terms of his identity as a monk, and specifically, as a monk at Gethsemani, he was in the mid to late 1960s more content at the monastery than he had ever been. In the fall of 1966, after the tumultuous summer with Margie Smith, Merton wrote about his place within the monastery and within the church. After commenting favorably about the good there was at Gethsemani, both in the individual monks and in the community itself, Merton wrote: "I count myself lucky to be here. There really is no other place in the Church now where I would rather be. I see so evidently that my hermitage is my true place in the Church. And I owe this to my community. Also, let's face it, to my Abbot, of whom I am so easily critical" (Jv, 146: October 4, 1966). Although correspondents like Rosemary Radford Ruether told Merton that he should leave the monastery, Merton bristled at such suggestions: "I really have no desire to leave" (Jv, 276: August 14, 1967).

In his letters, he was similarly clear about his feelings about the church and his own identity as a Catholic monk and priest. In a circular letter he sent to friends in 1967 (he would send these circular letters when he felt overburdened by correspondence and couldn't respond personally to everyone who wrote to him), Merton addressed the topic of a priest named Fr. Charles Davis who made the decision to leave the church; evidently, his correspondents had brought the issue up with him in their own letters to Merton, and some perhaps suggested that this might be a step Merton should take. Merton began his comments on the issue by acknowledging the legitimacy of the arguments Fr. Davis made against what he perceived to be abuse of authority in the church: "I do not think these criticisms were altogether baseless or unjust. The present institutional structure of the Church is certainly too antiquated, too baroque, and is so often in practice unjust, inhuman, arbitrary and even absurd in its functioning . . . I certainly respect Fr. Davis's anguish—who of us does not sometimes share it?" (Lii, 95: Septuagesima Sunday 1967). As we have already seen, Merton frequently echoed Fr. Davis's arguments about the institutional church in his own journals and letters, and so he could not but be sympathetic to Fr. Davis's predicament. At the same time, however, Merton could not agree entirely with Fr. Davis, and his comments about this illustrate how seriously Merton took his own identity as a Catholic monk and priest. Despite his issues with the church, Merton wrote that "I cannot follow him in his conclusion that the institutional Church has now reached the point where it can hardly be anything other than dishonest, tyrannical, mendacious and inhuman" (Lii, 95: Septuagesima Sunday 1967). As he continued, Merton opened up to his friends about his own self-understanding of himself as well as his understanding of a church that too often falls short of its calling to be Christ's presence in the world.

> In actual fact I have never seriously considered leaving the Church, and though the question of leaving the monastic state *has* presented itself, I was not able to take it seriously for more than five or ten minutes . . . Being a Catholic and being a monk have not always been easy. But I know that I owe too much to the Church and to Christ for me to be able to take these other things seriously. The absurdity, the prejudice, the rigidity and unreasonableness one encounters in some Catholics are nothing whatever *when placed in the balance with the grace, love and infinite mercy of Christ in His Church*. And after all, am I not arrogant too? Am I not unreasonable, unfair,

demanding, suspicious and often quite arbitrary in my dealings with others? (Lii, 96: Septuagesima Sunday 1967; emphasis mine)

Merton found himself attacked by his fellow Catholics, particularly American Catholics, for his positions on war—at one point, Catholics in Louisville held an event to burn Merton's books (see Liv, 161: TM to Ernesto Cardenal; March 15, 1968)[9]—and he also was harshly critical of what he understood to be an overemphasis on an institutional, juridical, and authoritative conception of the church. But Merton viewed the church primarily through a theological and sacramental lens, no doubt because of his own daily celebration of the Mass, a celebration that we have seen meant a great deal to him. Despite the church's faults, Merton experienced in the church "the grace, love and infinite mercy of Christ," and he was not about to abandon that for the sake of his own discontentment with other facets of the church. He wasn't oblivious to the very real faults of the church. In reply to the author Czeslaw Milosz's criticisms of the church, Merton's reply is clear. "You can say absolutely nothing about the Church that can shock me," he wrote. "If I stay within the Church it is out of a disillusioned love, and with a realization that I myself could not be happy outside" (Liv, 85: TM to Czeslaw Milosz; March 15, 1968). The triumphalism on display in *The Seven Storey Mountain* was long gone by the 1960s. But his love for the church remained. It was, as he described it, a disillusioned love, but it was a love rooted in his ongoing experience of God's merciful love within the church.

9. The following letter by Robert H. Jutt to the editor of *The Record*, the newspaper of the Archdiocese of Louisville, gives an indication of the opposition Merton faced: "I am 65 years old and consequently do not have a draft card, but I assure you that I would rather die than burn it if I had one. However, there are some items that I do have that I am burning, among them is 'Seven Storey Mountain' and all the other books that I have that were written by this publicity seeking 'devout' priest" (*The Record*, March 14, 1968).

Merton Travels East

Pursuing Deeper Solitude in Alaska and California

Dom James Fox was consistently reluctant to allow Merton to travel. Despite Merton's repeated requests to accept invitations from various places throughout the United States and abroad, Dom James was unmoved apart from two exceptions. In 1956 Merton was permitted to travel to a conference of monastics at St. John's Abbey in Minnesota alongside of the abbot, and in 1964, Merton travelled briefly to New York in order to meet D. T. Suzuki. However, in 1968, Dom James retired. On January 8, 1968, Merton made his first reference to being invited by Jean Leclercq to an ecumenical conference of monks in Bangkok to take place in December, but he wasn't sure whether the soon-to-be-elected abbot would be more open to travel than Dom James. On January 13, 1968, Flavian Burns, one of Merton's former students, was elected as the successor to Dom James, and it became clear quickly that Dom Flavian was more open to travel for Merton than the previous abbot. In May, Merton travelled to California to lead a retreat for the Cistercian nuns at Redwoods Monastery, and in June Dom Flavian gave permission for Merton to travel to Asia in the fall.

Not only did Dom Flavian see Merton's voyage as an opportunity for him to engage more directly in dialogue with adherents of Eastern religions, but it was an opportunity for him to look for another place to live as a hermit. Although Merton's hermitage was secluded in the woods about a mile away from the monastery, too many people knew where it was and would pop in unannounced. "I am not really living like a hermit," he wrote. "I see too many people, have too much active work to do, the place is too noisy, too accessible . . . All I have is a certain privacy, but real solitude is less and less possible here" (Jvii, 82: April 18, 1968). By June, Dom Flavian encouraged Merton to look for places where he could live as a hermit perhaps in California or New Mexico, all while still maintaining his stability at the Abbey of Gethsemani. That is, he would remain a monk of Gethsemani even while living as a hermit elsewhere. By the end of July, with plans now set for travelling to

New Mexico, Alaska, and California before his voyage to the East, Merton wrote in his journal about hoping to find a place where he could live as a hermit in these states, or even in Asia. But he was absolutely clear, as he was in his journal entry the night before his departure from the hermitage, that he was not looking to break ties with the Abbey of Gethsemani even if he was a hermit elsewhere: "I am not starting out with a firm plan never to return or with an absolute determination to return at all costs. I do feel there is not much here at the moment and that I need to be open to lots of new possibilities. I hope I shall be! *But I remain a monk of Gethsemani*" (Jvii, 166: September 9, 1968; emphasis mine). His insistence that he had no plans to be anything but a monk of Gethsemani was reiterated in letters to Gethsemani sent from both Alaska and Asia. Given the rumors spreading around about why Merton had left the monastery, Merton wrote from Asia to his secretary, Br. Patrick Hart, to instruct him to "keep telling everyone that I am a monk of Gethsemani and intend to remain one all my days" (Liii, 399: TM to Brother Patrick Hart; September 26, 1968). And one month before his death, he wrote to his abbot that he was keen to live as a hermit away from the monastery, but insisted that he would still always be "a member of my monastic family there" (Liii, 411: TM to Abbot Flavian Burns; November 9, 1968). He wanted to be canonically tied to the monastery, to remain a monk and priest of the Abbey of Gethsemani, but both he and his abbot believed that true solitude as a hermit could only occur elsewhere.

After spending the night at Bellarmine College (now University), Merton flew to New Mexico on September 11 where he met Georgia O'Keefe and spent a few days at the Apache reservation. On September 16 he left for Alaska, having been invited by the Archbishop of Anchorage to give a retreat to contemplative nuns in his archdiocese. When he received the invitation in August, Merton's first thought was that Alaska could be a perfect location to live as a hermit, and the archbishop was open and enthusiastic about this possibility (see Jvii, 153: August 13, 1968). Merton was impressed with both the beautiful geography and the people, and could envision himself living as a hermit in this environment. "I think that unless something very definite comes up to change things," Merton wrote to his abbot, "this would be the obvious place to settle for real solitude in the United States." He continued: "I can't say with certitude that I am called to be a hermit here, but I do believe it is a very real possibility and that I must keep it in mind and look into it further and perhaps make a decision on my return from Asia" (Liii, 401: TM to Abbot Flavian Burns; September 26, 1968). As he explained further to the abbot, the archbishop of Anchorage wanted contemplatives in his archdiocese, and the local church would see to Merton's material needs. Merton wasn't interested in being anything other than a Trappist monk and a priest. He was, however, interested in greater solitude in order to live out his calling as a hermit more fully than he was able to do at Gethsemani, and he felt that the archbishop of Anchorage, as well as the priests and people of the archdiocese, were offering him precisely this possibility.

While in Alaska, Merton gave a series of conferences for a community of contemplative nuns, and these conferences, given less than a month before travelling to Asia, indicate his esteem for the local Catholic community. Moreover, in these conferences Merton explained his reasons for going to Asia and expounded on the contemplative life in such a way that shows that his interest in interreligious dialogue did not confuse or compromise his understanding of contemplation or his sense of who he was as a Catholic contemplative. For example, in a talk to the Alaskan nuns called "Prayer, Tradition, and Experience," Merton delved into the importance of having a clear theology of prayer, "a theology that supports prayer, that goes with prayer and gives it structure" (TMA, 115), and to illustrate his point he drew the nuns' attention to the early Desert Fathers and the ways in which they were formed theologically and spiritually. He focused on how each monk was trained and formed in relationship with other monks, and particularly, under the guidance of a spiritual director who guided them as they entered into the life of prayer. Merton noted that this kind of formation occurs less frequently in Catholic monastic circles than in the past, but that it is still present in Buddhist monasticism, and it was to explore this formation, as well as to learn from their spiritual practices, that Merton was going to the East:

> The reason my Abbot has allowed me to go over there is so that I can give people a rundown on what these Asian traditions are about that would be useful because they do have techniques of meditation that work. They are not theological but it is good psychology. The Buddhist idea is strictly psychological purification. It is deliberately confined to psychology, there is no theology in it whatever, and Buddha absolutely refused to give any kind of theological message. (TMA, 126)

As these comments illustrate, Merton wasn't going to the East to become a Buddhist. Rather, in agreement with his own abbot, he was going to the East because he felt that Catholics—and particularly monks—could learn something from their Buddhist counterparts about meditation and their methods of spiritual formation.

That Merton continued to take seriously his own identity as a Catholic monk and priest is on display in these conferences to the nuns. In them he emphasized such points as needing to have a robust theology of the Holy Spirit and the Spirit's transforming work in prayer if we are to understand the purpose of the Christian conception of contemplation, which he described as being inextricable from "the Christian experience of sonship, the Christian experience of being risen with Christ, the Christian experience of having received the Spirit" (TMA, 89). Contemplation is nothing else, he continued, but "the Christian experience of Christ living in our hearts" (TMA, 79). And when asked about praying before the Blessed Sacrament, Merton commented on how valuable this practice had always been for him and continued to be, as well as on how important Christ's eucharistic presence was for him at the hermitage:

> For some people—for me—it is a help. I didn't realize how true this was until I moved into my hermitage and was not allowed to have the Blessed Sacrament. This went on for a couple of

years, and I didn't even think about it really until somehow or other the issue came up again and I was given permission to have the Blessed Sacrament reserved at the hermitage. I found it was a great help. One of the things that was nicest about it—well, I would lie in bed and if I woke up, there was the tabernacle. This is a real, simple, naïve sort of thing, but actually it made me feel quite different at night, just the sense of this Presence. There is nothing nicer than that. (TMA, 90–91)

Merton left Alaska for California with the sense that he would return after his trip to Asia to live as a hermit in Alaska. "It is clear I like Alaska much better than Kentucky," he wrote in his journal, "and it seems to me that if I am to be a hermit in the U.S., Alaska is probably the place for it" (Jvii, 193: September 27, 1968). At the same time, he continued to look for possible hermitage sites while in California, though with less success than he had in Alaska. He also gave conferences on the contemplative life to the Cistercian nuns at Redwoods Monastery. On October 15, Merton boarded a flight in San Francisco that would take him to Asia and his final earthly destination.

Merton's Dialogues in Asia

Merton left for Asia hopeful that this trip would transform him deeply. In the plane somewhere over the Pacific, he wrote: "We left the ground—I with Christian mantras and a great sense of destiny, of being at last on my true way after years of waiting and fooling around. May I not come back without having settled the great affair" (Jvii, 205: October 15, 1968). Precisely what he meant by "the great affair" isn't clear, but any sense that he was reconsidering his identity as a Trappist monk and priest is discounted by his own words about remaining a monk of Gethsemani in the months and weeks leading up to his departure for Asia, including what he wrote in his journal and letters while in Alaska.

Merton travelled extensively during his nearly two months in Asia, spending most of his time in India. Not long after arriving in Calcutta in October, Merton attended a conference organized by an interfaith organization called the Temple of Understanding at which he gave a talk on monasticism and dialogue between Eastern and Western religions. He prepared a text for his talk, but chose instead to speak more informally. His prepared text illustrates Merton's understanding of both the benefits and the limitations of interreligious dialogue. From his perspective, dialogue on a deep level can occur between contemplatives from different religions because such dialogue can transcend the merely doctrinal so as to focus on the experiential. "On this existential level of experience and of spiritual maturity," Merton wrote, "it is possible to achieve real and significant contacts and perhaps much more besides" (AJ, 312). At the same time, he was clear that he was not proposing the idea that all contemplative or mystical experiences are essentially the same regardless of genuine religious differences:

> Without asserting that there is complete unity of all religion at the "top," the transcendent or mystical level—that they all start from different dogmatic positions to "meet" at this summit—it is certainly true to say that even where there are irreconcilable differences in doctrine and in formulated belief, there may still be great similarities and analogies in the realm of religious experience. (AJ, 312)

As we have already seen, Merton was wary of any kind of dialogue that disregarded differences as irrelevant or inconsequential. "There can be no question of a facile syncretism," Merton wrote in the prepared text, "a mishmash of semireligious verbiage and pieties, a devotionalism that admits everything and therefore takes nothing with full seriousness." Rather, he insisted "there must be a scrupulous respect for important differences" (AJ, 316). At the same time, for those who have entered into their own religious tradition seriously, and here Merton particularly has in mind monastics who are fully immersed in their monastic traditions, interreligious communication can take place on a deep level. Such communication involves more than simply sharing ideas. Rather, "the kind of communication that is necessary on this deep level must also be 'communion' beyond the level of words." And when such communion happens, one has the capability "to meet a discipline [*sic*. Should read "disciple"] of another, apparently remote and alien tradition, and find a ground of verbal understanding with him" (AJ, 315).

It was not a question for Merton of abandoning one's own religious tradition or of disregarding interreligious differences. Instead, even while acknowledging differences, Merton insisted that it was possible to learn from, and even identify with, someone from another religious tradition. But this can only occur if each person takes their own tradition with utter seriousness. In his informal talk at the conference, which he gave in place of his prepared remarks, Merton emphasized that in order for communication on the deepest level to occur, those in dialogue need to be "faithful to their own calling, to their own vocation, and to their own message from God." And when they engage in dialogue from this foundation, it is possible for them to discover a fundamental unity that exists and that allows for genuine communion to occur even while acknowledging difference. "My dear brothers, we are already one," he said, "but we imagine that we are not" (AJ, 308).

Both Merton's prepared text and his informal presentation for the Temple of Understanding conference further show that he didn't come to Asia for the purpose of abandoning his identity as a Catholic monk and priest in order to adopt an Eastern religious identity. That said, he believed that he could learn from his Eastern religious counterparts and so wanted "to drink from ancient sources of monastic vision and experience" in order "to become a better and more enlightened monk" (AJ, 313). But such exploration did not mean that Merton would be anything other than a Trappist monk.

Merton's dialogue with Buddhists, particularly Tibetan Buddhists, throughout the rest of October and November appeared to involve precisely the kind of communication and communion that he talked about at the Temple of Understanding conference. Perhaps his most famous dialogues were with the Dalai Lama, which took place over three meetings during November. Their conversations were wide-ranging—they discussed epistemology, meditation, as well as Western monastic life—and after their final meeting, Merton remarked that he felt that there existed a "real spiritual bond" between them (Jvii, 266: November 8, 1968). And when describing his conversations with other Buddhists, he wrote that he experienced precisely what he described in his talk at the Temple of Understanding conference: "So far my talks with Buddhists have been open and frank and there has been full communication on a really deep level. We seem to recognize in one another a certain depth of spiritual experience, and it is unquestionable" (Jvii, 264: November 7, 1968).

However, while he found his dialogue with Buddhists enlightening and deeply meaningful, his thoughts were never far away from Gethsemani. In the same journal entry in which he described his first meeting with the Dalai Lama, Merton wrote about how much his appreciation for the hermitage at Gethsemani had grown during his time in India, in no small part because he was finding solitude hard to come by even in the mountains. And as he contemplated the future, he wrote frequently in his journal that he could not see himself living as a hermit in Asia, but that he saw Alaska or California as being the most likely place for him to live out his life as a hermit. Interestingly, he even suggested that he might just go back to Gethsemani permanently: "I suppose I ought essentially to end my days there. I do in many ways miss it. There is no problem of my wanting simply to 'leave Gethsemani.' It is my monastery and being away has helped me see it in perspective and love it more" (Jvii, 282: November 17, 1968).

Moreover, as a circular letter he wrote in November shows, far from making him question his identity as a Catholic monk, his dialogue with Buddhists seemed to be leading him even more deeply to experience the indwelling presence of Christ. After describing his many dialogues with Buddhist leaders, Merton concluded the letter as follows: "I wish you all the peace and joy in the Lord and an increase of faith: *for in my contacts with these new friends I also feel consolation in my own faith in Christ and His indwelling presence.* I hope and believe He may be present in the hearts of all of us" (Lii, 121: November 9, 1968; emphasis mine).

Merton's Experience at Polonnaruwa

In early December, Merton flew to Sri Lanka for a brief visit. There he would have a profound experience. On December 2, Merton visited Gal Vihara, one of Buddhism's most sacred sites located in the ancient city of Polonnaruwa. Gal Vihara was constructed in the twelfth century and its primary attraction consists of four massive statues of the Buddha carved out of granite. In previous chapters, I wrote about two experiences of the transcendent that Merton had, one being at the Church of St. Francis in Havana and the other at the corner of Fourth and Walnut in Louisville. Merton's description of what happened to him at Gal Vihara in Polonnaruwa indicates that he experienced something truly profound while looking at the giant statues of the Buddha, and it is important that we delve into this experience. His description begins as follows:

> I am able to approach the Buddhas barefoot and undisturbed, my feet in wet grass, wet sand. Then the silence of the extraordinary faces. The great smiles. Huge and yet subtle. Filled with every possibility, questioning nothing, knowing everything, rejecting nothing, the peace not of emotional resignation but of Madhyamika, of *sunyata*, that has seen through every question without trying to discredit anyone or anything—*without refutation*—without establishing some other argument. For the doctrinaire, the mind that needs well-established positions, such peace, such silence, can be frightening. I was knocked over with a rush of relief and thankfulness at the *obvious* clarity of the figures, the clarity and fluidity of shape and line, the design of the monumental bodies composed into the rock shape and landscape, figure, rock and tree. And the sweep of bare rock sloping away on the other side of the hollow, where you can go back and see different aspects of the figures.

As Merton continued to gaze at the Buddhas, something extraordinary occurred:

> Looking at these figures I was suddenly, almost forcibly, jerked clean out of the habitual, half-tied vision of things, and an inner

clearness, clarity, as if exploding from the rocks themselves, became evident and obvious . . . The thing about all this is that there is no puzzle, no problem, and really no "mystery." All problems are resolved and everything is clear, simply because what matters is clear. The rock, all matter, all life, is charged with *dharmakaya*—everything is emptiness and everything is compassion. I don't know when in my life I have ever had such a sense of beauty and spiritual validity running together in one aesthetic illumination. Surely, with Mahabalipuram and Polonnaruwa my Asian pilgrimage has come clear and purified itself. I mean, I know and have seen what I was obscurely looking for. I don't know what else remains but I have now seen and have pierced through the surface and have got beyond the shadow and the disguise. (Jvii, 323: December 4, 1968)

Much has been made of this experience. Claims have been made that Merton attained here the first level in becoming a bodhisattva, a figure who has attained Buddhist enlightenment, or that he became an "Incarnate Buddha."[10] Given that he used Sanskrit terms to describe his experience, and given that he had this experience while gazing at the ancient statues of the Buddha, are we to assume that Merton had some sort of conversion experience to Buddhism at Polonnaruwa? In his biography of Merton, William H. Shannon referred to various interpretations of this experience "that pull the event out of the total context of Merton's life and give it a weight of meaning that it cannot bear—for instance, making it the climax of his life that nothing past or future could possibly match." I cannot help but agree with Shannon when he writes that such "an evaluation hardly seems warranted."[11]

10. See Park, *Thomas Merton's Encounter with Buddhism and Beyond*, 41–46, for a description of how Merton's Polonnaruwa experience has been variously interpreted. The above examples are ones to which Park draws attention and they are from Donald Grayston, "In the Footsteps of Thomas Merton: Asia," *The Merton Seasonal* 33 (Winter 2008): 26; and Edward Rice, *The Man in the Sycamore Tree: The Good Times and Hard Life of Thomas Merton* (New York: Doubleday, 1970), 172.

11. William H. Shannon, *Silent Lamp: The Thomas Merton Story* (New York: Crossroad, 1992), 277. For an overview of Merton's experience that also references

In the first part of his description, Merton appears to use the Sanskrit term *madhyamika* to describe his opposition to dogmatism, an opposition he expressed many times prior to this experience. As we have seen, Merton was not opposed to the study of theology. In fact, he understood the importance of such study, not only in his role as a teacher to the novices, but as someone who took his faith seriously and understood the importance of doctrine. He regularly admitted to correspondents that he was something of a traditionalist when it came to theological matters,[12] and his writings demonstrate how significant the Trinity, Christology, eucharistic theology, and Mariology were to him. At the same time, we've seen that he opposed an approach to doctrine that privileged orthodoxy over the human person, and that he had little patience for an approach to Christianity that saw it more as a series of tenets one needs to believe than as a life to be lived out rooted in the experience of the indwelling Christ. It was this emphasis on experience over rigid orthodoxy that attracted him to Buddhist thought. From Merton's perspective, the focus in Buddhism was not on simply knowing about the reality of things preached by the Buddha, but on experiencing that reality. It is this point that Merton seems to be drawing out by referencing *madhyamika*. Merton understood the Buddhist concept of *madhyamika* to refer to the Buddhist critique of dogmatism, of the refusal to understand that absolutisms cannot fully encompass the totality of reality.[13] Something about the statues, and particularly the expressions of the faces of the Buddhas, brought this concept to mind. Indeed, while gazing at the Buddhas, he *experienced* the concept in such a

various interpretations of it, see Donald Grayston, "Thomas Merton in Asia: The Polonnaruwa Illumination," in *Thomas Merton: Monk on the Edge*, ed. Ross Labrie and Angus Stuart (Vancouver: Thomas Merton Society of Canada, 2012), 135–54.

12. For example, see his letters to Rosemary Radford Ruether (Li, 500–501: February 14, 1967) and June J. Yungblut (Li, 637: June 22, 1967).

13. See Joseph Quinn Raab, "*Madhyamika* and *Dharmakaya*: Some Notes on Thomas Merton's Epiphany at Polonnaruwa," *The Merton Annual* 17 (2004): 196–99, for a fuller examination of Merton's use of *madhyamika*.

way that he felt relief and joy. But while his experience of the idea was unique, his rejection of dogmatism as expressed above was not.

In terms of the second part of Merton's description, Shannon notes that one "can make too much of it, or too little" (Shannon, 278). Certainly, if we compare his account of his Polonarruwa epiphany and his epiphanies in Havana and at the corner of Fourth and Walnut, there exists a similarity in tone. In all three Merton described the experiences as occurring suddenly and forcefully, bringing with them insights about the nature of reality. Moreover, without minimizing the profundity of Merton's experience, Shannon points out that Merton's reference to finding "what I was obscurely looking for" was used by Merton when describing other events in his life. For example, he talked about finding something he had been looking for when describing his visit to a church in Rome as a teenager, when given permission to use an old toolshed in 1953 as a temporary hermitage, and when given permission to become a hermit in 1965 (Shannon, 278). That said, we need to take Merton seriously when he wrote that "I have now seen and have pierced through the surface and have got beyond the shadow and the disguise." Merton had been convinced that deeper exposure to Buddhism, particularly to Buddhist monks, could help him become a better monk, and he felt it was possible to engage in genuine communion with practitioners of another religion. Before Polonnaruwa, he experienced such communion with Buddhist monks, including the Dalai Lama. At Polonnaruwa, he experienced this kind of communion with the Buddhist tradition itself while gazing at these enormous statues of the Buddha. As was the case with his dialogue with Buddhist monks, this communion did not lead him to question his own identity as a Catholic monk and priest. The same can be said about his experience of communion at Pollonaruwa. This was a moment in which he came more fully to understand the Buddhist tradition and Buddhist teaching experientially, and in which he came to understand existentially the commonalities between this tradition and his own. As such, "this very significant experience can be understood within the context of the larger narrative of his Catholic life" (Raab, 195).

This was not a moment of conversion from Catholicism to Buddhism. To read this event in such a way would be to disregard all that Merton said and wrote in days, weeks, monks, and years leading up to this experience. As Julius Lipner wrote in his review of *The Asian Journal* for *New Blackfriars*, "Not for a moment does he give the impression of diluting or turning his back upon what is lasting and valid in the treasures of his own Christian tradition."[14] That Merton used Buddhist terminology to articulate his own experience doesn't point to his adoption of Buddhism, but rather to his ever-deepening understanding of the commonalities shared by Buddhism and his own Catholicism, commonalities that Merton was keen to affirm even while recognizing the clear differences between the two. He used Buddhist terminology to describe an experience he had while gazing at statues of the Buddha, similar to the way he used Islamic terminology to explain Christian ideas to his Sufi correspondent, Abdul Aziz. But as Tyler Anderson pointed out, "It was a Buddhist setting and he used a few Buddhist terms, but for the most part the language is about as tradition-neutral as one could get."[15] Merton was not articulating a moment of conversion, but a moment of transcendence that clearly transformed him. He had travelled to the East to have a deeper understanding of Buddhism and of the relationship of his own Christianity to it, and Polonnaruwa marks a moment of attaining just such an understanding.

Conclusion

Three days after his Polonnaruwa experience, Merton flew to Singapore where he met Lee Beng Tjie, a professor of philosophy at the University of Singapore. He celebrated Mass in the home of Lee Beng Tjie and his wife. The next day he flew to Bangkok where he would attend the conference of interreligious monastics to which he had been invited by Jean Leclercq earlier in the year.

14. Julius Lipner, Review of *The Asian Journal* in *New Blackfriars* 56 (1975): 473.
15. Tyler Anderson, "What Matters Is Clear," *The Merton Annual* 23 (2010): 77.

His last entry in his private journal is on December 8, and his final lines in the entry refer to his plans to say Mass for the feast of the Immaculate Conception before leaving for the Red Cross compound where the conference was to take place. On December 10, Merton gave his talk, titled "Marxism and Monastic Perspectives." His talk revolved around what both Eastern and Western monasticism have to say constructively regarding Marxism, but he concluded the talk by referring to the importance of interreligious dialogue from his perspective as a Catholic monk:

> I believe that by openness to Buddhism, to Hinduism, and to these great Asian traditions, we stand a wonderful chance of learning more about the potentiality of our own traditions, because they have gone, from the natural point of view, so much deeper into this than we have. The combination of the natural techniques and the graces and the other things that have been manifested in Asia and the Christian liberty of the gospel should bring us all at last to that full and transcendent liberty which is beyond mere cultural differences and mere externals. (AJ, 343)

In these final words, Merton again signaled that his interest in such dialogue was not to facilitate his own eventual conversion to an Eastern religion, but to enable himself and other Christian monastics more deeply to understand and experience the fullness of their own tradition.

Merton was someone with a deep and abiding interest in non-Christian religious traditions, particularly Eastern religious traditions, and he travelled to Asia with the express purpose of learning about those traditions and of discovering further points of convergence between his own contemplative tradition and Buddhism. But he made no secret of the fact that vast differences exist between Christianity and Buddhism that cannot and should not be ignored. More than once he spoke out against syncretism and indifferentism, recognizing that both not only violated Christian distinctiveness but also the distinctiveness of non-Christian traditions. Merton did not travel to Asia looking for a new religious tradition. Rather, as a monk steeped in his own tradition, Merton sought to understand more thoroughly not only what his own contemplative tradition offered to the world, but what contemplative traditions—both Eastern and Western—offered to a world that too often seems bent on its own destruction. At a time when divisiveness manifested itself in racial injustice and when it seemed all too likely that that divisiveness might result in nuclear holocaust, Merton endeavored to find lines of connection with other religious traditions as a means to counter the divisiveness that he understood to go against God's purposes for humanity. And he did so as a Catholic monk and priest who understood that he was called to work for this unity by his own Catholic tradition.

CONCLUSION

MERTON THE CATHOLIC

Thomas Merton died tragically on December 10, 1968, shortly after giving his talk in Bangkok at the conference to which he had been invited. The circumstances of his death were strange, involving a fan with an apparent electrical short. And while suggestions have recently been made that his death was suspicious, there is no reason to believe that it was anything but accidental. His body was flown back to the United States, and on December 17, the Abbey of Gethsemani received his coffin, celebrated the funeral mass, and buried him in a grave just outside the walls of the abbey church.

His personal effects were shipped to the monastery a month later by the American embassy in Thailand, and an inventory of these effects is in the Merton Center. In addition to the usual things one would expect anyone to have while travelling, there were personal items that Merton carried with him around Asia that illustrate what he considered essential. In addition to the Cistercian breviaries he used to pray the offices of prayer while travelling, Merton carried with him a rosary as well as a small icon of the Virgin and child, to which I've already referred. Perhaps most interesting are these lines from the inventory: "Brown Leather Snap Case with Zippered Base Section containing various pills, medication. *Zippered section contains what appear to be relics.*"[1]

---

1. American Consulate in Bangkok, "Inventory of Effects, Estate of Thomas James Merton," December 23, 1968, *Thomas Merton Center*, Bellarmine University. Emphasis mine.

Throughout his monastic life, Merton showed a deep love for relics. His journals reference the various relics he managed to acquire over the years—they were usually sent to him as gifts—and after moving to the hermitage, he recorded the relics he kept there. These included relics of Sts. Paul, Gregory of Nazianzus, Bede, Teresa of Avila, John of the Cross, and Louis (Jv, 333: n.d.). Sr. Mary Luke Tobin, a Sister of Loretto who was made an official observer at the Second Vatican Council, wrote the following anecdote that illustrates Merton's love for relics:

> I recall his taking us (the retreatants) up the back hill to see his hard-earned hermitage. With obvious pleasure, he showed us all his little treasures, including bongo drums given him by a friend, a stole sent to him by John XXIII, and various relics he cherished. I remember writing him from Rome asking if he would like a first-class relic of the newly canonized Lebanese hermit, Charbel. "Oh yes," he answered, "I'm a great relic man!"[2]

He never wrote specifically about relics nor about why he valued them enough to carry eight of them with him on his pilgrimage to the east. His saintly companions on his voyage were Sts. Bede (d. 735), the learned Benedictine monk; Romuald (951–1057), founder of the Camaldolese Order; Peter Damian (1007–1072), a reforming Benedictine monk and Doctor of the Church; Bruno of Cologne (ca. 1030–1101), founder of the Carthusian Order; Thomas Becket (1118–1170), the English martyr; Nicholas of Flüe (1417–1487), a Swiss hermit; Charbel Makhluf (1828–1898), a Lebanese hermit; and Thérèse of Lisieux (1873–1897), to whom Merton maintained a consistent devotion. That Merton carried these relics with him on his journey east is further evidence of how immersed he was in his own Catholic tradition.

---

2. Mary Luke Tobin, "Introduction," in Thomas Merton, *Springs of Contemplation: A Retreat at the Abbey of Gethsemani*, ed. Jane Marie Richardson (New York: Farrar, Straus and Giroux, 1992), viii–ix.

On October 3, 2020, the vigil for the feast day of St. Francis of Assisi, Pope Francis signed his social encyclical, *Fratelli Tutti*. Written and published in the midst of the Covid-19 pandemic, *Fratelli Tutti* focuses on the imperative of love and openness to others in a world that appears to be fracturing. Pope Francis begins the encyclical by bringing up the example of St. Francis of Assisi (ca. 1181–1226), specifically pointing to an episode in his life when he visited Sultan Malik-el-Kamil in Egypt: "Francis went to meet the Sultan with the same attitude that he instilled in his disciples: if they found themselves 'among the Saracens and other nonbelievers,' without renouncing their identity they were not to 'engage in arguments or disputes, but to be subject to every human creature for God's sake.'" Pope Francis praised his namesake for his "openness of heart, which knew no bounds and transcended differences of origin, nationality, colour or religion."[3] As I read the pope's description of St. Francis, I could not help but think that Thomas Merton also exemplified precisely this kind of openness of heart, an openness that was firmly rooted in his own Catholic identity rather than opposed to it.

There are those who are attracted to the early Merton of *The Seven Storey Mountain* and its account of a man and a monk who portrayed Catholicism in glowing terms, depicted other religions and Christian traditions somewhat judgmentally, and described his entrance into the Abbey of Gethsemani as an escape from the influences of an evil and pernicious world. Many of those attracted to the early Merton are wary of the later Merton who dove headlong into interreligious and ecumenical dialogue, and who opened himself up to a world that he had previously rejected.

But as I have endeavored to demonstrate in this book, the transformation of the early, more insular, Merton to a monk open to the world and to others did not involve a repudiation of Catholic tradition, but rather a deepening understanding of and engagement with

3. Pope Francis, *Fratelli Tutti* 3, Vatican website, October 3, 2020, http://www .vatican.va/content/francesco/en/encyclicals/documents/papa-francesco_20201003 _enciclica-fratelli-tutti.html.

it. He came to understand, as Pope Francis is himself trying to teach Catholics today, that our faith—and particularly our understanding of the meaning of the Eucharist—calls us to a radical openness to others.

Pope Francis writes in *Fratelli Tutti* that the Covid-19 pandemic has exposed our "false securities," revealing the fault lines in our societies and in the church (7). He specifically mentions the "hyperbole, extremism and polarization" that have become so much a part of our political and theological landscape (15). In these circumstances, Pope Francis calls us as Christians to follow the path of dialogue and encounter, a path by which we engage others in a love rooted in the dignity that each person possesses by virtue of their humanness. Such dialogue does not mean watering down one's own beliefs. As Pope Francis emphasizes, "A false notion of tolerance has to give way to a dialogic realism on the part of men and women who remain faithful to their own principles while recognizing that others also have the right to do likewise" (221).

Thomas Merton provides us with an example of a Catholic who was deeply immersed in and transformed by his own tradition, and who opened himself radically to the world and to others in precisely the way that Pope Francis calls us to do. In a time when polarization continues to fracture us as citizens and as Christians, Merton's life and thought, his example of genuine encounter with others, provides us with a way forward. It is a way characterized by love, by an understanding of the inviolable worth of each person, and it is rooted fundamentally in the love God manifested to us in the incarnation.

INDEX